Negotiating a Perilous
Empowerment

Ohio University Press

Series in Race, Ethnicity, and Gender in Appalachia
Series Editor:
Marie Tedesco

Memphis Tennessee Garrison: The Remarkable Story of a Black Appalachian Woman,
edited by Ancella R. Bickley and Lynda Ann Ewen

The Tangled Roots of Feminism, Environmentalism, and Appalachian Literature,
by Elizabeth S. D. Engelhardt

Red, White, Black, and Blue: A Dual Memoir of Race and Class in Appalachia,
by William R. Drennen Jr. and Kojo (William T.) Jones Jr., edited by Dolores M. Johnson

Beyond Hill and Hollow: Original Readings in Appalachian Women's Studies,
edited by Elizabeth S. D. Engelhardt

Loving Mountains, Loving Men,
by Jeff Mann

Power in the Blood: A Family Narrative,
by Linda Tate

Out of the Mountains: Appalachian Stories,
by Meredith Sue Willis

Negotiating a Perilous Empowerment: Appalachian Women's Literacies
by Erica Abrams Locklear

Negotiating a Perilous Empowerment

Appalachian Women's Literacies

ERICA ABRAMS LOCKLEAR

OHIO UNIVERSITY PRESS
ATHENS

Ohio University Press, Athens, Ohio 45701
www.ohioswallow.com
© 2011 by Ohio University Press
All rights reserved

To obtain permission to quote, reprint, or otherwise reproduce or distribute material from Ohio University Press publications, please contact our rights and permissions department at (740) 593-1154 or (740) 593-4536 (fax).

Printed in the United States of America
Ohio University Press books are printed on acid-free paper. ∞

20 19 18 17 16 15 14 13 12 11   5 4 3 2 1

Library of Congress Cataloging-in-Publication Data

Locklear, Erica Abrams.
 Negotiating a perilous empowerment : Appalachian women's literacies / by Erica Abrams Locklear.
   p. cm. — (Series in race, ethnicity, and gender in Appalachia)
 Includes bibliographical references and index.
 ISBN 978-0-8214-1965-6 (acid-free paper)
 1. American literature—Appalachian Region—History and criticism. 2. Literacy in literature. 3. Women—Appalachian Region. 4. Sex role in literature. 5. Women in literature. 6. Appalachian Region—In literature. I. Title.
 PS286.A6L63 2011
 810.9'3522—dc22

2011000731

*For my parents, Bert and Darlene Abrams.
And for my husband, J. Mark Locklear.*

"Everything added meant something lost, and about as often as not the thing lost was preferable to the thing gained, so that over time we'd be lucky if we just broke even. Any thought otherwise was empty pride."

—Charles Frazier, *Cold Mountain*

"Literacy is not a neutral activity. It does change self-identity, family relations, and politics. Resistance to literacy may be for many students an intuitive effort to preserve culture, self, and family and is *not* then a simple matter of anti-intellectual or remedial behavior. It may be, from one point of view, a heroic defense of another form of literacy valued by one's family and community."

—Miles Myers, *Changing Our Minds: Negotiating English and Literacy*

Contents

Introduction   1

Chapter 1. Appalachia on Our Pages: Situating
      Appalachian Literacy and Literary Analysis   23

Chapter 2. Shaping Biscuit Dough and Rolling Out Steel:
    Responding to Literacy Commodification
    in *The Dollmaker*   56

Chapter 3. Narrating Socialization: Linda Scott DeRosier's Memoirs   92
      Interview with Linda Scott DeRosier   127

Chapter 4. "Overcoming" Backgrounds:
      Competing Discourses in *The Unquiet Earth*   142

Chapter 5. Invasion of the Mountain Teachers:
      Literacy Campaigns and Conflicts in Lee Smith's Work   174
      Interview with Lee Smith   212

Epilogue   229

Notes   235

Works Cited   240

Index   251

Acknowledgments   255

List of Illustrations

Figure 1.1	"Isn't It About Time for School?"	36
Figure 1.2	"Out of the Fog"	37
Figure 1.3	Edith Vanderbilt	38
Figure 1.4	"Take a Full Bath More Than Once a Week"	40
Figure 1.5	Moonlight School Commencement	41
Figure 1.6	"First Lesson"	42
Figure 1.7	Minerva Clark Sprouse	43
Figure 1.8	Textbook Illustration of a Community Party	47

Introduction

In 2000, Appalachian author Lee Smith paired with longtime friend and high school teacher Debbie Raines to edit and publish an oral history of Smith's hometown titled *Sitting on the Courthouse Bench: An Oral History of Grundy, Virginia*. Students in Raines's senior English class collected the stories, enjoying a rare opportunity to work with one of Appalachia's best-known writers. Raines's students received high school credit for their work and were also able to add an impressive credential to their college application packets. When I interviewed Smith in October 2007, she told me the story of one of Raines's talented female students who applied to several colleges and had been accepted to all of them. For various reasons the student chose to study at Berea College, and when Smith met the girl's mother at a banquet celebrating the senior class's accomplishments, she was shocked by the mother's reaction to her daughter's success. Smith recalls, "I said, 'I guess you're just really proud of your daughter,' and [the mother] just burst into tears. She said, 'It won't never be the same after this.' She said, 'She'll go off, and then she'll come back and she won't know us no more.' And I said, 'What do you mean?' And she said, 'She just won't really know us anymore. It'll all be different from now on. I've only got,' whatever it was, 'six more months with her'" (2007).

Several months later, in June 2008, Smith delivered a keynote address at the third annual Mountain Heritage Literary festival at Lincoln Memorial University, sharing a slightly different version of this same story with her audience. During the address she added, "All I could do was hug that mother tight. I could not say, 'That's true. Though she will always love you, and she may well appreciate you even more, she *won't* be exactly like you anymore, and she will feel guilty, the way we all do, and she will suffer for it, the way we all do, and she will be forever formed by this extraordinary childhood" (2008, 313).

This mother's concerns are not uncommon; after all, with the start of every semester, worried parents say tearful good-byes to their children on the steps of college dormitories across the nation, but what this mountain mother laments—and ultimately, what this book argues—is something different. For Appalachian women, the transformative powers of education, and more specifically, literacy, are no doubt empowering, but they can also be perilous. Gaining new technical, social, and cultural literacies, especially ones that might not be shared by those in the learner's home community, almost always comes at a price. Usually this entails a palpable distancing from home, loved ones, and the mountain community that first nurtured the one who has chosen to leave (physically, mentally, or both), but the severity of that cost varies depending on the individual, the learning situation into which she enters, and a number of other factors.

Despite these variances, this project contends that while positive, gaining new literacies never happens easily, and for Appalachian women in particular, the process often results in the constant negotiation of self-identity. In some instances, such negotiation opens a space for creative expression through literate practices that helps bridge the gap between the learner and her home community, while in other cases it allows learners to communicate the vexing nature of literacy acquisition to audiences who might not otherwise consider how new literacies can and do affect mountain women.

In recent years several literacy studies have focused on Appalachia, yielding important ethnographic data about the effects of literacy on identity.[1] While findings from each study varied, one constant remained: many Appalachian participants expressed a fear of "getting above their raisings," a phrase characterized by alienation from family and home culture as a result of literacy attainment, formal education, or a return to school. In the above-mentioned keynote address, for example, Lee Smith says, "We were all brought up not to 'get above our raising.' How many times have you heard this? So the guilt involved when we seem to have done it is simply immense" (2008, 315).

Similarly, in Katherine Kelleher Sohn's work, participants freely discussed the many advantages literacy and formal education provide, but they were also clear in asserting that those advantages came at a price—once participants became aware that their way of speaking, acting, and thinking was sometimes at odds with that of mainstream society, they also faced dilemmas about their own identity. Interestingly, once participants in Sohn's study completed college, none elaborated on their past fears of getting above their raising, despite the fact that their pursuit of a postsecondary education drastically altered some of the women's personal lives, even ending one woman's marriage in divorce. Sohn makes clear, however, that these alterations were not necessarily negative. One recently divorced interviewee (Sarah) tells Sohn, "With college, I could say, 'I'm a person too. I don't have to take this nonsense from my husband.' Primarily, I feel that college contributed to my sense of independence and financial security, which in turn threatened my husband and had a direct effect on the divorce" (2006, 131–32). As this comment illustrates, the results of literacy attainment are highly individualistic and complex in nature, yet despite the personal freedom this woman experiences, it seems odd that none of the interviewees comment on their previous fears of losing their common sense or of sounding "citified" as consequences of their educations (24, 35).

As explained in greater detail in the following chapter, one primary reason Appalachians remain reluctant to discuss the loss sometimes associated with literacy attainment is because doing so would only further bolster pervasive stereotypes that cast the region as illiterate, notions residents understandably want to avoid. As linguistic anthropologist Anita Puckett explains in her article about gender and literacy in an Appalachian eastern Kentucky community, many mountain residents "are hesitant to risk an affront to their public image or name" (1992, 143).

Conversely, as this project posits, characters created by Appalachian authors enjoy far more agency in exploring the identity conflicts associated with literacy attainment than do "real-life" learners. By discussing the obvious merits and the less frequently recognized pitfalls of literacy acquisition, this study analyzes the ways mountain writers depict the negotiation that takes place as Appalachian women learn to juggle entrance into disparate worlds via literate practices. In the following chapters I analyze this negotiation in works by Harriette Simpson Arnow, Linda Scott DeRosier, Denise Giardina, and Lee Smith. As the authors and characters in this study illustrate, that negotiation generally achieves two things: First, it places the learner in a liminal space, what Lee Smith calls the state of "an exile" (2007), which can allow for a negotiation between multiple discursive worlds that might not otherwise be possible. Second, such negotiation provides an opportunity for authors to creatively chronicle the dilemmas associated with literacy, ultimately granting insights that add to what we already know about Appalachian literacies from ethnographic research.

What both real-life learners in Appalachia and fictional characters in Appalachian literature must contend with, however, is the notion of exceptionalism. As scholars like Henry Shapiro, Allen Batteau, and others have convincingly argued, in many ways the notion of Appalachia as a place apart often functions as more of a social construct than reality, one begun by late nineteenth-century Local Color writers including but not limited to Mary Noailles Murfree, James Lane Allen, and John Fox Jr., as well as turn-of-the-century anthropologists and missionaries.[2]

In *Appalachia in the Making: The Mountain South in the Nineteenth Century*, for example, scholars Mary Beth Pudup, Dwight Billings, and Altina Waller contend that none of the essays in their collection "[claim] that the patterns described were necessarily unique to the highland South or general to the whole mountain region," and instead they "seek to place the study of Appalachia within the wider compass of comparative regional histories of the United States through which common themes of American history are nuanced by geographical difference" (1995, 3). Likewise, people around the world—certainly not just those in Appalachia—can and oftentimes do experience the kind of identity conflicts that new literacies introduce and that this study explores. And yet this phenomenon is, in fact, different for Appalachian people not because they are exceptional, but rather because Appalachians are well aware that much of the rest of America conceives of them as such.[3]

As discussed in the following chapter, during the last century Appalachia has become a national repository for many cultural concerns, most notably for this project, illiteracy. Consequently, when an Appalachian person, and especially an Appalachian woman, experiences personal conflict directly resulting from the acquisition of a new literacy, the urge not to discuss that conflict is strong, since doing so would only further bolster the notion of exceptionalism that most any Appalachian would prefer not to support. In other words, the misguided notion of exceptionalism in some ways makes these Appalachian learners exceptional in their reactions to it. As also discussed later in the project, Appalachian women often find that while certain literate activities are sanctioned by their communities, those that threaten established gender norms (typically ones that privilege male superiority) are not well accepted, thus heightening an already troublesome conflict introduced by new literacies. While the dilemmas introduced by new literacies warrant careful scholarly attention wherever and to whomever they occur, considering how these conflicts play out for Appalachian women tells us not only about their individual trials, but also about how America still conceives of the Appalachian region, how Appalachians react to that conception, and how Appalachian writers work to establish Appalachia as a literate place by empowering their female characters with new literacies that sometimes result in painful consequences.

Defining Literacy and Literacies

On the surface, literacy seems like a fairly simple concept to explain. If asked, most Americans would respond that literacy means the ability to read and write. But upon a more careful inspection, notions about what literacy means—and what qualifies an individual as literate—begin to break down. In the 1970s literacy theorists began this discussion, and since then many more literacy scholars have continued working toward a definition of this culturally and politically loaded term. In the 1970s Walter Ong, Jack Goody, Ian Watt, Eric Havelock, and other strong-text theorists explained literacy as an autonomous skill set that individuals use to decode meaning from printed text and inscribe meaning onto paper through writing. In the 1980s and 1990s, a body of literacy scholarship emerged that became known as New Literacy Studies (NLS). NLS scholars like Shirley Brice Heath, James Paul Gee, and Brian Street began a trend in which literacy researchers considered the social context surrounding literacy acquisition, a significant contribution to the strong-text theories of the previous decade. The effects of family, culture, and community on learners became primary sites of investigation, and a careful focus on localized literacy narratives by scholars like Deborah Brandt offered more concrete ways for discussing how a person gains the complex thing we call literacy.

In this study I rely most heavily on the assertions of one NLS scholar in particular: James Paul Gee. In *Social Linguistics and Literacies: Ideology in Discourses*, Gee proposes a definition of literacy that takes a person's discourse community membership into account. He first explains that "Discourses are ways of being in the world, or forms of life which integrate words, acts, values, beliefs, attitudes, and social identities, as well as gestures, glances, body positions, and clothes. A Discourse is a sort of identity kit which comes complete with the appropriate costume and instructions on how to act, talk, and often write, so as to take on a particular social role that others will recognize" (1996, 127).

Gee explains that primary discourses are those that individuals are born into, consequently learning the language and social practices of their family and home community. Once individuals move outside this realm, they necessarily enter into secondary discourses, and Gee contends that "any socially useful definition of literacy must be couched in terms of these notions of primary and secondary Discourse. Thus, [he defines] literacy as *mastery of a secondary Discourse*" (1996, 143 [italics in original]). In many (if not most) cases, this transition from primary to secondary discourse involves textual literacy, but not always. This is a crucial distinction to recognize when considering the characters and authors I discuss in this project, because it means that when authors or characters leave their mountain communities and learn new ways of being that are sometimes at odds with those established at home, they have gained a new literacy. Reading and writing are often intimately involved in this process, but so too are the transitions between discourse communities that Gee identifies.

Equally important to this project is the notion that literacy is not singular: individuals acquire multiple literacies throughout a lifetime, some of which challenge long-held identity markers of regional and cultural heritage. Gee is not alone in insisting that "literacy is always plural" (1996, 143); in a recent collection of essays about literacy, Victoria Purcell-Gates also posits that "*literacy* is now pluralized to *literacies*" (2007, 2 [italics in original]); and James Collins and Richard Blot distinguish between the notion of literacy and literacies by explaining that literacies are "relativist, sociocultural . . . intrinsically diverse [and] historically and culturally variable" (2003, 4). They also posit that "it seems that there is no single literacy, instead a multiplicity of practices and values get the same label. Indeed, the label 'literacy' can be and is extended to areas that have no or little connection to text, or at least to processes of decoding entextualized information" (3).

Similarly, the approach established by Kim Donehower, Charlotte Hogg, and Eileen E. Schell provides a useful working definition of *literacy* for this study. In their work on rural literacies, they describe literacy as "the skills and practices needed to gain knowledge, evaluate and interpret that knowledge, and apply knowledge to accomplish particular goals" (2007, 4). But not all literacy scholars agree that definitions of literacy should extend beyond reading and writing. Researcher David Vincent, for example, argues that the word *literacy* "is daily extending its application," that "literacy has become too promiscuous," and that "in both popular and learned discourse the term is attached to a proliferating body of conditions and activities" (2003, 341). Vincent goes on to admonish that "scholars of written communication should be especially alert to the meaning of words, and the indiscriminate application of the term threatens to empty it of any precise meaning," wryly commenting that "for accuracy, scholars of written communication perhaps should now refer to 'literacy literacy' to describe their field of study" (342–43). In a time when "literacy" seems to apply to all manner of skills, from information literacy to financial literacy to computer literacy to emotional literacy, Vincent has a point. Even so, this study contends that the careful application of the term to discourse transitions precipitated by new literacies—whether technical, social, or cultural—strengthens meaningful definitions of the term, especially when applied to Appalachians, a group of people so long beleaguered by assumptions of illiteracy.

For the Appalachian women analyzed in the following chapters, the skills and practices they use to gain knowledge—that is, new literacies—simultaneously empower and threaten the relationships they have with their home communities. While these theoretical discussions about the meaning of literacy are helpful, and indeed necessary, concrete examples of learning processes also illustrate nuances of literacy that often escape abstract discussions about such a complex term. To address this fact, in the following chapter I consider how one historical account of adult literacy schooling in Western North Carolina can help define what literacy meant in the earlier part of the twentieth century for both educators and students, as well as what it means now in contemporary discussions about literacy in literature.

Contextualizing Appalachian Women's Literacies

Native American and Appalachian Literacies

To best understand the problems that literacy and continued education can introduce into the lives of Appalachian women, it is helpful to first consider how literacy functions for other marginalized groups. A brief look at the history of Native American[4] boarding schools provides an extreme example of literacy-induced alienation from one's home community. Numerous scholars have explored the effects of Native American boarding schools on Indian identity, and it is not my purpose to restate what many scholars have already written; yet I do believe that considering the Native American boarding school example alongside accounts of Appalachian literacy acquisition allows us to discern striking similarities that span both space and time, connections that further illuminate what literacy can mean for groups who operate, or are perceived to operate, outside the hegemonic norm.[5]

As historian David Wallace Adams explains, the Indian boarding school story began in 1875, when Lt. Richard Henry Pratt was made responsible for transporting seventy-two Native American prisoners of war from Fort Sill, Indian Territory, in present-day Oklahoma to Fort Marion, in St. Augustine, Florida (1995, 36). The prisoners "were a mixed lot, composed of thirty-four Cheyenne, two Arapaho, twenty-seven Kiowa, nine Comanche, and one Caddo" (36–37). Once Pratt moved the prisoners to Florida, he experimented with whether he could make the Indians "civilized," and he went about this process by requiring structured schooling in the morning and vocational training in the afternoon. Apparently it mattered little to Pratt that his civilization process targeted Native Americans from distinct tribes with their own linguistic, social, and cultural practices; his primary goal was to wipe away the learners' first heritage and replace it with one that he believed superior. Not surprisingly, English literacy skills provided the most direct route to such civilization.

Prisoners followed the academic and vocational regimen while they were held captive, and when they were released three years later in 1878, twenty-two of the men stated that they wanted to pursue further education (Adams 1995, 44). Pratt's search for a school to accept the Indians was not an easy one, especially since Custer's Last Stand at Little Big Horn had occurred just two years previously. Pratt eventually located a school that would accept the group: the Hampton Normal Institute, founded in 1868 by Samuel Chapman Armstrong to educate newly freed African Americans during Reconstruction. It should be noted that Armstrong's parents were missionaries, a thread that links the literacy stories of many marginalized groups along a common trajectory. Native Americans, African Americans, many immigrant groups, and Appalachians were the object of great attention from generally well-intentioned missionary groups eager to teach literacies that encouraged homogenization and a rejection of home culture, assuming that home culture was judged deviant.

Such submission was necessary for the proper Americanization many religious institutions promoted in the late 1800s and throughout the twentieth century. Coincidentally, the eventual promoter of the controversial "cast your bucket" methodology, Booker T. Washington, served as the Indian dormitory supervisor (Adams 1995, 252), and while African American and Native American students learned alongside one another without major dispute, funding was eventually pulled from Native American students because funders feared a commingling of the races, even though interracial dating was not allowed (326–28).

Pratt received funding to start his own school, and he founded what was soon to become the infamous Carlisle Indian Industrial School in Pennsylvania. As Adams explains, Pratt favored the "Kill the Indian in him and save the man" mantra, a principle that proved detrimental to many students' sense of Indian identity (1995, 52). Yet, as with the acquisition of any new literacy, the process was not wholly negative, and as Native American scholar Ernest Stromberg points out, the acquisition of English literacy enabled native writers like Francis La Flesche and Zitkala-Ša (Gertrude Simmons Bonnin) "to achieve a great deal of success in the terms of the dominant culture" (2006, 98). Pratt and administrators at other boarding schools were criticized for their recruitment and treatment of students, which often involved persuading them away from their home reservations with enticing stories of the abundant fruit and bounty in the East, shuttling them like so many cattle on an east-bound train, systematically cutting their hair, assigning them new English names (some as ridiculous as Rip Van Winkle) (Adams 1995, 237), and more often than not subjecting them to living conditions that encouraged the spread of communicable diseases including tuberculosis, influenza, and trachoma.

Yet despite the sometimes deplorable situations in which Indian students found themselves, many successfully assimilated and returned home with positive reports about their experiences. But seldom were student accounts so simple. Memoirs by Zitkala-Ša and Polingaysi Qoyawayma provide narratives that clearly reflect the complex nature of literacy acquisition, as well as the identity consequences that ensued. A brief consideration of their stories helps better situate the Appalachian authors that I discuss at length later in this project, especially when thinking about how these writers portray their literacy-initiated dilemmas in creative form.

Zitkala-Ša

Dakota Sioux Zitkala-Ša was born in 1876 and received her formal education from several different day and boarding schools, as well as a college.[6] For many proponents of Indian boarding school education, Zitkala-Ša was the model success story. She was a successful student, she won writing and oratory prizes in college, and she even taught at the Carlisle Indian Industrial School for eighteen months (Spack 2002, 145). In 1921 she published *American Indian Stories*, a collection of her previous work that reveals mixed feelings about her educational experiences, making clear that while valuable, those experiences distanced her from a cherished home and culture. What make her stories worth discussing here are the common threads that link her experiences to the feelings and emotions experienced by Appalachian authors and characters considered in this project. In both cases learners are enthralled with the benefits of literacy but also simultaneously wary of its power to distance learners from their home culture.

In *American Indian Stories* Zitkala-Ša remembers that missionaries who came to her reservation to recruit boarding school pupils persuaded potential students with tales of a faraway land where, after enjoying an exciting trip aboard an "iron horse," Indian children could pick apples from the trees (1921, 42). In the same way that Lee Smith's missionary character, Gertrude Torrington, regales Ivy Rowe, protagonist of *Fair and Tender Ladies*, with stories of big-city life, the missionaries who visit Zitkala-Ša's reservation paint such a beautiful picture of life away from the reservation that like many of the other Indian children, Zitkala-Ša begs her mother to go. Her mother grudgingly agrees, but once Zitkala-Ša is aboard the train headed eastward she writes, "When I saw the lonely figure of my mother vanish in the distance, a sense of regret settled heavily upon me. I felt suddenly weak, as if I might fall limp to the ground" (44–45). The regret that Zitkala-Ša mentions here occurs repeatedly in both real-life and fictional literacy narratives. The distancing between parent and child, particularly between mother and daughter, caused by further education is a trope that knows no cultural boundaries, though those from marginalized groups, like Native Americans and Appalachians, experience it more frequently and more intensely.

The focus of this project's third chapter, Linda Scott DeRosier, demonstrates a strong connection to the grief and regret Zitkala-Ša experiences upon leaving her home to attend school. As discussed at length in that chapter, DeRosier's extended educational experiences strain the relationship she has with her mother, and both Zitkala-Ša and DeRosier remake their identities in one of the most powerful exertions of self-identity possible: they both change their names. In his foreword to *American Indian Stories*, Dexter Fisher explains that Zitkala-Ša was first named Gertrude Simmons, carrying the surname of her half brother. She identified herself as Gertrude Simmons until her sister-in-law became angry with her "because [she] insisted upon getting an education" and had "deserted home," so she changed her name to Zitkala-Ša, a Lakota name that means "Red Bird" (Zitkala-Ša 1921, x).

Similarly, well-known Dakota Indian Luther Standing Bear chose Luther as his first name only because he was forced to do so as a student at Carlisle. In his memoir he recalls that students had to choose from a list of English names written on the chalkboard, and "when [his] turn came, [he] took the pointer and acted as if [he] were about to touch an enemy" (1928, 137). The effects of name changing on an individual's identity are myriad and complex, and in chapter 3 I explore a similar decision by Linda Scott DeRosier when she morphs from Linda Sue Preston to Lee Preston to Lee Scott to Linda Scott to Linda Scott DeRosier.

All of these narratives share the fact that although gaining new literacies was painful for each of these learners, it also allowed them to exert their cultural heritage in a way that would not have been possible without formal education; they were able to share their experiences with a larger audience because they learned new discursive practices in which they could communicate more broadly.

As literary scholar Amelia Katanski points out, "Even after [Zitkala-Ša's] supposed indoctrination into Western culture through her schooling, she maintains an identity in her repertoire that she associates with her Indianness, and she uses the literacy in English that she gained in the school to present this Sioux identity to the world," reflecting what Katanski aptly calls the "situational self" (2007, 114). In the same way that Katanski proposes to analyze "how American Indian boarding school students developed complex self-definitions and turned their ability to read and write in English to their own uses despite a curriculum that made English literacy the marker of lost tribal culture and achievement of 'civilization'" (6), this study seeks to explore how the perilous nature of literacy acquisition—an acquisition that can fracture homes, relationships, and even communities—also simultaneously empowers the owners of that literacy to bear witness to the cultural landscape from which they come.

A heavy focus on gender also permeates both Native American and Appalachian literacy narratives, and in the case of Native American narratives, we find a marked emphasis on education for women. Upon close inspection it becomes clear that such emphasis was calculated and purposeful: literate mothers presumably made better mothers, who would in turn raise better children and, consequently, children who resembled American citizens, since Native Americans were not granted such citizenship until the Indian Citizenship Act (or Snyder Act) of 1924. As discussed in more detail in the following chapter, literacy and American nationalism are so deeply entangled that it is impossible to explore one without considering the other. Likewise, gender so closely informs this project's study of literacy acquisition and authors' portrayal of it that considering how it functioned in Indian boarding schools is a worthwhile and even necessary endeavor.

In the January 17, 1890, issue of *Indian Helper*, the periodical published by the Carlisle Indian Industrial School, Thomas Morgan was quoted in a piece titled "Which Should Have the Best Chance for Education: Indian Boys or Girls?" He concluded that girls should receive the best chance for education, saying, "I would give it to the GIRLS because they need it the most. They make the home and train the children. Why are white children so happy? It is because the white women are educated. If we educate the Indian women to make happy homes, to train their children to industry and thrift, we redeem the Indian race through them."

In *Managing Literacy, Mothering America*, literacy scholar Sarah Robbins explores a similar phenomenon in what she calls the "domestic literacy narrative" (2004), and as mentioned previously, linguistic anthropologist Anita Puckett explores how gender affects literacy in a rural eastern Kentucky community. What Morgan encourages and what Robbins and Puckett discover is that with marginalized groups, literate activity is often more closely associated with women than it is with men, and in Puckett's study, participants even claim that it is "more natural" (1992, 139) for a woman to engage in literate activity than a man. Thus logic would follow that these women experience more dilemmas about their own identity as a result of acquiring literacies, abilities their community initially assumed were "natural."

Polingaysi Qoyawayma

Polingaysi Qoyawayma (Elizabeth Q. White) was a Hopi woman who was born in 1892, sixteen years after Zitkala-Ša. Qoyawayma's work does not receive the same critical attention that Zitkala-Ša's does in Native American studies, but Qoyawayma's memoir echoes many of the same dilemmas Zitkala-Ša and other students of Indian boarding schools wrote about and, by extension, the same dilemmas that comprise the works by mountain authors I consider in this study. What distinguishes Qoyawayma's account of education is that in addition to focusing on the sadness of losing ties with her home community, she carefully chronicles the difficulties she faced when reentering her community, mostly because after her time at the Sherman Institute, she judged her home culture as inferior.

In her memoir she talks about herself in third person, explaining to Vada F. Carlson, who recorded Qoyawayma's story, that "she almost dreaded the day when her four years at Sherman would come to a close and she would return to her home. She was certain she would not like it. She had outgrown village life" (1964, 64). And she later recalls that "this life was not for her. She would never again be happy in the old pattern. She had gone too far along the path of the white man," and she "became almost a stranger within her own home" (69, 74). At one point she even chastises her parents for eating their meals on the floor and not sleeping in beds (69). While a note of sadness colors Qoyawayma's memoir, her frustration with her home culture's insistence on maintaining Hopi traditions appears to outweigh any sorrow she feels upon reentry.

As with some of the mountain women discussed in this project, once Qoyawayma gains new literacies and returns to her community, the domestic notion of "home" emerges as a highly contested site of debate, especially concerning previously accepted ideas about a woman's place. Her mother is horrified to learn that upon returning to the village, Qoyawayma has no immediate plans to marry or bear children. As Qoyawayna explains when she tells her story in third-person narration, "She was not yet willing to become a living seed pod for her Hopi people. She loved children, but was not ready to assume the role of mother," going on to assert that "for no man ... would she grind corn on her knees" (1964, 70). Equally shocking to her family, Qoyawayma expresses interest in building her own house, which she eventually does, to the astonishment of most everyone around her.

While not all the authors and characters in this project rebel against communal gender norms as a result of literacy acquisition, several of them do. In *The Dollmaker* Harriette Simpson Arnow sends a powerful rhetorical message to readers, enjoining them to avoid the rigidity of limiting gender binaries. And like Qoyawayma, Linda Scott DeRosier learns to resist the restraints bound up with socially constructed notions of gender. Both women ultimately become teachers, Qoyawayma an educator in Indian schools, and DeRosier a professor of psychology at various universities and colleges, most recently Rocky Mountain College in Billings, Montana. Likewise, Denise Giardina's protagonist uses her literate prowess to write about and for the people of her community, and Lee Smith's main female characters gradually gain empowerment through a sometimes painful distancing from the homes they love.

Like the majority of authors and characters discussed in the following chapters, both Zitkala-Ša and Qoyawayma use the new literacies they have gained to pay homage to the culture from which those literacies ultimately distanced them. In Qoyawayma's case, she presages the theories espoused decades later by literacy theorist Paulo Freire in *Pedagogy of the Oppressed*. Instead of teaching her Hopi students stories from white culture to which Hopi children could not relate, she insists on drawing from common Hopi stories and legends. Such materials privilege a Hopi way of life and also teach her students skills that will benefit them both inside and outside the village.

Yet another connection between Appalachian and Native American accounts of literacy exists when we consider how unlikely it was that students at Indian boarding schools were honest when chronicling their experiences, at least with boarding school administrators. Doing so would have only undermined their chances for further success while at the school, and Katanski points out that "the educators ignored or were unaware of much of the actual students' responses to their experiences" (2007, 41). Katanski goes on to assert that "students learned to parrot the views of the teachers in order to be successful, in order to survive, even if those views denied the students' own experiences and caused them to appear to support the obliteration of their own cultural heritage" (88). The mountain subjects of ethnographic researchers often find themselves in a similar situation, though theirs is not a case of survival, at least not in the literal sense. Instead, many Appalachian people who discuss their learning processes with literacy researchers freely narrate the benefits associated with learning while skimming over or altogether ignoring the difficulties associated with academic endeavors.

In the foreword to *No Turning Back*, Qoyawayma expresses the same sentiment almost verbatim when she writes, "Hopi people are exceedingly sensitive to ridicule, and I am no exception to this rule. It has been a ball and chain, preventing me from expressing myself, especially along the line of my painful experiences as a pioneer in Indian education, both as a student and a teacher" (1964). Likewise, for mountain residents talking at length about how it felt to leave home, to learn new things, and to return changed—sometimes to the point of being unable to function within the limits of acceptable community behavior—would not send the message that mountain residents want to communicate.

As already briefly mentioned and discussed further in the following chapter, during the late 1800s and early 1900s the notion of Appalachia as a place apart began to take root in the American conscience; portrayals of rugged, individualistic, American mountaineers were also countered with ugly depictions of ignorant, toothless, lawless, illiterate moonshiners with a penchant for incestuous trysts with their cousins. In the same way that discussing the negatives associated with learning would only damage the delicate relationship Indian students maintained with boarding school teachers and administrators, for mountain residents, talking about the perils of literacy acquisition with literacy researchers would only provide more fodder for already exaggerated portraits of an illiterate Appalachia.

African American Literacies, Appalachian Literacies, and Questions of Ethnicity

If stories from Native American boarding schools provide the most startling account of literacy-initiated loss, then a brief consideration of African American literacies reveals literacy narratives of marginalized peoples couched in drastically different historical and critical terms. Unlike the Native American boarding school example, where students were seen as the focus of regulated educational uplift supported by the United States government, for African Americans literacy was seen as something forbidden that was worth fighting for, the fundamental building block for freedom and perhaps equality.

When abolitionists like William Lloyd Garrison, Wendell Phillips, Lydia Maria Child, and authors like Harriet Beecher Stowe began promoting slave narratives and literature in the mid-nineteenth century, with it they also promoted textual literacy skills for African Americans, both enslaved and free. Anyone remotely familiar with Southern history knows that teaching a slave to read and write in the South was punishable by law, and many masters considered textually literate slaves a serious threat to plantation security.

In his well-known account of slavery, Frederick Douglass provides a moving account of the effect literacy had in terms of his ability to envision life as a free man, proclaiming that because his mistress (Mrs. Auld) had taught him the alphabet, she had given him the inch, and "no precaution could prevent [him] from taking the ell" (1960, 64). This phrasing resonates with readers because he chooses these words in response to Mr. Auld's earlier abominably racist comment that "if you give a nigger an inch, he will take an ell" (58). Moreover, African Americans who were literate were also capable of showcasing their reasoning and logic skills in written form, a fundamental tactic in dismantling misguided Enlightenment beliefs based on models of scientific racism.

Similar spotlights on literacy dominate the majority of slave narratives from this time period, prompting literary critic James Olney to assert that literacy, identity, and freedom are "the omnipresent thematic trio of most important slave narratives" (1984, 55). Yet, as literary scholar Katherine Clay Bassard (1992) notes, this supposed literacy-initiated freedom was not equally available to slave women, even when those women were textually literate. Certainly Harriet Jacobs presents literacy as one of the most clever, subversive vehicles to her freedom in *Incidents in the Life of a Slave Girl* (2000). She explains that one of the ways she was able to hide in her grandmother's garrison for seven years, away from her promiscuous master, was through her ability to read and write: she would write her master letters, send them with someone northward, and have them mailed to her master from a northern destination. This strategy led him to believe that she was miles away, when in fact she was hiding in close proximity. But Bassard also asserts that women like Jacobs were "keenly aware of the limits of literacy-as-freedom ideology," and "they express everything from mild tension to outright suspicion of the power of the Written Word to provide freedom, economic security, and a restructuring of social formations of power" (1992, 120).

Similarly, even though researchers like Anita Puckett (1992) found that in some mountain communities residents thought it more "natural" for women to engage in literate practices than men, Appalachian women know that engaging in those practices can be viewed as problematic by members of their home communities, especially when the acquisition of new literacies results in behavior deemed aberrant by community gender standards.

But like the mountain authors discussed in this project, African American women also rely on the empowerments provided by new literacies to counter any losses they might experience. When writing about the ways in which literacy emboldened African American women to enact social change, scholar Jacqueline Jones Royster contends that "African American women writers use the power of language to resist simplification, stereotyping, and other disempowering effects. They use language to resist value systems that would render their knowledge and experiences irrelevant and immaterial, or that would erase the specificity of their material conditions" (2000, 72). For the purposes of this study we could replace "African American" with "Appalachian" in this quote, because the mountain writers in this study use their literacies to the same effect. To take Royster's point even further, we should also remember that for the Native American, African American, and Appalachian cases discussed thus far, the power of language that Royster identifies is almost always accompanied by dilemmas about identity, community affiliation, and allegiance to home.

Moreover, we must keep an obvious fact in mind: Native Americans and African Americans can also be Appalachian. The very necessity of discussing this topic points to the ways in which whiteness and Appalachia are deeply embedded in the national mind-set; many Americans have long been invested in the myth of a white Appalachia. In 1914, for example, geographer Ellen Churchill Semple wrote that mountaineers were thought to be "the purest Anglo-Saxon stock in all the United States" (1995, 150), a reassuring racial heritage when scores of European immigrants were entering the country in record numbers and many Americans feared national racial degradation.

Literary critic Chris Green posits that the American Missionary Association (AMA) played a major role in creating the notion of a white Appalachia. In *The Social Life of Poetry: Race, Appalachia, and Radical Modernism*, Green discusses the creation of the "mountain white" category, explaining that "mountain whites were understood to be equivalent to . . . other minorities via their exclusion from and exploitation by the forces of American and international capital and government" (2009, 18). His research also directs readers' attention to the October 1883 issue of *The American Missionary*. In a report on the Bureau of Woman's Work, Miss D. E. Emerson, the secretary responsible for reporting such activity, wrote that at the upcoming annual AMA meeting a special Woman's Meeting would be held where reports would be given on the missionary work with the Chinese of the Pacific Coast, the Native Americans at the Santee School in Nebraska, and the mountain whites in Kentucky (310). In this instance and in many more that would follow, Appalachian people were categorized and viewed as a separate ethnicity, an exceptional population to which the AMA could minister. But by referring to mountain residents as "mountain whites," the AMA and others created a construction of race that blatantly ignored the first residents of Appalachia—Cherokee Indians—and also obfuscated the presence of African Americans.

Appalachian historian John Alexander Williams points out that in 1860 there "was only one county in Appalachia with no slaves."[7] The notion of a homogeneously white Appalachia also overlooked the varied groups of immigrants who came to coal fields in central Appalachia in the early twentieth century to find work. And yet the term "mountain white" served the AMA well, allowing them to focus on uplifting a population of "pure Anglo

Saxons" who were conceived of as different from other white Americans. In some ways it seems conceivable to say that Appalachians were different, given the geographic isolation of many mountain communities, but in recent years scholars like David Hsiung (1997) have shown that Appalachia was far more connected with the greater United States than previously believed.

For the purposes of this study, it is crucial to consider how ideas of Appalachian ethnicity affect our perceptions of Appalachian women's literacies and authors' portrayal of it. Perhaps most importantly, we must recognize the fact that regardless of the racial designation of a mountain native, Appalachians are still often viewed as a separate ethnicity by non-Appalachian Americans and are thus subject to the same prejudices directed toward ethnically marginalized peoples. In the forward to Sohn's (2006) *Whistlin' and Crowin' Women of Appalachia: Literacy Practices Since College*, scholar Victor Villanueva writes that "Appalachian is a color, even if not recognized as such. . . . There's a racialization to Appalachia, something more than a class reference, something akin to 'ethnicity'" (xiv–xv). It is this sort of ethnic designation that so closely links the literacy narratives of Appalachian people with other marginalized groups, including Native Americans and African Americans.

Figuring Social Class

In the same way that the acquisition of new literacies proves both empowering and problematic for groups marginalized by race and ethnicity, the same concept applies when thinking about social class, which never functions separately from race or gender. As with the other case studies already discussed, numerous scholars have written about how social class affects learning; writers including bell hooks (2000), Mike Rose (1989), and Richard Rodriguez have emphasized gains and losses inherent in the educational process, and in Rodriguez's highly criticized autobiography, *Hunger of Memory*, he writes that he eventually "accepted the fact that education exacted a great price for its equally great benefits" (1983, 160).

Scholars who specialize in Working Class Studies have also written much about the tensions that emerge between children and parents when children from working-class backgrounds acquire postsecondary education and work in academia.[8] In the introduction to *This Fine Place So Far from Home: Voices of Academics from the Working Class*, for example, Carolyn Leste Law writes, "In my trajectory from working-class family of origin to the threshold of middle-class professional status, I have suffered a loss my present context doesn't even recognize as a loss; my education *has* destroyed something even while it has been re-creating me in its own image" (Dews and Law 1995, 1).

Virtually all of the authors and characters in this study who acquire new literacies face a similar dilemma: the Nevels children in *The Dollmaker* must either forsake their Appalachian identity or reject the new literacies offered by Detroit; Linda Scott DeRosier constantly monitors herself both in the academy and at home; in Giardina's *The Unquiet Earth* frequent reading ironically results in the novel's protagonist (Jackie) initially discounting and undervaluing the culture from which she comes; and in Lee Smith's *Fair and Tender Ladies* Ivy Rowe feels ashamed of her grandmother when she unexpectedly encounters her in town. The Appalachian women considered in this study embody a multiplicity of identities, identities that operate under a triple burden of ethnicity (Appalachian), gender (female), and class (working class). Certainly there are plenty of Appalachian residents who are middle- to upper-class, but those are not the stories represented by the authors considered in this project, with the possible exception of DeRosier when she becomes a professor.

Differentiating Appalachian Women's Literacies

Although many connections between Appalachian residents and other marginalized groups exist, this book contends that the particular case of Appalachian women's literacies deserves special attention. While the comparisons just established make clear that the Appalachian example is in many ways not unique, the long-held idea of Appalachia as an illiterate region—and residents' keen awareness of that label—sets Appalachian women's literacies apart as something worth exploring on their own. A critical analysis of this loss lies at the heart of this study, and it is one that is seldom acknowledged by educators and researchers for various reasons which I explore in the following chapter.

As already discussed, although some mountain communities consider it more "natural" for women to develop literate skills, as literacy scholar Sara Webb-Sunderhaus points out, "literacy, particularly academic literacy, become[s] a dangerous force, one that [can] distance students from family members and loved ones" (2007, 15). Similarly, the women in Sohn's study were afraid that if they became too educated they may be "severed from their families," and one woman's in-laws did not support her college aspirations because "they felt that [she] should be home doing cooking, cleaning, and caring for the children" (2006, 78, 104). As illustrated by these examples, domesticity and the acquisition of new literacies can function in opposition to one another, particularly when the pursuit of new literacies impedes the performance of duties deemed appropriate by societal gender standards. Yet at the same time, new literacies empower these women—both fictional and real—to communicate the losses embodied in that empowerment to a larger audience. As Lee Smith speculates, "Perhaps exile can be a crucible of creativity and change, as well as art" (2008, 316).

Negotiating a Perilous Empowerment

CHAPTER 1

Appalachia on Our Pages: Situating Appalachian Literacy and Literary Analysis

Remembering Illiterate Depictions, Considering the Consequences

Since the beginning of the twentieth century, the Appalachian region has been associated with illiteracy, and the longevity of that association still influences contemporary mountain authors. In an interview published in *Appalachian Journal*, for example, Appalachian writer Ron Rash discusses the thematic emphasis on education in his novel *The World Made Straight*, explaining that "education's the way you get out. Any minority culture knows that" (Bjerre 2007, 220). His deceptively simple statement encapsulates much about what lies at the heart of this project; for those doing the "getting out" that Rash references, education oftentimes results in a loss of acceptance within one's home community. By recognizing Appalachian people as a minority culture, Rash highlights differences between people of the mountain South and other Americans that seem obvious to most Appalachians but perhaps not to non-Appalachians. Education can bring these differences to the forefront, resulting in difficult identity decisions on the part of the educated. Of course literacy—most commonly defined as the ability to read and write, though as this project works to illustrate, it is never that simple—undergirds the kind of education Rash references, and he notes that with "Appalachia in particular, there are pervasive stereotypes about no one being able to read, no one having an education, and that's obviously not true" (220–21).

Certainly illiteracy exists in some parts of Appalachia (Rash even refers to his paternal grandfather who could not read or write), but for a number of historical and political reasons discussed later in this chapter, many Americans regard Appalachia as the most illiterate region in America. Rash even recalls an instance when a non-Appalachian asked him whether his family read his writing, and he reflects that "the assumption was that they couldn't read, or even if they could, that they would not be remotely interested in it. And that struck me as remarkable, particularly from someone who would probably have considered himself very liberal and open-minded. I was kind of stunned, really, that someone would make that kind of broad assumption" (Bjerre 2007, 221). These types of judgments are commonplace among many Americans, and they produce a host of beliefs that influence the way the rest of the nation conceives of Appalachia, as well as the ways in which Appalachian people conceive of themselves.

Literary representations of Appalachia date back to the early part of the twentieth century, when Local Color writers, missionaries, and education officials were deeply invested in securing the image of Appalachia as a fixed entity, one to be kept in its place as a politically useful repository of social aid. Many education officials and missionary organizations deemed earlier reform efforts in the Deep South unsuccessful and hoped for less racial tension in the Appalachian mountains. While the AMA cast Appalachia as an area replete with mountain whites in need of social aid, Local Color writers like Mary Noailles Murfree and John Fox Jr. exoticized the region and its inhabitants through the stories they published. Oft-cited Appalachian scholar Henry Shapiro argues that such writing helped secure "the otherness of the southern mountain region . . . as fact in the American consciousness" (1978, 18).

As with other travel writing commonly read during that time, the vast majority of stories written about Appalachian people during the late 1800s and early 1900s characterized mountaineers as fundamentally different from other Americans, while virtually no fictionalized accounts by native Appalachians were published or read on a large scale. As geographer Stephen Hanna notes, there were a few exceptions to this rule, including Samuel Johnson's 1908 "Life in the Kentucky Mountains, by a Mountaineer," but such pieces were uncommon and rarely reached a wide audience.[1] Consequently, America's initial encounter with fictionalized accounts of the mountain South portrayed it as quaint, violent, and most important for this project, illiterate.

As memoirist John O'Brien explains, for readers of magazines like *Atlantic Monthly*, *Lippincott's*, and others that published Local Color writing, "contrasting an imagined Victorian world, of which [readers] believed themselves to be a part, with an imagined hillbilly world helped convince middle-class Americans that they had indeed reached the peak of Western civilization" (2001, 173). Unfortunately, many readers assumed that the stories of wild hillbillies that populated Local Color writing were true, reading "the books as journalism" while "reviewers gave them the status of sociology" (173). Shapiro even points out that "the short stories of Mary Noailles Murfree's *In the Tennessee Mountains* (1884) remained the principal text used to understand the peculiarities of mountain life" (1978, xv).[2] As such, the region seemed especially susceptible to literary mythmaking, and many of the stories about illiterate, filthy, degenerate mountaineers written to entertain actually "educated" the reading public about the assumed ways of Appalachian people.

Moreover, these stories defined a literary history for the region, one that the authors in this study steadily reshape, realign, and repute. In their considerations of regionalist writing, literary critics Judith Fetterley and Marjorie Pryse state that they "understand [regionalist writing] as the site of a dialogical critical conversation" (2003, 2), and certainly that assertion applies to the conversation in which Appalachian women writers like Arnow, DeRosier, Giardina, and Smith engage when they write in response to Local Color writing. Unlike their Local Color predecessors, the authors whose work I explore in this study seem far less concerned with establishing mountain people as the epitome of ruggedness, individualism, and American nationalism. Stephanie Foote argues that "regional writing was responsive to the nationalizing demands of the era that produced it" (2001, 13), while the authors in this study are far more concerned with establishing their own literary niche while also revising the one that predicated it.

Arnow, DeRosier, Giardina, and Smith, of course, were not the first Appalachian writers to write against the Local Color tradition of portraying Appalachia in an expected, stereotypical way. As the twentieth century progressed, Appalachian writers slowly started publishing their own work, as when in 1940 James Still published *River of Earth*, a text many scholars consider one of the most important works of Appalachian fiction. Roughly twenty years later, native Appalachian Cratis Williams wrote the first dissertation about Appalachian literature, and since then new mountain writing and criticism have continued to flourish. These writers have often focused on literacy in their writing, but women writers in particular have repeatedly depicted the consequences of literacy attainment in their stories and memoirs, signaling a persistent anxiety over literacy tropes. The authors considered in this study continually return to scenes in which characters gain new literacies that produce significant internal and external conflict.

The tradition of Otherness from which these authors work also provides an important backdrop for my purposes in revealing the identity conflicts that literacy attainment often causes for Appalachians. The notion of Appalachia began well over a century ago, and a number of scholars, including Henry Shaprio (1978), Allen Batteau (1990), and John Alexander Williams (2002), have posited varying theories about the events that led to the conception of Appalachia as markedly different from the rest of the American South. Perhaps the most ubiquitous and most often challenged idea argues that as industrialization crept its way southward during the Reconstruction years, the majority of mountainous regions in the South remained agricultural, if only because the steep hillsides and deep valleys of Appalachia did not readily lend themselves to the kind of frequent travel that characterizes industry and commerce. Reason would follow (though certainly not all Appalachian scholars, such as David Hsiung, agree on this point) that as the rest of the nation became modernized, the people living in these remote areas continued with their isolated existence, and their relative geographic seclusion stymied the kinds of economic, cultural, and intellectual advances other Americans were making. Around the turn of the century, this vein of logic—whether imagined or real—characterized most speeches and essays written to promote Appalachian spiritual and educational uplift, and mission and education groups generally portrayed mountaineers as homogeneously violent, ignorant people worthy of pity and outreach.

Politically influential individuals like Berea College president William Goodell Frost frequently described mountain people as remnants of a simpler, purer time in American society, and as such they showed great hope for the rest of the nation. In his 1899 essay titled "Our Contemporary Ancestors," Frost claims that mountaineers were "in the pioneer stage of development," and that "Appalachian America may be useful as furnishing a fixed point which enables us to measure the progress of the moving world!" (313). As scholar Tommy Thompson notes, "Frost saw the mountaineers as terribly backward and wanted to reshape them into the mold of what he considered mainstream American life" (1993, 181). Thompson explains that Frost initiated a Bible reading program in which a woman deemed appropriately qualified and educated rode through the mountains teaching "correct" Bible interpretations (181).

Frost fancied that he knew Appalachian people and what was best for them better than they could possibly know themselves, echoing the approach Lieutenant Pratt took with Native Americans when he established the Carlisle Boarding School in Pennsylvania. In the same way that Indian education officials used photographs and newspaper articles to present Native American savagery to the larger public to appeal for financial backing for their work, Frost systematically publicized Appalachians' every flaw nationwide to attract monetary and moral support for his efforts at bringing civility to mountaineers. His campaigns contributed to the permanent image of an illiterate Appalachia, and his strategically romantic portrayals of mountain people objectified them, making their illiteracy a useful deficiency that missionaries and educators could work to solve.

Similar views permeated (and still permeate) media depictions of the region, as evidenced by Dan Rather's comment in a 1989 *48 Hours* episode that despite the federal government's spending of more than three billion dollars to improve the roads leading into and out of Appalachian Kentucky in the 1960s, "like a lot of things in the hills, it didn't change much."[3] While some residents of Appalachia appear to hold the same beliefs, as when one of the Bowling children in Rory Kennedy's 1999 HBO documentary of an Eastern Kentucky family laments that he does not have running water and it "seems like it just never changes," as DeRosier points out in her writing, this hardly presents a complete picture of Appalachia. Literacy scholar Katherine Kelleher Sohn notes that "no place is monolithic" (2006, 3). As DeRosier illustrates in both *Creeker* (1999) and *Songs of Life and Grace* (2003), media images of the mountains have always favored depictions of the socially disadvantaged, oftentimes glossing over middle- and upper-class Appalachians.

A particularly revealing instance of this trend appears in Jack Weller's 1965 study, *Yesterday's People: Life in Contemporary Appalachia*. In his introduction he acknowledges that "there is a middle class as well as a professional class in the mountains," but since people in those classes are generally not a part of the stereotypical "folk culture" that he seeks to document, "one might even go so far as to say that any Appalachian person who is willing to read such a study as this hardly qualifies to be included in it" (5, 7). As a document written during the War on Poverty, contemporary readers can almost begin to understand—if not forgive—Weller's fixation on "the folk," but that fixation still lingers in contemporary representations of Appalachia.

On February 10, 2009, CBS aired a *20/20* special hosted by Diane Sawyer titled *A Hidden America: Children of the Mountains*. In it, camera crews documented the impoverished lives of several Appalachian children, repeatedly referring to the region in which they lived as Appalachia. The broadcast presented a clear image of Appalachia—a region notoriously difficult to quantify, classify, or define—as a place rife with poverty-stricken addicts. While the stories the *20/20* special captured were no doubt accurate for particular individuals, like most popular media representations of the area, it failed to mention middle- and upper-class Appalachian families (with the exception of one local coal baron), made barely any mention of urban Appalachian cities like Knoxville, Asheville, Huntington, or Birmingham, and glossed over the racial and ethnic diversity the region offers.

As John O'Brien points out, "Reporters and writers come [to Appalachia] expecting hillbilly squalor and they find it at the exclusion of everything else" (2001, 113). Yet writers like DeRosier contest those representations, and despite the prevalent belief that Appalachia never changes, the female authors considered in this study work to subvert the notion of a docile, unchanging Appalachia through their poignant depictions of identity change wrought through literacy acquisition.

In theoretical terms, Appalachia's portrayal as Other has been compared with the dominance of Western hegemony over the Orient that Edward Said sets forth in *Orientalism*, and several scholars have noted similarities between Appalachia and other colonized regions.[4] Discussing similarities between Appalachianism and Orientalism, Rodger Cunningham notes that "the exteriority of the representation is always governed by some version of the truism that if the Orient could represent itself, it would; since it cannot, the representation does the job" (1989, 21). Frost helped perpetuate this kind of mythic representation, and it had long-lasting effects for the Appalachian region and its people, especially the notion that the region teemed with illiterate mountaineers. Literacy scholar Peter Mortensen (1999) notes that his own conclusion about the impact of such depictions is "ironically resonant" with Harvey Graff's literacy myth[5] that "*il*literacy enabled the social advancement of those willing to use it as the conceptual capital to their turn-of-the-century charitable and professional enterprises. Gleaning the fields of rustic illiteracy has left a legacy no less devastating to rural livelihood than blight or drought" (1979, 163).

The legacy of devastating Appalachian stereotypes Mortensen notes has continually influenced the region's writers, and although the female authors considered in this project respond to it in various ways—ranging from rhetorical warnings to readers to flexibly negotiate new discursive worlds to depictions of the identity dilemmas that result from literacy acquisition—literary treatments of literacy remain a central thread in the works discussed in this project. In some instances these fictionalized portrayals align with literacy theories based on case studies of real people, but on other occasions authors focus heavily on characters' struggles with literacy attainment, vividly portraying the identity dilemmas that can and oftentimes do ensue.

Reading, Writing, and God's Word for Mountain Women

When discussing the projection of illiteracy onto Appalachia, it is helpful to remember that the works considered in this project are written accounts of literacy attainment, powerful testaments to the literary prowess of the region and its women writers. And yet we must also consider that the reality for some Appalachian women is that literacy attainment seems impossibly out of reach for a number of reasons, including the isolated areas in which they sometimes live and the patriarchal systems that can govern their lives. In my interview with Lee Smith, she discussed the time she spent working with adult students in the literacy program at the Hindman Settlement School in Kentucky, and she noted that all of her students were women. She went on to comment that her students were able to attend those literacy classes only if they could "get away from their husbands who didn't want them to learn how to read or parents who didn't want them to learn how to read" (2007) or children who demanded all of their attention and time.

Even after overcoming these obstacles, some of Smith's students, like Kentucky ballad singer Florida Slone,[6] abruptly stopped attending the classes since the dominating men in their lives believed "all a woman needed to read was the Bible" (L. Smith, 2007). Although literacy researchers like Anita Puckett (1992) conclude that literate activity functions as a more acceptable part of a woman's life than a man's, Smith's discussion also illustrates that literate activity must be kept in check so that women do not find escape from their often oppressive roles as wives and mothers.

Author Lucy Furman clearly illustrates this dynamic in 1920s novels like *The Quare Women* (1923) and *The Glass Window* (1926), books that fictionalize Katherine Pettit and May Stone's founding of the Hindman Settlement School in Kentucky. In *The Quare Women*, for example, a character named Aunt Ailsie timidly asks her husband, Uncle Lot, for permission to learn to read, and he replies: "Hit allus been my opinion ... that women-folks hain't got no use for larning. Hit strains their minds, and takes 'em off of their duty" (1923, 42). He eventually consents to allow her to "larn jest enough ... to be able to read Scripter, and no more," since he believes "in [his] soul that larning in general is too much for a woman's mind" (87). As if these notions were not oppressive enough, he also forbids her to sing ballads, since he believes that they have connections with the devil and sin (110–11).

As the story between Aunt Ailsie and Uncle Lot progresses throughout *The Quare Women* and into *The Glass Window*, Uncle Lot undergoes a major ideological shift and appears to realize that his treatment of Aunt Ailsie is not only unfair but unfounded spiritually. But perhaps more interesting for this project is the fact that Aunt Ailsie subversively undermines Uncle Lot's decrees, secretly teaching her son Fult the old songs in *The Quare Women*, as well as singing them for Isabel, one of the women who help Virginia and Amy (representations of Pettit and Stone) found the school (1923, 112). In *The Glass Window* Ailsie sneaks into town to peruse the children's books Amy and Virginia leave with the current teacher, Giles, while they are away for the summer. Additionally, much of the book focuses on her plot to trick Uncle Lot into installing a glass window in their cabin. Near the end of the novel she regrets her calculating behavior but eventually gets her window, causing readers to wonder whether Furman may be using this scenario to suggest that such rebellion does, in fact, produce the desired effect in repressive patriarchal systems.

Contemporary readers, particularly feminist readers, of Furman's work are understandably appalled by Uncle Lot's rule over Ailsie, especially where matters of literacy and education are concerned, and we cheer Ailsie's resistance to her subjugated position. Yet Furman's 1920s representation of the potential empowerments and dangers of literacy still resonate today, including the warning one woman issues to unmarried Virginia and Amy in *The Quare Women* that "a woman that sets out to ketch larning is mighty apt not to ketch a man" (1923, 162). Ailsie has certainly caught her man, but when she wants to learn how to read and write, she realizes the implications of being married to a man whose thoughts align with Virgil Lively's, the man who convinced Florida Slone to stop singing ballads publically and to stop her campaigning for the benefits of adult literacy programs. Furman does not fully explore the identity conflicts such learning causes for Ailsie, but the main authors considered in this project continually depict women who seek and sometimes achieve such escape, only to find that along with substantial benefits, the new literacies they gain also often introduce or exacerbate already present familial conflicts in their lives.

The Moonlight School Example

Although Furman published her novels about the Hindman Settlement School in the 1920s, Katherine Pettit and May Stone began the school approximately two decades earlier, in 1902. Just nine years later, in 1911, Kentucky resident Cora Wilson Stewart started the Moonlight School project in Rowan County, roughly one hundred miles northwest of the Hindman location in Knott County. The program held night adult-education classes, focusing on teaching anyone eighteen years or older to read and write. Because these adult students worked during the day, either performing paid labor tasks or domestic duties in the home, nighttime was often the only time they had available in which to learn to read and write. Classes were generally held in the summer and fall, and students traveled to these classes by the light of the moon, hence the name Moonlight Schools. In many ways, a brief analysis of the program, as well as one of its offshoots, provides a useful historical basis for thinking about what literacy meant for educators and adult students in the first few decades of the twentieth century, as well as what it means now for contemporary discussions about literacy depictions in literature.

The program ultimately raised national census literacy rates for the state of Kentucky, and Stewart became the darling of newspaper reporters and education officials in the state and later the nation. In 1919, for instance, Hortense Flexner wrote an article titled "Are You Too Old to Learn?" (his conclusion was that no matter your age, you are not), in which he praised Stewart's efforts and included photographs of adult pupils with one caption that read "Rugged roads to travel, hills to climb, streams without bridges to cross, children to lead and smaller ones to carry, but they came—1,200 strong!" (13). With the goal of eliminating adult illiteracy across the state by 1930, Stewart's campaign garnered national attention, and numerous other states adopted her program and its materials before she founded the National Illiteracy Crusade in 1926 (Baldwin 2006). But along with this kind of praise, Stewart also received her fair share of criticism. Her highly visible efforts at eradicating adult illiteracy had the effect of casting the people of Kentucky and much of the Appalachian region as unable to read and write.

As historian Yvonne Honeycutt Baldwin notes in her biography of Stewart, "By calling attention to widespread illiteracy in the Kentucky mountains and elsewhere, [Stewart] held the commonwealth up to a national scrutiny that many politicians and school leaders at home [in Kentucky] found uncomfortable" (117), since her campaign further highlighted negative portrayals of the mountains. Though the goal of increasing literacy rates was no doubt admirable and much needed, in many ways Stewart relied on the increasingly popular stereotypes set forth by Local Color writers and missionary groups to raise funds for her illiteracy campaign. As previously mentioned, she hailed from Rowan County, Kentucky, the home of the Martin-Tolliver feud, and as Baldwin observes, "like Berea college president William Goodell Frost and other purveyors of missionary education in the mountains, Cora used that notoriety to further the campaign against illiteracy" (15).

In purposely playing into the stereotypes Local Color writers and missionaries used to characterize the region as drastically different and as "a strange land and a peculiar people" (Harney 1873), Stewart's campaigning techniques conflated fact with fiction, and Baldwin notes that "the romanticization and overstatement of [Appalachians'] condition was part of the rhetoric of the crusade, meant to entice financial and moral support from the educated community and to play on public sympathy for the benighted mountaineers, worthy whites more deserving of uplift than blacks and immigrants" (2006, 48). As a native Appalachian, Stewart strategically continued stereotypes marking Appalachians as illiterate, since this marking was meant to garner much-needed financial support for her Moonlight School project. For her purposes, relying on labels of Appalachian illiteracy was worth the financial rewards reaped by her campaign.

In 1922 Stewart published a book about her experiences with the project titled *Moonlight Schools for the Emancipation of Adult Illiterates*. In the opening chapter she repeatedly highlights mountain people's desire to learn, but she also echoes William Goodell Frost when she claims that "they are a people of arrested civilization" (2). She goes on to explain that she began her schools with three groups of people in mind: illiterate mothers who needed to communicate with children no longer living in the community; middle-aged men "shut out from the world of books"; and illiterate young people of both sexes who have "rare talents, which if developed might add treasures to the world of art, science, literature and invention" (13).

Later in the book Stewart places heavy emphasis on World War I soldiers who cannot read or write letters, men whose illiteracy results in a serious communication handicap during wartime. She casts her program as part of the solution, and the connections she draws between the Moonlight School and patriotism in general become increasingly clear. Literate citizens, she concludes, are better citizens, even writing that "to teach them would not only enrich them as citizens but in the words of the prophet Isaiah would, 'increase the nation and extend all the borders of the land'" (1922, 186). In several sections Stewart presents her agenda as a nationalistic one, emphasizing that the core of patriotism and loyalty to country begins with the ability to read and write.

As was common during the Progressive Era, notions of citizenship were also bound up with religion. At one point in *Moonlight Schools for the Emancipation of Adult Illiterates*, Stewart proudly describes a community gathering in which Moonlight School students publicly presented their new skills and were rewarded with a Bible at the ceremony's conclusion. Stewart makes clear that students' newfound ability to read and write combined with possession of God's Holy Word provided the potential for moral improvement, writing that "when the Jezebel of the community came forward and accepted her Bible and pledged herself to lead a new life forevermore, there was hardly a dry eye in the house" (1922, 53). As discussed later in this chapter, ideas about literacy, citizenship, and religion were so intertwined that discussion of one topic necessitates discussion of the others.

In addition to making emotionally charged patriotic appeals to the Kentucky public, Stewart also relied on a simplistic definition of literacy to further her cause, something that the authors considered in this project avoid. Shunning the practice of using grade-level reading proficiency to gauge literate ability, Stewart devised her own teaching materials geared toward a rural-based adult audience: Once students completed the second set of materials, which, as Baldwin notes, "could be accomplished in two six-week sessions of night school," Stewart declared pupils literate (1922, 137). This system produced a remarkable rise in Kentucky literacy rates thanks to the Moonlight School program, but Stewart encountered trouble with her methods when she entered the national literacy crusade arena. Around this time New Deal politicians were committed to establishing a sixth-grade reading level as the standard for literacy, which would deem most Moonlight School graduates illiterate, a fact that greatly concerned Stewart since this move would significantly diminish the perceived success of her project.

Perhaps even more remarkable, even though politicians were pushing for the sixth-grade reading standard as the new hallmark of literacy, "crusade rhetoric masked the fact that illiteracy lacked a public policy definition.... No one had identified the stage at which an individual passed from illiteracy to literacy. The standard varied from state to state," and these levels ranged from completion of second grade to sixth grade (Baldwin 2006, 137). This quandary continues to create conflict among educators, politicians, and policymakers, and deciding when an individual becomes literate—and indeed, what literacy means—remains hugely important for both historical and contemporary portrayals of Appalachia.

Despite the problematic nature of some aspects of Stewart's program, and her methods of publicizing that program, when we consider the life-changing impact her campaign had for many mountain residents, it becomes difficult to demonize the totality of her work. Instead of teaching adult pupils from primary readers, for example, Stewart created a newspaper from which students read. She explains that the newspaper served several purposes, one of them being "to enable adults to learn to read without the humiliation of reading from a child's primer with its lessons on kittens, dolls and toys" (1922, 23). Articles in the newspaper readers were also meant to relate directly to the lives of residents, reinforcing pedagogical strategies later espoused by literacy theorists Paulo Freire and Donaldo Macedo, though the papers were eventually traded for books as the program grew.[7] In some ways it seems clear that Stewart's intentions were benevolent at their core, especially when we consider passages like this one: "The youngest student was aged eighteen, the oldest eighty-six. It was a scene to bring tears to the eyes, but surely one to make the heart rejoice, to see those hoary-headed old people and those robust young people seated at their desks studying together, or standing on a row in class to spell, or lined up at the blackboard to solve problems or to write" (18).

Yet Stewart still harbored inherent judgments about the residents she taught. In her chapter titled "Dealing with Illiterates," Stewart brags about the change in mountain speech the program promoted, writing that "'ing' was restored to its proper dignity," "the most glaring monstrosities of pronunciation were weeded out," and that "a language conscience was created where none had existed before" (1922, 27). This kind of conscience—one that surely caused internal strife—lies at the heart of this project. Plenty of letters from pupils who learned to read and write in the program survive, but these are letters written to Stewart and other teachers, usually thanking them for learning how to read and write. In a rhetorical sense these letters were not the proper venue for student criticisms of the program, nor were they likely to reveal the identity conflicts that were likely caused when teachers criticized and corrected mountain speech patterns.

Moonlight Schools in Western North Carolina

Two notable biographies (one by Willie Nelms and one by Yvonne Baldwin Honeycutt) have been written about Stewart and her work, yet little research has focused on programs that emulated Stewart's in the rest of Appalachia but were outside her jurisdiction. One particular example in Western North Carolina provides much insight into the workings of such programs and the effects they had on students.

In 1914, three years after Stewart began the Moonlight School program in Rowan County, Kentucky, the state superintendent of education for North Carolina, Dr. J. Y. Joyner, began organizing an adult literacy campaign in his home state (Stewart 1922, 125–26). In 1915 he even designated the month of November as Moonlight School Month in North Carolina (Day 1938), and according to Stewart, "The North Carolina Legislature of 1917 appropriated $25,000 annually for moonlight schools and in 1919 the work was made a part of the public school system of the state" (1922, 128). Around this same time, Stewart's Moonlight School model was also gaining attention in other states, and in 1915 Alabama followed Kentucky's model and mandated Moonlight Schools statewide (125).

Meanwhile, a woman named Elizabeth Morriss from Selma, Alabama, had graduated from Peabody College in Nashville in 1898, become a teacher, and was presumably aware of her home state's focus on Moonlight Schools (Cattell 1932, 670). At some point she became interested in educating adults in Appalachia, and she moved to Buncombe County, North Carolina. Historical records explaining precisely how Morriss became interested in Moonlight Schools and how she chose Western North Carolina are vague at best and incomplete at worst, but thanks to archival documents housed in the North Carolina Collection at Pack Memorial Library, we do know that in 1919 Morriss began volunteering in Asheville, North Carolina. By 1920 she was the chairperson of Adult Illiteracy in the State Federation of Women's Clubs, and she also became the Director of Adult Education in Buncombe County. She served in this position for ten years, during which time she helped establish Moonlight Schools in Buncombe County, in both urban and rural areas. Once she stepped down from the position, Della (or J. M., Jesse M.) Day, a woman who had taught in the program and worked for Morriss, assumed the responsibility of directing the program. In 1931 the night school budget was

Figure 1.1 This newspaper cartoon appears in the front of Della Day's scrapbook, housed in the North Carolina Collection, Pack Memorial Library, Asheville, North Carolina. It was drawn by Billy Borne, a cartoonist for the *Asheville Citizen-Times* newspaper. Copyright 2000, Asheville, NC Citizen-Times, Reprinted with permission.

canceled because of local bank failures, but Day continued to operate the program (Day 1933). By 1933 the Works Progress Administration ran the classes, and eventually the program was absorbed into the school system.

Day kept a scrapbook of photographs, letters, and newspaper articles related to her Moonlight School experiences, and on the first page of the scrapbook she pasted a cartoon image that indicates the level of public attention focused on eradicating illiteracy for American citizens during this time (see fig. 1.1). The cartoon artist (Billy Borne) casts illiteracy as an enormous, none-too-intelligent-looking man, one whose shoes are so worn that his toes are visible. Accompanied by wretchedness and inefficiency, he looks curiously over his shoulder at the figure of Uncle Sam,

Figure 1.2 "Out of the Fog," by Billy Borne, published in the July 1, 1927 edition of the *Asheville Citizen Times* newspaper. Copyright 2000, Asheville, NC Citizen-Times, Reprinted with permission.

who beckons him from the schoolhouse. Not only does this cartoon capitalize on stereotypes of poor citizens (particularly hillbillies) with patches on their clothes and inadequate shoes, but it also reflects the connections between literacy and citizenship that Stewart referenced in her book about the Moonlight School project.

Perhaps an even more telling image, also by cartoonist Billy Borne, appears in the July 1, 1927, edition of the *Asheville Citizen Times* newspaper (see fig. 1.2). Here, Borne depicts a man and woman using a rope labeled "Buncombe Co. Adult Schools" to climb out of the fog of illiteracy toward a

Figure 1.3 Photograph of Edith Vanderbilt, taken June 24, 1923, from Della Day's scrapbook. North Carolina Collection, Pack Memorial Library, Asheville, North Carolina.

better existence, which he draws as the sun, shining its knowledge on these mountain folk. Lest viewers misunderstand the identity of these climbers, Borne attaches a tag to the back of the man's shirt that reads "Illiterate Mountain Folks," and he blocks the woman's face from view with a traditional bonnet. This kind of demeaning characterization of adult learners, particularly Appalachian ones, was not uncommon during this time, even though Morriss and other educators appeared to have good intentions.

Like Stewart, Morriss was proud of her students' accomplishments, and on June 24, 1923, a commencement ceremony was held for graduates of the program at the Biltmore Estate in Asheville, which was and still is America's largest privately owned home. Edith Vanderbilt presided over the affair (see fig. 1.3), and as seen in the photograph taken of her on that day, posters were displayed with large captions that read "Undelivered!," under which a Bible was pictured with a tag that read "To the Nations of the World." Although it made quite the philanthropic statement that the Vanderbilt family held a night school graduation ceremony on their property, images from that day belie the fact that learners were seen as the undelivered, people who must be raised up out of the fog of illiteracy, as Borne would draw the situation four years later.

As part of the ceremony students also participated in a poster contest, and the winner (see fig. 1.4) created a poster that admonished viewers to "take a full bath more than once a week." The fact that Western North Carolina adults had learned to read and write certainly deserved celebration, and the commencement ceremony provided just that. It even made logical sense for organizers to create competitions in which learners could compete to show the depth of knowledge they had attained. But as this photograph illustrates, learners were cast as previously ignorant of things like personal hygiene. As Stewart explains in her book, and as Morriss (1927) includes in the textbooks she eventually wrote for use in the program (*Citizens' Reference Book*), cleanliness was a frequent topic of instruction. But photographing a grown man holding a poster with instructions for bathing contradicts the educators' claim that they treated learners with respect and dignity.

The question that drives the foundation of this book asks, "How did this man feel about being photographed with his poster? Was he proud? Was he ashamed? Can we presume that he already knew how to keep himself clean?" Of course we cannot know how this particular person would have answered these questions, nor can we glean such answers from student letters, since those letters were generally written to teachers to thank them for their work. Even contemporary interviews with mountain residents who

Figure 1.4 This photograph is of a night school student taken June 24, 1923 at the Biltmore estate commencement ceremony. He is holding his prize-winning poster, which instructs viewers to "Take a Full Bath More than Once a Week." From Della Day's scrapbook, North Carolina Collection, Pack Memorial Library, Asheville, North Carolina.

have recently gained technical literate skills cannot fully answer questions like these since, as previously discussed, mountain people are always aware of stereotypes and the dangers of reinscribing those if they discuss the pitfalls of becoming literate. But through the careful construction of fictional worlds, ones not so intimately connected with reality, the Appalachian women writers considered in this project tackle these questions head-on, revealing that internal strife almost always accompanies the acquisition of new literacies, certainly ones that would necessitate making a poster about cleanliness and being photographed with it.

It is also worth noting that the commencement ceremony celebrated the achievements of urban Western North Carolina residents, since the first big push into rural areas did not occur until early July of that same year. Adult students from all across the county attended the event, as seen in figure 1.5. Even a quick glance at this particular image overturns stereotypical images of poor, barefoot, ignorant hillbillies. Instead, the men pictured here are dressed in suits and ties, the women in elaborate dresses and hats. In many

Figure 1.5 Photograph of commencement ceremony held at the Biltmore Estate on June 24, 1923, from Della Day's scrapbook. North Carolina Collection, Pack Memorial Library, Asheville, North Carolina.

Figure 1.6 Here Della Day is pictured standing behind pupils Obadiah Surrett and his wife; the woman and child on the left are not identified. The photo's caption reads "First Lesson" and is housed in Della Day's scrapbook in the North Carolina Collection, Pack Memorial Library, Asheville, North Carolina.

ways, this image provides a startling juxtaposition to the idea that these people needed deliverance or instruction on bathing, though it must also be remembered that Morriss's efforts did introduce reading and writing skills to a large number of people who otherwise would not have had access to those skills. This is a distinction that deserves attention, since the powers of literacy are not easily dismissed. As with all matters concerned with Appalachian literacy, the effects for learners were both positive and negative.

Soon after the commencement ceremony, Morriss extended her programs to rural locales, and perhaps one of the most successful Moonlight School endeavors in Western North Carolina took place in the Big Sandy Mush community, about twenty miles northwest of Asheville. As with the Moonlight Schools in urban areas, newspaper articles praised the interest and support local residents had in the program, as evidenced by article titles such as "Much Interest in Sandy Mush." According to information Day kept in her scrapbook, as many as seventy-five people attended the first session at Liberty Hill School on July 3, 1923, and more than fifty people came to the initial session held at Chestnut Grove.

By this time, Morriss had a staff of teachers working for her, and Della Day worked with residents in Big Sandy Mush. Day collected numerous photographs of Sandy Mush residents, as well as letters from those students. In figure 1.6 she

Figure 1.7 Moonlight School student Minerva Clark Sprouse is pictured here holding a bible. From Della Day's scrapbook. North Carolina Collection, Pack Memorial Library, Asheville, North Carolina.

is pictured standing behind Sandy Mush resident Obadiah Surrett and his wife. This was presumably either the first or an early visit made to the Surrett family, since she wrote "First Lesson" underneath the image. A photograph taken on that same day shows Minerva Clark Sprouse (see fig. 1.7) holding a Bible that she soon learns how to read. While these images stand in stark contrast to the photograph of the graduates at the commencement ceremony held at the Biltmore Estate, they are also similar in that they subvert Local Color notions of barefoot, benighted hillbillies who have no desire to learn.

Obadiah, his wife, and Minerva are not formally dressed as are those in the Biltmore House photograph, but with good reason: these photographs were taken while they were at home, going about life as usual, not when they were attending what by all accounts would be considered a major ceremony at the Vanderbilt residence. Minerva (or Aunt Nervie, as she was also called) has on a clean dress, her shoes seem perfectly functional, her glasses appear to be in good condition, and her hair is clean and neatly arranged.

It can be tempting for scholars to argue that women like Cora Wilson Stewart, Elizabeth Morriss, and Della Day capitalized on images of mountain people to portray them as in dire need of educational intervention, and in some ways they did; certainly such arguments have been made regarding the American Missionary Association and their coining of the term "mountain white" so they could minister to the needs of Appalachian residents. But after researching the primary documents about the Moonlight Schools, it appears that these women were *primarily* interested in teaching adults how to read and write, and they projected that image of their work publicly (in newspaper articles and reports) and privately (in personal scrapbooks and letter collections) in a reasonably objective manner, poster competitions withstanding.

They did not ask Aunt Nervie to remove her shoes to be photographed. Such an idea may seem absurd to contemporary researchers, but as Baldwin illustrates in her history of Cora Wilson Stewart, missionary workers were willing to sacrifice the image of mountain people in order to support their work: in 1928, for instance, missionary supporter Mary Swain Routzhan commented that "perhaps in real life Lizzie Ann is no longer barefooted, but if we show a picture of Lizzie Ann wearing shoes and stockings, it is doubtful whether she will appeal so greatly to the hearts of whose gift the [literacy] work depends" (quoted in Baldwin 2006, 16).

Fortunately, this does not seem to have been the approach taken by Morriss and her staff, though some educators writing about her work did hold the view that she ministered to those in need of deliverance. In 1927, for example, L. R. Alderman published an article titled "Buncombe County's Excellent Work for Adult Illiterates" in *School Life*, a publication of the Bureau of Education. In it he calls adult mountain learners "primitive people," writing that Morriss "contrasted the native beauty of the country with the backwardness of the people" (177-78). Yet other writings about Morriss's work contrast statements like Alderman's. Miss Willie Lawson, for example, the deputy state superintendent for the State of Arkansas Department of Education, visited the Sandy Mush community with Della Day, and upon her return to Arkansas she wrote a letter to her, thanking her for the experience. In her letter she seems sincere in her compliments of her hostess's (Mrs. Garrett) cooking, and she asks Mrs. Day to "tell Leona King that I am not forgetting that she is to write me a letter. Give my best wishes to all of the pupils, please, and tell them how much my visit with them helped me" (Lawson 1924).

Perhaps the best testament against the supposed backwardness of these people lies in a brief analysis of the letters they wrote after learning to read and write. Della Day kept many such letters written to her by students. Taken in their totality, the letters clearly illustrate how thankful participants were to learn to read and write, and most inquire as to whether Day would continue her teaching in their respective communities. A letter to Mrs. Day from E. L. Jones, dated January 3, 1924, is written in hopes of starting another night school in Sandy Mush: "Mrs. Day I will write you a few lines to let you know that I haven't forgotten you. I am sorry the night school is out. I have got up a petition for another school at Liberty Hill. I got sixty-eight names. I hope you will be one of our teachers. I have sent the petition to Mrs. Morriss so I will close." As evidenced by this writer's support for the program and willingness to start a petition to continue the program, residents supported the learning that was taking place. Such evidence from Day's scrapbook clearly demonstrates the positives of such learning, but what of the negatives? Like Stewart's students who were tasked with restoring language to its "proper dignity" (1922, 27), in what ways did these experiences result in identity conflict?

Like Cora Wilson Stewart, Morriss developed her own materials for students. She recognized that attending school as an adult was often a difficult—and for some shameful—decision, and she did not want to exacerbate that shame by subjecting students to childlike lessons. In 1927, almost eight years after she arrived in Asheville, she authored a two-volume set titled *Citizens' Reference Book*, a textbook for adult learners published by the University of North Carolina press with an introduction by distinguished sociologist Howard Odum. This followed a much smaller publication of similar material by the state superintendent of public instruction in Raleigh, North Carolina, in 1922. The first line of the preface to the 1927 volumes reads, "*The Citizens' Reference Book* has been prepared primarily to meet the interests and needs of native adult beginners" (v).

It would seem that the lessons in the book would draw from adult themes, but readers might be discouraged to learn that part of the first lesson instructs pupils to recite, "I work. I play. I work and I play. I like to work. I like to play" (Morriss 1927, 1). But a closer inspection of the text reveals illustrations that depict adults seated at desks, writing, or in chairs, reading. Moreover, in many instances the lessons seem to serve a dual purpose for both child and parent. Lesson eight, for example, asks students to write: "I work in the day. I play in the day. I go to the night school. I sleep at night. I do not stay late at the night school. I do not work late at night. My sister likes to sleep late in the day. My father and mother go to night school," while a later lesson includes practice sentences such as "My wife and I have a son. My wife and I have a daughter" and "My husband reads to me. I like for him to read to me" (8, 12, 13). The text does not include as many references to mountain life as we might expect, but the introduction to the text by both Morriss and Odum makes clear that they intended this book for a national audience, which might help explain (though not excuse) why we find no mention of tobacco, ramps, creasy greens, or molasses in vocabulary lists.

What we do find, however, are lessons written with a clear nationalistic agenda. Following World War I it comes as no surprise that patriotism was stressed in these materials; certainly that was a frequent theme in Stewart's text. Volume 2 in the series has an overt focus on the ideal American citizen, one who has an awareness of American history, bathes regularly, and eats a balanced diet. Such goals were common during the Progressive Era, and it is true that a sizable percentage of the American population during that time needed instruction in personal hygiene and health issues. But judging from the already clean state of learners like Obadiah Surrett, his wife, and Minerva Clark Sprouse (see figs. 1.6 and 1.7), it seems that such instruction was not necessary.

So while Morriss and her staff may not have blatantly relied on stereotypical images of mountain people to do their work, the pedagogical approach they advocated for teaching "native-born" adult students reveals that assumptions of inferiority were still at work, though they were not as blatant as the ones espoused by people like L. R. Alderman. This observation is not meant to devalue or discredit the very good and important work of Morriss and her staff; instead, I want to consider how these teaching methods may have catalyzed identity conflicts for mountain students learning to read for the first time.

Volume 1, for example, instructs students to write a letter addressed to a friend, inviting her or him to a community party (1927, 45). The illustration for such a party depicts streamers, Chinese lanterns, formally dressed attendees, and slices of fancy cake (see fig. 1.8). While it appears that the Sandy Mush residents pictured in Della Day's scrapbook lived reasonably comfortably, it is also relatively safe to assume that they did not have streamers or Chinese lanterns in their homes. Although historian Kirstin Hoganson (2007) explains that an "Orientalist craze" did "[sweep through] the nation from the 1870s to the turn of the century," explaining that "in the last decades of the nineteenth century . . . a wider section of the American public had access to non-European imports" (17, 19), it seems unlikely that

Figure 1.8 This illustration appears in Citizens' *Reference Book: A Textbook for Adult Beginners in Community Schools* by Elizabeth Morriss. Copyright © 1927 by The University of North Carolina Press. Used by permission of the publisher. www.uncpress.unc.edu. The illustration portrays a party image that seems unlikely in a rural, Appalachian locale.

Sandy Mush residents would have spent hard-earned savings on such decorative items. Given what researchers know about the power of literacy, what effect would such images and party descriptions have for adult mountain residents? Would they cause pupils to question or even devalue their mountain heritage in favor of this more mainstream model of Americana?

Applying Moonlight School Examples to Literary Representations of Literacy

In theoretical terms, the assertions of sociolinguist James Paul Gee prove particularly helpful when speculating about the effects such learning might have had for mountain residents in the 1920s and certainly for the fictional representations of more contemporary mountain women that this project considers. In *Social Linguistics and Literacies: Ideology and Discourses*, Gee discusses the kind of conflict such literacy acquisition can entail, and he asserts that "the conflicts are real and cannot simply be wished away. They are the site of very real struggle and resistance" (1996, ix). In the same way that researcher Katherine Kelleher Sohn documents the fears that contemporary women in her study have about getting above their raising, decades earlier Stewart encountered the same quandary when promoting her adult literacy education program. As Stewart biographer Yvonne Honeycutt Baldwin explains, "In Stewart's part of the country [Rowan County Kentucky], there was a distinctive prohibition against 'getting above one's raising,' a nebulous and difficult-to-define injunction that did not necessarily preclude success but meant that one should never forget his or her roots" (2006, 118).

One of the authors considered in this project, Linda Scott DeRosier, struggles with this dilemma repeatedly when moving between her home community of Two-Mile Creek, Kentucky, and the larger discursive world of academia. In most university arenas academic discourse favors a more homogenized speech that does not carry markers of a regional identity, yet as later discussed in chapter 3, DeRosier stubbornly refuses to consciously alter the way she speaks, because as Sohn notes, "language is closely tied to the way women define themselves and create community, and changing that language is a method of erasing culture" (2006, 37). Although DeRosier acquires what Gee would call a secondary discourse in her academic endeavors, she remains tied to and proud of her home community of Two-Mile Creek.

Sohn explains that loss of mountain accents comprises just one of many worries her participants have about entering college and consequently gaining new literacies through mastering secondary discourses. At one point, Sohn reflects that "in spite of its promises that I had bought into, literacy can be a two-edged sword" (2006, 76), particularly for Appalachian women since they are marginalized both by region and by gender. Making a similar observation, researcher Janice Lauer notes that the literacy attainment process "generates increasing tension between husband and wife, within families, and between friends, as gender roles are unmasked in their grimness, and as alternatives are highlighted in literature and theory" (Hamilton 1995, xii). Linda Scott DeRosier chronicles her exposure to these alternatives in her memoir, and even though her first husband does not oppose her continued education (in fact, he encourages it), her educational path combines with a host of other factors to permanently change the dynamics of their relationship, and her first marriage eventually ends in an amicable divorce.

A similar tension exists between first cousins Rachel and Dillon in Denise Giardina's (1992) *The Unquiet Earth*; and in Lee Smith's (1988) *Fair and Tender Ladies*, readers cannot help but notice that Ivy Rowe's mother shows little excitement over the educational achievements Ivy makes while under Miss Torrington's direction. Ivy's mother senses the increased strain Ivy's education places on their relationship, and Sohn notes that some parents "have unrealistic expectations that their children will return to them unchanged by education," which explains "the fear [Sohn's] students often communicate to [her] of becoming alienated from their families" (2006, 128). Marcia Egan notes the same phenomenon in her study when she reports that the family of one of her subjects "feared that by going to school, she was choosing school over her family" (1993, 272). Yet despite these fears, the women Sohn studies do enter college, and she reports that "going to college assisted the women in the Preston County study to become somebody and make their voices heard" (2006, 38). Furthermore, she asserts that the women's "acquisition of academic literacy did not destroy family or community" (44).

When considering the types of resistance identified by literacy scholars like James Paul Gee, Henry Giroux, Paulo Freire, and others, it seems surprising that Sohn does not uncover that kind of resistance with the participants in her study once they begin college; instead, the majority of their fear of alienation manifests before actual schooling begins. Yet, as noted earlier, the women's reluctance to discuss the costs of literacy attainment is closely bound with stereotypes of mountain illiteracy: Discussing those fears before going to school might be acceptable, but chronicling the costs of literacy attainment once they finished their studies would only support the fixed image of an illiterate, ignorant Appalachia, a perception most native Appalachians would prefer to avoid. Linda Scott DeRosier's personal reflections about her own literacy attainment seem similarly divided. During our interview she did not discuss a tangible sense of loss resulting from her education, though sections of *Creeker: A Woman's Journey* and *Songs of Life and Grace* imply otherwise, once again suggesting that written works provide a crucial, if ironic, space in which authors can consider the cost of literacy attainment.

The fictionalized accounts of literacy acquisition considered in later chapters depict struggle, resistance, and loss at almost every turn. Two of Harriette Simpson Arnow's (1954) characters (Reuben and Cassie) stubbornly refuse to forsake any facet of their Appalachian identities in favor of city-approved behaviors; Denise Giardina (Douglass 2006) laments that losing ties with her home has permanently marked her; and one of Lee Smith's characters (Ivy Rowe) claims that her daughter (Joli) has "fair broke [her] heart" and has "travelled far beyond [her]" in becoming an author and moving away from home (1988, 268, 271). At the same time, these authors painstakingly devote pages of their works to describing the literate abilities of their characters. In many cases, these female Appalachian authors seem caught between overturning stereotypes of illiteracy by portraying literate characters and revealing the various kinds of painful identity negotiations that literacy attainment often requires for Appalachians and Appalachian women in particular.

While Sohn presents a remarkably optimistic view of literacy acquisition, literacy scholar Andrea Fishman theorizes perhaps more accurately about the costs incurred by literacy attainment in her study of Amish literacy practices. At odds with both Sohn's and DeRosier's conclusions, Fishman states: "We need to realize that our role may not be to prepare our students to enter mainstream society but, rather, to help them see what mainstream society offers and what it takes away, what they may gain by assimilating and what they may lose in that process. Through understanding their worlds, their definitions of literacy, and their dilemmas, not only will we better help them make important literacy-related decisions, but we will better help ourselves to do the same" (1990, 38).

Similarly, Janet Carey Eldred argues that we can teach "what [Patricia] Bizell calls 'rhetorical literacy'; that is, we can deemphasize *failure* to enter successfully some new world, and instead emphasize analysis of discursive arenas, of the difficulty of choice, and of possibilities for new or reformed cultural and discursive spaces" (1991, 697–98; italics in original). Yet in a region like Appalachia—one that Frost described as slumbering in a "Rip Van Winkle sleep" (1899, 6)—the sort of opportunity for resistance Fishman encourages seems unlikely at best if Appalachian people ever hope to change their negative image. No doubt such resistance would be viewed by many Americans only as obstinate, stubborn, and further proof of backward hillbilly culture.[8]

Conversely, Appalachian authors have more leeway in exerting creative license in the construction of their characters and stories. In DeRosier's case, she has more control over the ways in which she tells her literacy narrative. Her authorship allows her to rhetorically situate her story so that it does not bolster the stereotypes she works against, but the people researched in literacy studies do not wield that kind of authorial power. Instead, their stories are transcribed and reinterpreted by a literacy scholar who may or may not understand their explanations of literacy-initiated losses. When participating in a study, subjects understand that these complex dynamics are at work and may give researchers generally positive reports about their journeys to literacy.

Despite the freedom that fiction and memoir writing grant authors in depicting the costs of literacy attainment, as demonstrated by the impact of the Local Color movement, stories can be dangerous in shaping national perceptions of an area and its people. No doubt aware of this possibility, the Appalachian authors considered in this study deal with that potential pitfall in interesting and varied ways. Denise Giardina (1992) places the novel's hope in Jackie, a formally educated woman who has left the mountains of West Virginia and then returned to help salvage the area from the destruction of strip mining; Lee Smith (1983) relies on stereotypes of mountain women in her depiction of *Oral History*'s Dory Cantrell as the essence of a mountain flower, but then creates an articulate and intellectually curious character in *Fair and Tender Ladies*' (1988) Ivy Rowe; Harriette Simpson Arnow (2003) exerts much energy describing the resistance of her characters, but her portrayal also concedes the necessity of conforming to some degree, and despite the stark division between resistant or pliable portrayals, she depicts all of her characters as aware of the difficult identity choices at stake. Unfortunately, as Douglas Reichert Powell observes, artistic portrayals of mountain people are "caught in the irony that they need the legibility, the recognizability of the stereotypes they propose to undermine in order to get the audience [or readers] undermining the stereotypes along with them" (2007, 212).

In recent years literacy scholars have begun to trace autobiographical accounts of literacy acquisition, and as Janet Carey Eldred and Peter Mortensen note, "literacy narratives . . . play a part in how we view our artists and how they construct and tell their stories as artists" (1992, 530). Certainly both the autobiographical and fictional literacy narratives considered in this study contribute to how we view Appalachian women writers. As literacy scholar Morris Young notes, "The literacy narrative has emerged in many instances when marginalized peoples have been forced to prove their legitimacy as citizens or potential citizens through a demonstration of their literacy, education, and often a (cultivated) desire to join a dominant culture" (2004, 34).

Although Appalachians have always been conceived of as American, as the 1989 CBS *48 Hours* broadcast proved with its title—"Another America"—even in the latter part of the twentieth century, Appalachian people were (and still are) considered deviant from mainstream American society. Moreover, as Peter Mortensen notes when writing about the Hindman Settlement School in Kentucky, "children and adults throughout the southern mountains, like those at Hindman, were schooled to accept their otherness precisely as it was understood by those [namely missionaries] who had invented it" (1994, 110).[9] Writing out of and within that tradition of otherness, the women writers and the characters they envision analyzed in this study create literacy narratives that "act to confirm, transform, or even reject [authorial and character] participation in culture, raise questions about community identity and membership, or encourage participation of not only the writer but also the reader in making meaning from the narrative" (Young 2004, 35).

As noted with the Local Color movement, the meanings that readers take away from these stories influence public perception in addition to individual conclusions about the region and its people. Thanks to the long tradition of the illiterate mountaineer, readers expect to encounter that sort of character in Appalachian literature. In some cases even contemporary Appalachian authors rely on these well-established tropes (as with Lee Smith's characterization of Dory Cantrell, which in turn operates as clever rhetorical commentary on caricatures of mountain women), but more often than not, the writers considered in this project use their autobiographical and fictional representations to turn away from what readers expect. Not only are the majority of characters considered in this study literate, but they are also the bearers of multiple literacies that produce both joyous and tragic consequences, particularly where identity issues reside.

Literary critic Casey Clabough asks, "How much does contemporary literary regionalism reveal the true essence of a distinctive place and its people? How much is merely an act—a formulated drama unfolding on a set, draped partially in nostalgia, that no longer exists save within the confines of the writer's mind?" (2007, 301). Whereas Local Color writers sustained American readers' nostalgic longing for romanticized representations of a simultaneously exotic, noble, degenerate, and illiterate Appalachia, contemporary mountain writers like the ones considered in this project work against the seemingly fixed notion of "Another America." Instead of crumbling under the oppressive weight of Otherness so long projected onto the Appalachian region, the native Appalachian women authors considered in this project use that tradition to inform their work in exciting and interesting ways. Through analyzing the ways in which Appalachian women authors write about literacy acquisition, including the identity-related dilemmas of that acquisition, we can better understand the saturation of illiteracy stereotypes, the effects of those misconceptions on Appalachian people, and the subsequent empowerments and perils mountain women encounter when gaining new literacies.

Upcoming Chapters

To illustrate the kinds of conflicts inherent in literacy attainment, this project begins its literary analysis by considering one of the most devastating accounts of literacy acquisition in Appalachian literature: Kentucky-born Harriette Simpson Arnow's *The Dollmaker*. In this work, first published in 1954, Arnow painstakingly renders how the Nevels family copes with the drastic change of moving from a rural life in Kentucky to an urban, proletarian existence in Detroit. Arnow's depiction of character reactions to this change fall along sharp lines of allegiance: characters represent either home, Kentucky, and Appalachia (Gertie, Reuben, and Cassie) or Detroit (Clovis, Clytie, and Enoch). Arnow grants her characters no negotiation between these vastly different worlds, and this rigidity extends to the submissively feminine role that Arnow's main character, Gertie, assumes in following her husband to Detroit against her better judgment. Ultimately, Arnow's portrayal of these "either-or" situations revolving around a gendered literacy sends a rhetorical warning to readers to avoid such rigidity in their own lives. Even so, Arnow's repeated emphasis on the literate skills of her mountain characters reveals a steady attention to mountain literacy that helps overturn stereotypes of Appalachian illiteracy; as with the other authors considered in this project, Arnow demonstrates an obvious thematic preoccupation with literacy, illiteracy, and representations of both.

The following chapter explores two works by eastern Kentucky-born writer Linda Scott DeRosier: her (1999) memoir, *Creeker: A Woman's Journey*; and her (2003) work of creative nonfiction, *Songs of Life and Grace*. In each of these accounts DeRosier emphasizes the importance of setting down an accurate written record of Appalachia and its people. In doing so, she frequently returns to themes of literacy and illiteracy, and she carefully depicts the costs associated with becoming socialized away from her home community of Two-Mile Creek into the new discourse community of academia. Despite the difficult nature of such a transition, she largely accepts these changes, managing to negotiate her identity between two disparate discursive worlds.

Unlike *The Dollmaker*'s Gertie Nevels, DeRosier resists limiting gender expectations by extending her education beyond what was once considered appropriate for women, and she consequently achieves the kind of identity compromise Arnow's characters never attain. In both works DeRosier portrays what it means for a mountain woman to leave home and also be able to return home changed but still able to function acceptably among loved ones. Her decision to write in memoir and creative nonfiction forms bridges the space between Appalachian and non-Appalachian audiences, and each of her works operates as a hybrid of the literacy narrative and narrative of socialization.

This project's fourth chapter considers West Virginia writer Denise Giardina's (1992) novel *The Unquiet Earth*. Media images of Appalachia made popular since the War on Poverty figure prominently in this novel, and Giardina's characters generally learn about outsiders' perceptions of them through classroom situations in which literacy acquisition plays a crucial role. Ironically, for Giardina's main character, Jackie (a biographical representation of Giardina), gaining the technical ability to read discourages writing, since Jackie encounters either a complete absence of Appalachian representation or negative portrayals of the region. In both Giardina's life and in the novel, exposure to traditional literary conventions and settings results in the idea that "real" writers do not come from Appalachia, but this notion changes as Jackie acquires new literacies, which in turn results in a loss of connection with her mountain home that is eventually bridged through the very act of writing. Giardina's thematic preoccupation with loss stems from her own life, and fiction writing operates as an outlet through which Giardina can write about those experiences while also transmitting her political messages about the destruction and devastation unethical coal mining practices inflict upon mountain environments and communities.

Chapter 5 investigates *Oral History* (1983) and *Fair and Tender Ladies* (1988), two novels by Virginia-born writer Lee Smith in which literacy acquisition continues to introduce difficult identity situations, especially for female characters. By considering these novels together, readers can trace the path from oppressive silence to public voicing, from Dory Cantrell to Sally Cantrell to the Cline Sisters, to Ivy Rowe, to Ivy's daughter Joli. When considering this progression, audiences understand that the painful distancing Joli endures remains necessary for the public voicing of Appalachian women's stories. Relying on a popular trope established during the Local Color movement, Smith introduces a teacher from outside each of the main characters' respective communities (Richard Burlage in *Oral History* and Miss Torrington in *Fair and Tender Ladies*).

Even though in some ways these teachers offer intellectual freedom from the sometimes stifling mountains in which the female protagonists of both works live (Dory Cantrell in *Oral History* and Ivy Rowe in *Fair and Tender Ladies*), each teacher also functions as an authority figure whose teachings cause characters to question their allegiance to their mountain-based identities. Smith's portrayal of Burlage's and Torrington's entrance into each novel's mountain community casts the Appalachian region as a feminized, womblike space that outside interests (whether timber and coal companies or teachers like Richard Burlage and Gertrude Torrington) invade, often with dire consequences. Smith's focus on private writing and public authorship in both novels also draws readers' attention to issues of audience access, a clever rhetorical strategy that causes readers to question what they know about Appalachia and how they know it.

CHAPTER 2

Shaping Biscuit Dough and Rolling Out Steel: Responding to Literacy Commodification in *The Dollmaker*

> I suppose it was because I was young with a rather stupid look. I don't know why, but this woman with an accent very different from the ones I knew, more like those of our teachers at Berea, was watching the work. She came around and watched me for a while and then she said, "Can either of your parents read or write?" My reaction was violent. I didn't move. I just tried to imagine my parents, my home, my grandparents, my great-grandparents, both great-grandfathers—there were stories of their books and their books still around—without books and newspapers like those poor, pitiful people unable to read who would come to get my mother to write letters—but I only had one wish: to get that woman away from me and I felt that if I said, "Of course they can read," she might ask more questions, so I said, "No, neither can read or write." She was satisfied. She had guessed correctly.
>
> (Eckley 1974, 33)

In this interview excerpt from Wilton Eckley's study on Harriette Simpson Arnow, Arnow retells the details of an incident that occurred during her years as a student at Berea College in the mid-1920s. While acknowledging the existence of illiteracy in Appalachia by referring to "those poor, pitiful people unable to read," Arnow pointedly rejects generalizations that cast the region as wholly illiterate. Arnow describes her understandable reaction to the woman's casual assumption of illiterate lineage as "violent," since

Arnow's family had an established tradition of literacy. Even so, she hides her feelings from her observer, and in doing so she avoids explaining the supposed anomaly of literacy in an Appalachian place. After finishing her studies at Berea, Arnow briefly taught junior high and high school but quit teaching in the mid-1930s to devote as much time as possible to writing, temporarily working as a waitress to support herself.

Over the next thirty years Arnow published two novels (*Mountain Path* and *Hunter's Horn*), wrote another novel (*Between the Flowers*), and published several short stories. In 1954—roughly three decades after her experience at Berea—she published *The Dollmaker*. The novel won wide critical acclaim during its time and was nominated for the National Book Award in 1955, losing only to William Faulkner's *The Fable* (Eckley 1974, 44). Critic William Schafer insists that the book is "too big and too serious to ignore" (1986, 50); and Tillie Olsen laments that as a woman's "book of great worth [*The Dollmaker* suffers] the death of being unknown, or at best a peculiar eclipsing" (1978, 40).

Set during the Second World War, the novel portrays the painful relocation of Clovis and Gertie Nevels, along with their five children, from a relatively happy, if poor, life in the Kentucky mountains to a depressingly bleak existence in Detroit. As with other texts in this project, literacy operates as a central theme in *The Dollmaker*, ultimately demonstrating that adopting a new set of values (oftentimes values perpetuated through literate activity in a city classroom) results in a tangible sense of loss for those who reject many aspects of their Appalachian identities in favor of city-approved behaviors, speech, and familial codes. Critical consideration of this text also helps further establish a working definition of the term "literacy," one that builds upon the Moonlight School example discussed in the previous chapter, as well as definitions established by literacy theorists, to demonstrate that literacy extends beyond the technical ability to read and write.

Perhaps most importantly, the fact that Arnow chose to represent the struggles of the Nevels family through literacy tropes once again connects Appalachians with other marginalized groups discussed in the introduction to this project. Like any number of immigrant peoples who settled in Detroit and elsewhere, the Nevels family was expected to conform to the cultural requirements of the city, and literacy operated as a potent vehicle for transmitting the requirements of such conformity. Theorists have long argued that cultural assimilation occurs in degrees, often resulting in code switching, and this process seldom erases a person's previous cultural ties.

Likewise, literacy acquisition operates in a similarly gradual fashion. One might be tempted to argue that ignoring the nuances of this literacy-induced transition stands out as the novel's biggest flaw, but in this chapter I contend that by setting up unrealistic binaries that result in "all or nothing" decisions for her characters, Arnow's depictions encourage readers to notice and consider the various kinds of identity conflicts that literacy can introduce.

In *The Dollmaker* characters experience no dialectical learning process like the one theorized by literacy scholars including Deborah Brandt (1990, 2001), Paulo Freire (1970, 1987), and James Paul Gee (1996), in which literacy acquisition results in some negotiation between old and new; no manner of compromise between mountain and city-based literacies appears in Arnow's text. Instead, either she depicts pliable people who completely accept their new community's requirements and consequently bear no signs of their previous mountain lives, or she describes stubbornly resistant characters unwilling to negotiate between the competing discursive worlds of Appalachia and Detroit. Gertie's husband, Clovis, must make a similarly dichotomous choice between Appalachia and Detroit, and although Arnow sets up a viable avenue for negotiation through Clovis's union activity—a space in which he could potentially gain some sense of agency in the alienating world of Detroit—he fails to pursue it.

Arnow also extends this rigidity to characters' perceptions of gender boundaries demarcating socially acceptable roles for women and men. By granting Gertie feminine as well as masculine traits, Arnow suggests the flexibility of Gertie's gender identity, yet in some (but certainly not all) ways Gertie continues to assume the role of submissive female, a decision that has dire consequences. Although none of the novel's characters recognize the literacy-based and gendered negotiations available to them, readers do. We also recognize the ways in which Arnow's characters seem blind to them. As such, the novel sends an important rhetorical message, enjoining readers to avoid such rigidity in their own lives. The novel ultimately operates as a cautionary tale warning readers away from the plight of Arnow's characters, who are trapped in an "adjust or abandon" situation that is anything but dialectical.

One popular interpretation of *The Dollmaker* identifies it as "one of the great proletarian novels of the age" (Denning 1996, 264). Cratis Williams, for example, writes that as a proletarian novel, *The Dollmaker* should be "on the list of required reading for the social worker who seeks to understand the problems of the mountain migrants in adjusting to civilization in contemporary America" (1976, 349). With its focus on lower-working-class characters and the powerfully negative effects of industrialization for the Nevels family, the proletarian label does seem to fit: Clovis works in a factory plagued with strikes, Gertie reluctantly uses unfamiliar tools to produce and sell more of her dolls, and the family constantly struggles to buy an ever-increasing number of products purchased on payment plans. However, the novel lacks the sense of collaborative revolution that has often been considered the hallmark of proletarian fiction.

Although literary critic Barbara Foley writes that 1930s Marxist critics responsible for defining proletarian literature cited no formula for the proletarian novel, they also believed "proletarian literature, as a 'weapon,' should be revolutionary rather than reformist," and "proletarian texts should convey ideas and attitudes that would impel readers to take action against existing social conditions—that is move them leftward" (1993, 118). Although *The Dollmaker* teems with capitalistic injustice, the novel lacks the sort of didacticism that might qualify it as a weapon. Arnow's biographer also comments on Arnow's negative reaction to issues of *Masses* and *Daily Worker*, proletarian literature she explored while living in Cincinnati: "What she found . . . disappointed her. Or perhaps it would be better to say what she did not find: she did not find people treated as individuals, only faceless masses. Her own background in the hills had taught her that even illiterate humble people could carry on an organized and meaningful life and that such people were not without insight or emotion" (Eckley 1974, 37).

Even though the novel does not have revolutionary implications, it does send an important social message that revolves around literacy, one that until now has gone largely unnoticed by literary critics. While physical acts of labor render the adults of the novel urbanized, industrialized, and homogenized, the children undergo a similar transformation resulting from exposure to dominant, school-based literacies. More specifically, the literacies Arnow presents operate within two parallel factory models that function as sites of both resistance and loss: the Nevels children attend schools that operate as factories of homogenization and "adjustment," which some (Reuben and Cassie) resist, while the others (Clytie, Enoch, and Amos) accept; and Gertie loses her only source of enjoyment when she stops whittling in order to produce identical dolls in the factory-like space of their apartment. In repeatedly focusing on the losses incurred as a result of Detroit-based literacy attainment, Arnow criticizes the kind of literacy, and the identity choices it entails, valued by an urban environment. As such, Arnow's novel has much to teach us about the fictional portrayal of literacy attainment, lessons that the contemporary authors in the remainder of this project routinely integrate into their novels as well.

Reconfiguring Literacy

Near the novel's beginning Arnow establishes many of her characters as literate, especially Gertie. After forcefully stopping a car carrying army officials, Gertie demands that they help save her sick and choking baby, Amos, by driving him to the nearest doctor. As Gertie convinces the army officer and soldier to help her, an important conversation emerges. While performing an emergency tracheotomy on Amos, Gertie talks about her whittling talent with the army officer, and she tells him about her intention of someday carving a man from her prized block of wild cherry wood. She goes on to name several biblical characters that might serve as models for her piece, prompting the officer to comment that she seems "to be quite a student of the Bible" (*TD*, 18).[1] When Gertie explains, "Th Bible's about th only thing I've ever read," readers know it is a familiar text. They later realize that Gertie has also read the Constitution, as well as a variety of poems and other literature (18, 59, 130). Arnow returns to Gertie's literate ability frequently, but by presenting it as a normal—and even expected—part of Gertie's repertoire, Arnow succeeds in depicting Gertie's literacy as a typical mountain skill. Such attention to Gertie's literacy near the novel's beginning discourages readers from reinscribing stereotypes about mountain illiteracy, especially later in the novel when some members of the Nevels family resist acquiring new skills demanded by the city.

In her depiction of Appalachia, Arnow's continued focus on literate events configures literacy as a normal, if not universal, part of mountain life. The emphasis that the Nevels family and much of the surrounding community place on the daily arrival of mail, especially letters from those writing home about their war experiences abroad, showcases the centrality of literate activity for many of Arnow's characters. Genuinely interested in placing the physical location of her loved ones, one community woman, Mrs. Hull, orders a world map and hangs it at the joint store and post office location. Although some of the women speak fearfully of foreign places in "hoarse whispers" because of their unwillingness or inability to conceptualize the vast geographic distance between themselves and those at war, others speak "casually, as they had used to speak of the next creek or hill, of the Aleutians, New York, Paris, Calcutta, Hampton Roads, Okinawa, Louisville, London, Cincinnati, Kelly Field, Oak Ridge" (*TD*,114). In scenes such as these, Arnow emphasizes both the literate ability and the intellectual curiosity of this Appalachian community, perhaps because she did not always witness such curiosity in her childhood mountain home.

In his biography of Arnow, Wilton Eckley explains that as an adolescent Arnow was influenced by World War I, especially the frequent letters soldiers sent home. According to Eckley, she was appalled that some members of her own community could not read those letters, and likewise, that there were "parents who had sons in France, yet had no idea what or where France was because they could not read a map" (1974, 26). Considering the biographical relevance of this passage, it becomes clear that this inclusion operates as a fictional corrective for Arnow, one that rejects common assumptions connecting Appalachia with illiteracy. As in the passage included at the beginning of this chapter, Arnow avoids denying the existence of illiteracy in Appalachia, but she also illustrates the literate skills of mountain people as well.

Building upon these representations of traditional types of literacy, Arnow also develops several scenes in which Gertie conducts reading lessons with her children in their Kentucky cabin. Once again Arnow appears to draw from her own life when constructing such character interactions. From 1918 until 1919, Arnow's mother (Mollie Jane Simpson) taught Arnow and her siblings at home, since the family lived in a remote area of Lee County (Eckley 1974, 27–28). Arnow presumably draws from these experiences when fictionalizing the learning that takes place in the Nevels cabin. In these scenes Arnow focuses most on Cassie, and even though five-year-old Cassie lacks the technical ability to read and write, she demonstrates her familiarity with narrative conventions. During one reading session, Cassie plays with the family dog, Gyp, instead of reading. When Gertie scolds her, Cassie replies, "Where's Gyp? This is a lion. He's about to choke to death on gingerbread" (*TD*, 88). Cassie's older sister, Clytie, corrects Cassie, saying, "You're all mixed up. . . . Th lion I've been a readen to you uns in that old language book had a thorn in its paw" (89).

In this instance Cassie has devised a new version of one of Aesop's fables, one infused with a more familiar, personal tone that results in a sense of ownership over the story, its characters, and its outcome. Even when Clytie challenges Cassie's story, Cassie undauntedly responds, "My lion . . . is choked on gingerbread" (*TD*, 89). In the same way that Cassie retells a classic fable, Arnow redefines traditional definitions of literacy. In this seemingly innocuous scene, Arnow lays the groundwork for the ways in which we can read her treatment of literate practices throughout the remainder of the novel, a reading that proves crucial when considering the identity conflicts the family later faces in Detroit.

To even better prepare readers to think about various kinds of literacy, Arnow grants Cassie similar creative license when Cassie reads an entire story to Gertie based on a book's pictures instead of its printed words. After Gertie asks Cassie to read from her primer, Cassie recounts the story's events without looking at the book's text. However, when Gertie points to a word and asks Cassie to read it, Cassie cannot. Cassie's lack of one-to-one correspondence illustrates a cognitive gap between the printed letters of a word and its meaning, and she bridges this noncommunicative space by memorizing and retelling the story, complete with her own twists and turns. Her technical inability to read allows a creative narrative redirection, a shift that parallels the transition Arnow demands of her readers when they define literacy. Just as Cassie's verbal telling of the story operates as a viable form of literacy, so too does the children's ability to read the Detroit school system. It is equally important to recognize that while encouraging readers to reconsider their notions about literacy, Arnow also establishes the traditionally literate skills of Gertie and several of her children early in the novel, lest any reader be tempted to equate nontextual literacies with illiteracy.

Before the family moves to the city, Arnow depicts most literacy events as shared experiences, often highlighting the cognitive connections between the Nevels children. For example, when Clytie and Cassie debate the "correct" version of a fable, a socially interpretive space opens, one that disproves early literacy scholars' idea that literacy functions as a solely individual act. Unlike the strong-text theories of literacy made popular by early scholars like Jack Goody and Ian Watt, the act of reading, writing, and learning in the Nevels household is anything but autonomous. In *Literacy as Involvement: The Acts of Writers, Readers, and Texts*, Deborah Brandt insists that we should "see a text not as a fixed artifact but as the public social reality (the public context) in which writing and reading unfold" (1990, 39); and as readers become aware of the importance of shared learning for the Nevels children, Arnow prepares her audience to notice the drastic shift in literate activity once the family moves to Detroit, where such activity stops being dialectical.

While in Kentucky, Gertie's household work allows her to engage in the social activity of reading with her children. They feel comfortable participating in these literacy events in their home environment, and the work of both mother and child is accomplished. However, after the family's move, the children's family-based literacy events cease as the family struggles to adjust to their new, unwelcoming environment. This struggle results in a reliance on different types of literacies, ones that involve difficult decisions about maintaining or abandoning Appalachian identity within the new and threatening context of Detroit.

In Kentucky Gertie assumes most of the responsibility for ensuring that her children learn to read and write, and her role as matriarchal educator aligns with gendered literacy trends noted by literacy and Appalachian scholars. Shirley Brice Heath writes that in the white mill town of Roadville, "mothers take more interest in their children being good students than do fathers" (1983, 45), presumably because compared with the men of the community, Roadville women have higher levels of formal education. Similarly, Victoria Purcell-Gates (1995) writes about her experiences working with an illiterate urban-Appalachian mother who desperately wants her son to become literate, even though the child's father seems unconcerned about his son's battle with illiteracy. Arnow presents a similarly involved parent in Gertie when the narrator explains that the Nevels children attended a summer school taught by a young teacher from Lexington, and that after those sessions ended, they "played school" at home. Gertie usually supervises these activities as she completes domestic labor tasks, such as cleaning or churning butter.

At home the oldest Nevels child, Reuben, appears willing to participate in literacy events along with the two middle children, Enoch and Clytie, but the youngest child, Cassie, has more difficulty learning than the others. Arnow's fictional portrayal of Gertie's combination of motherly duty with pedagogical responsibility predates the later identification of gendered literacy trends by literacy scholars, just as her suggestion that we conceive of literacy as more than the ability to read and write appeared decades before this idea becomes popular in literacy studies. As a female Appalachian author writing in the 1950s, Arnow understood the implications of literacy attainment long before literacy scholars began discussing it in the early 1970s, and she draws from that understanding to create a novel that not only showcases the dilemmas introduced by literacy, but also urges readers to consider the universality of the book's theme: literacy can isolate, displace, and alienate learners, especially those from marginalized groups.

Just as Arnow pushes readers to conceive of literacy as more than the act of reading and writing, she does the same for the concept of illiteracy. In an early episode, Gertie's gullible willingness to believe misleading Help Wanted signs posted in Kentucky reveals that the act of reading alone does not suffice as an adequate form of literacy. After Gertie and the children arrive in Detroit, Gertie has a conversation with another traveler at the train station. Gertie soon learns about the woman's plans to leave Detroit for her original home in west Tennessee due to the intolerable living conditions near Willow Run, a Michigan-based airplane plant opened by the Ford motor company during World War II. When Gertie learns that the woman's husband spends many of his work hours "jist a standen till they [need him]" so the company can "make more plus," Gertie asks the woman what she means by "plus" (*TD*, 154). The woman explains that by hiring more workers, companies can claim increased costs in making a particular product. The government gives the companies more profit when production costs increase, and consequently the woman reasons, "Th more men, th more plus fer th owners, th more money an more men fer them unions" (154).

The woman's explanation helps Gertie revise her earlier understanding in light of a new, contextual literacy. She exclaims: "Th county paper an th radio an them signs on th trees allus said them men was bad needed at Willer Run—tu win th war" (*TD*, 154). In this scene Gertie learns the fallibility of printed materials; before coming to Detroit she accepted the message of those materials as true, and she (along with much of her community) genuinely believed that all workers who went north were desperately needed for the war effort. Arnow's decision to insert this scene in the Detroit train station forecasts that similar situations await the Nevels family. Although most of them already have the technical ability to read and write, they must work to develop new literate skills required by the city.

Other literacy events that occur within a mountain setting are less obvious. With these more subtle scenes, Arnow further prepares her readers to expand their traditional notions of literacy; such an expansion is necessary in understanding how the Nevels children later read their new world of Detroit. Arnow compares Gertie's woodcarving ability to literate ability, and throughout the novel it remains one of her most important competencies, particularly when her carving supports the family financially. Near the novel's beginning, when Gertie explains to the military officer that she has always whittled, Arnow compares the lines on Gertie's hands to pages from a book: "She looked down at the hand that held the poplar wood, the back brown and wrinkled, fingernails black and ragged, then at the palm, smooth with the look of yellowed leather. It was as if the hand were a page engraved with names" (*TD*, 17). This description occurs as Gertie tells the officer that she uses her hands to make practical farm items, like handles, yet the simile connecting her hand with a page engraved with names suggests that readers need to understand (and in fact, read) Gertie's whittling in a creative, literate context. Here Arnow also reveals Gertie's yearning to express her carving talents more creatively, yet readers soon learn that Gertie regards the acts of carving dolls and other playful items as "foolishness."

By revealing the potential for creative expression stifled by practical necessity, this scene forecasts the eventual commodification of Gertie's carving in Detroit. Gertie's whittling history encodes her hand, suggesting that just as she shapes the wood for various purposes, the act of carving similarly influences her world. Arnow thus compares the changes brought to Gertie's life through her carving with the changes the technical skill of reading and writing can introduce to people's lives. In signaling Gertie's hand as a piece of writing, Arnow creates a powerful literacy metaphor, and in urging readers to draw comparisons between the act of whittling and a literacy event, she primes readers to critique the way Detroit commodifies Gertie's talent.

In a gendered twist on the matriarchal literacy trends noted by Heath and Purcell-Gates, Gertie's father provides her with the majority of her literacy skills. When Gertie tells the army officer about her familiarity with the Bible she goes on to explain: "When I was a growen up my mother was sick a heap an my father hurt his leg in the log woods. I had to help him, an never got much schoolen but what he give me" (*TD*, 18). As an injured man, her father remained at home and educated his children, a task usually reserved for women during that time. Arnow presents a similar overlap in gendered roles when Gertie assumes masculine characteristics ranging from her choice of dress to her eventual role as breadwinner in Detroit, and a continual tension between Gertie and her mother remains throughout the novel, especially over the forms of literacy Gertie learned from her father.[2]

During one visit home Gertie's mother chastises the learning Gertie received: "Yer pop *would* learn you th Constitution an some a th Bible—an you been spouten em ever since like you was a preacher an a lawyer, too" (*TD*, 59). As she listens to her mother's ranting, Gertie longingly touches the whittling knife in her pocket, and the narrator explains that "her mother had ever hated the whittling, even in her father—and in a girl it had seemed almost a sin" (62). Here Arnow reveals that for Gertie's mother, acceptable forms of literacy are gender-dependent; according to Gertie's mother, by assuming the masculine activity of whittling, Gertie refuses her role as a woman. Yet later in the novel Gertie acquiesces to her mother's biblically supported proclamation that Gertie should follow Clovis to Detroit as part of her wifely obligation, even though she has just purchased a farm for the family in Kentucky with her own money. Just as characters remain blind to the literacy-based negotiations available to them between Appalachia and Detroit, Arnow suggests flexibility in gendered roles only to have her characters reinforce gender dichotomies in the novel. Readers are no doubt aware that this strategy stands in stark contrast to the path Gertie could have chosen, which in some ways rhetorically advises readers against such submission.

Although Gertie feels proud of her ability to help her family by carving practical things for farm use, she views her special whittling project as a guilty indulgence, perhaps because of her mother's constant criticism. Gertie repeatedly expresses shame over "her time-wasting ways" (*TD*, 82). At one point Clovis says to her, "If'n you must waste elbow grease on whittlen, couldn't you make an ax handle er somethen somebody could use?," and Gertie internalizes such criticism (34). Once readers compare Gertie's carving with a type of literacy, they also begin to understand why she would deem reading for pleasure a waste of time, at least when other "real" work awaits.

Again, Arnow's biography yields more parallels between her fictional strategies and her own life: according to Eckley, just as Gertie viewed whittling as a waste of time, writing "was frowned upon by [Arnow's] parents as a waste of time and energy" (1974, 30). Gertie mimics this disdain for pleasure reading when she chides Enoch for reading when he should have been helping prepare the new cabin for their arrival (*TD*, 129). Enoch defends himself by replying, "I saw all these books an I recollected you wanted us to study ever day like we was goen to school. So's I studied some spellen" (129). Here Arnow emphasizes both Enoch's literate skills and his desire to learn. Despite the family's poverty and their continued struggle to own their own land, Arnow refuses to equate financial need with illiteracy, and she instead endows Enoch with the literate skills necessary to foster a growing intellectual curiosity. In doing so she overturns assumptions about Appalachian ignorance, creating a character eager to fulfill the educational goals his mother holds for her family.

Arnow also highlights how Gertie embodies that same penchant for reading; as Gertie looks through the books, "many of the poems were familiar as old neighbors who, though moved away and not seen for years, seem neighbors still when seen again" (*TD*, 130). Arnow names Marie La Coste's "Into the Ward of White-Washed Walls," an 1864 poem lamenting the death of La Coste's fiancé in a Civil War battle, as one of the poems Gertie reads. The poem's sentiment parallels Gertie's grief from the recent death of her brother Henley in World War II, and Arnow allows Gertie to read for only a few moments before Gertie stops "with the guilty realization that she was wasting time" (130). Here the connection between literate activity (both whittling and reading) and perceived wasted time illuminates the division between pleasure and necessity in the lives of the Nevels family. This division must be strictly maintained, even when the dividing line shifts (as when Gertie begins carving "frivolous" crucifixes to support her family).

Arnow emphasizes that just as Gertie feels obligated to carve practical farm items instead of fanciful dolls, Gertie also encourages structured school lessons but discourages the spontaneous reading of poetry. Gertie's delineation between acceptable literate activities and wasted time once again foreshadows the transformation of Gertie's carving talent into a form of raw labor. She longs to devote carving time to her block of cherrywood but instead usually carves cheap crucifixes for profit. Perhaps even more important, in these scenes Arnow sets up her later depiction of the kinds of literacy valued by Detroit, as well as the decisions that valuing system demands, as when Gertie must carve for profit instead of for personal expression.

Appalachia versus Detroit: Which Side Are You On?

The time Gertie is able to devote to her children and their literacy skills vanishes when the family moves to Detroit. The entire family must learn a new system, that of urban industrial commerce. Even though Gertie arrives in the city with a substantial amount of cash, she gradually spends the money on clothing for the children, appliances for the apartment, and other necessities of urban life. With Clovis on strike more than often than not, Gertie struggles to buy food in addition to paying for things, like ice, that she never bought in Kentucky. The new electric stove bought on a payment plan, the cumbersome washer, and the inability to harvest her own food (with the resulting reliance on expensive fruit and vegetable vendors), all combine to consume the majority of her time at home. These new and overwhelming responsibilities suggest the fraught process of living in Detroit. The drastic transition from an agrarian lifestyle to one of urbanized industrialization forces Gertie to focus her energies solely on her family's financial survival.

Consequently, she relies upon one of her home-based talents, whittling, to earn money for the family while her children enter an entirely new discursive arena in the city school system.

The Detroit classroom functions as a site where the Nevels children are encouraged to become good producers. To achieve such results, the classroom requires that they read, understand, and acquiesce to the identity changes demanded by the city of Detroit. During the family's railway journey to Detroit, Arnow foreshadows the family's entrapment, including the children's imprisonment in the school system and the unfriendly ideology that awaits them. On the train Gertie longs to see the landscape, but the dirty windows on the train reveal little because they are "steamy on the inside, crusted with snow and dirt on the outside, and stout as for a prison, with two thick panels of glass" (*TD*, 146). Although trains typically represent mobility, in this scene Arnow encourages readers to see that the locomotive symbolizes the hardships of industrialization for the family and the eventual death of Cassie.

The family's cab ride to their new tenement housing in an area ironically named Merry Hill also foreshadows the grim living situation that awaits them. Each member of the Nevels family anxiously looks out the cab's window, hoping for a glimpse of their new home, but smoke, steam, and ice blur their fields of vision. Arnow's narrator describes how "the frost on the car windows was at times a reddish pink, as if bits of blood had frozen with the frost" (*TD*, 163). Here we see a dim progression of gloom from the snow- and dirt-encrusted windows of the train to the cab's windows speckled with a substance resembling blood. Arnow's decision to make the frost reddish pink might be read as suggestive of the cost of human suffering in Cassie's death, Reuben's departure, and the utterly painful transition the family faces in Detroit. In this way and in others throughout the novel, Arnow personifies the city.

From the family's arrival until the close of the novel, Arnow depicts the city as a forceful, living being that exerts a considerable amount of control over the family. The narrator also reveals Gertie's shock when she sees her new home: "She had hardly thought of [the houses] at all, they were so little and so still against the quivering crimson light, under the roaring airplane, so low after the giant smokestacks" (*TD*, 164). Here Arnow draws a clear connection between the Nevels family's home and their social status: like the tenements dwarfed by the factory smokestacks, the family cowers in the presence of a capitalist system that requires either adjustment or abandonment. Arnow leaves no room for any middle ground between these two choices. While she depicts the act of reading, writing, and learning in the Kentucky cabin as a peaceful event that unfolds in a shared context, her descriptions of Detroit set up a much different literacy situation that soon presents difficult, divisive choices for the Nevels family.

Perhaps one of the most tragic aspects of *The Dollmaker* is that the Nevels family moves to Detroit with high expectations of the public school system. Gertie and her children envision a gymnasium, a sprawling library, and hot food served at lunch. The reality that awaits them presents a much different picture of "opportunity," as Arnow demonstrates in Gertie's first encounter with the school building: "Below the flag she saw a black roof streaked with snow, and under the roof two rows of empty windows set in the dark soot-stained walls of a two-story brick building that rose high and straight out of the dirty, trampled, paper-littered snow. The bit of yard was separated from the street by a high iron fence, like the fences she had heard were about penitentiaries" (*TD*, 194). This impression of the school immediately challenges Gertie's initial belief that a school could provide a better education for her children than she could at home.

Most readers would agree that Arnow portrays city life—including participation in its educational system—as undesirable, but read within a literacy context, this passage also encourages readers to see the empty windows of the school as representative of the young minds of Gertie's children. To take this reading even further, the paper strewn about the snow might be read as suggestive of the children's previous literacies that they will necessarily leave behind to function within the city school system.

Equally disturbing, as Gertie nears the building, she sees "two little flimsy-looking houses" that remind her of "the makeshift railroad workers' houses she had seen in the Valley" (*TD*, 194). Once she learns that these structures function as portable classrooms, she begins to seriously doubt the validity of her first assumptions about superior Northern schooling. In comparing the classrooms to railroad housing, Arnow once again links the imprisonment of the train, the city, and the city's school system. To be sure that readers understand the relationship between factories and schools, Arnow describes Gertie's reaction to the sound of the school: "Once outside, she stopped and turned around and stood for a long time staring at the gray building in the square of the dirty snow. A look of listening was on her face, for from [the school] there came between the sounds of distant trains and traffic a faint humming—like that from factories she had passed" (203). Arnow emphasizes that in addition to looking and functioning like a factory, the school even sounds like one, further highlighting the transition its students endure in having their literacies commodified like any other factory product.

The faith that Gertie places in the school system wavers when she sees the building, and it only deteriorates from that point on. Several literacy scholars note similar trends when formally uneducated people have unrealistic expectations for school systems or in the results of learning to read and write. Juliet Merrifield's study, for example, notes that "all the [Appalachian] people we profiled value education and literacy, perhaps having unrealistic expectations of the difference it could make in their own and their children's economic situations" (1997, 87). Although the participants in this study seem most concerned with economic gain resulting from literacy, Gertie and her children focus instead on what they believe a city school can provide, including material luxuries absent from rural schools (things like access to large libraries and sports teams), as well as instruction from supposedly better-qualified teachers. While the school does function as a site of learning, its primary instruction trains the children to remake themselves into obedient factory workers. Arnow's framing of their choices leaves little room for any negotiated middle ground between Appalachia and Detroit.

Just as Shirley Brice Heath argues that "the school is not a neutral objective arena; it is an institution which has the goal of changing people's values, skills, and knowledge bases" (1983, 367), Arnow clearly depicts the goal of the Detroit school system—standardization. Before leaving Kentucky the older Nevels children already know how to read and write; it is the new required reading of Detroit that threatens to either destroy or remake them. Read within this context, Gertie's first encounter with the school building clearly foreshadows the way her children will face difficult decisions about self-identification in the city. The building's factory-like appearance prefigures the commodification of Gertie's children's learning: although the building will produce educated students, the implication is that each child will resemble all of the others, just as any viable industrial product would.

When she finally enters the school building, Gertie realizes that literacy functions differently in Detroit. She remembers that "all a body had to do in Kentucky was send their youngens to school the day the County Health people came" (*TD*, 198), but in Detroit Gertie must assume responsibility for having her children immunized before starting school. Similarly, the Detroit enrollment process asks that she read, understand, and sign documents, but Gertie hesitates because "she had never put her name to anything, joined anything, promised anything" (198). In the school office Gertie signs three times, once for each child, and leaves her children's birth certificates on the desk "as directed," a symbolic representation of relinquishing educational control to the Detroit school system (200). Although such formal documents are not necessarily used against the Nevels family, as they were and are for many marginalized people, the paperwork signals an altogether new way of life.[3]

In this scene Arnow also depicts typical assumptions about Appalachian illiteracy when Cassie's teacher, Miss Vashinski, assumes that an inability to read and write causes Gertie to hesitate in signing the documents, when instead Gertie pauses to ponder the consequences of outsourcing the educational training of her children. Here Arnow emphasizes an Appalachian character's literate ability while simultaneously highlighting Miss Vashinksi's misreading of Gertie's literacy, yet in this situation Miss Vashinksi (not Gertie) exerts control over the Nevels children. In scenes like this one, readers become aware of the kinds of literacy valued in Detroit as Arnow continues to reveal how the city's cultural value system differs from the Nevels family's mountain existence in Kentucky. Yet at the same time, Gertie's resistance to "joining anything" recalls stereotypical notions about stubbornly individualistic mountaineers. At this point in the novel readers begin to understand the inevitable standoff between Gertie and the city's survival expectations.

Foregrounding the required discursive shifts of the Nevels children, Arnow portrays Enoch's first walk to school as a kind of rite of passage that initiates him into a new, marginalized position in Detroit. First a neighborhood boy hits him and knocks his cap off, and then another boy throws the hat into a trash heap and yells: "Go to yu public school, yu hillbilly heathen, youse. We don't have to go to school with niggers an Jews and hillbillies" (*TD*, 187). Here the boy insults Enoch in three ways: he points out a class-based divide between children who attend public schools and those who attend more expensive private Catholic schools; he connects heathen with hillbilly, suggesting an inherent superiority of the Catholic faith, which isolates Enoch and his Protestant family; and he compares hillbillies with Jews and African Americans, insinuating a religious and racial divide based on Appalachian heritage.

Literary critic Rachel Lee Rubin claims that *The Dollmaker* "demonstrates how the meaning of 'Appalachia' or 'the Kentucky mountains' for one family changes from a regional description, with meaning fixed in the present ('home'), to be understood as a designation of ethnicity, signifying both the historical past and the family's point of cultural origin" (1998, 177). She also writes that after the family moves to Detroit, "displacement is the key quality in the makeup of their ethnic identity" (178). In insulting Enoch based on the displacement Rubin identifies, the boy schools Enoch in reading Detroit as a racialized text, and Enoch becomes aware of his inferior position within that text. Moreover, the boy's comment situates Appalachians alongside other groups marginalized by ethnicity, a move that once again places Appalachian literacy dilemmas within a larger context.

Certainly the bully sees "hillbilly" as its own ethnic marker. Scholar Anthony Harkins has traced the tradition of portraying hillbillies as their own separate ethnicity to the late 1800s, and by the time Arnow published *The Dollmaker* in 1954, she was all too familiar with popular hillbilly stereotypes, since she too moved from Kentucky to Detroit, where she lived in standardized housing.[4] The neighborhood boy's intermingling of a slur about race, religious affiliation, and common stereotypes about mountain people illuminates how many of the residents in Detroit conceive of the Nevels family—they are different and must be categorized with all other negatively "different" groups. The factories that initially draw the family to Detroit also appeal to a range of other ethnic groups, and the resulting workforce resembles a multicultural sampling; Schafer writes that "all kinds of people are pulled into the labor camps to be homogenized as assembly-line robots" (1986, 49). This variation sometimes produces tension among different groups, and in the scene Arnow describes, Enoch's encounter mirrors the diversity (and potential insults) his father faces by seeking industrialized factory work.

Arnow does little to conceal the racist ideologies of many of Detroit's residents. Exposure to such thinking causes the Nevels family to consider their place in the Detroit hierarchy of racial classification, and this realization works in tandem with the acquisition of various other literacies required by the city. Before Gertie and the children even exit the Detroit train station, they are called "hillbilly" twice (*TD*, 151, 156). Soon after entering their cold apartment, a neighbor child, Maggie, brings firewood and explains: "These houses, they're good and warm anu rent's cheap, and they're the only places in Detroit where they keep u niggers out, really keep um out—sagainsa law. The niggers got into u last neighborhood where we lived" (175).

Maggie's comments demonstrate that a shared fear and loathing of African Americans bonds the residents of the Merry Hill housing project, which seems to make Gertie uneasy, since she recently befriended a black woman from Georgia aboard the train to Detroit. Gertie soon learns that many neighbors dislike "hillbillies" almost as much as African Americans, and such a comparison once again reminds readers of the similar dilemmas marginalized groups face in an urban environment. Arnow also emphasizes Gertie's recognition of this prejudice to illustrate Gertie's understanding of a complex racial structure. By this point in the novel Arnow has not only endowed Gertie with the ability to read, write, and whittle, but Arnow has also given Gertie and Enoch the skills necessary to read the racial injustices of the city.

Moreover, through this reading Enoch eventually leaves behind all aspects of his mountain identity, revealing once again Arnow's polarized portrayal of discourse transitioning. It is worth noting that theories developed by literacy scholars like Gee do not account for how Arnow's characters react to the "either-or" dichotomy that she establishes in the novel. While literacy scholars theorize about how learners seldom lose all elements of their primary discourse when undergoing a transition like Enoch's, in her fictionalization of these transitions, Arnow has Enoch leave behind virtually all remnants of his mountain self. Her authorial decision to do so not only adds an alternative to the ways literacy scholars conceptualize literacy acquisition, but it also exaggerates the cost of new literacies for some of her characters, making it difficult for readers to ignore such consequences.

Shortly after depicting characters who think of the Nevels family as hillbillies, Arnow highlights a parallel, yet opposite, view of the family. When Gertie takes her children to school for the first time she carries necessary paperwork in a basket. Calling it a "beautiful basket," the art teacher, Mr. Skyros, exclaims that he has "never seen one like it" (*TD*, 200). Gertie explains that a man from home, "Ole Josiah Coffey," made the basket, and Mr. Skyros seems so taken with it that she temporarily leaves it with him and his students. Arnow spends little time developing this scene, but it says much about the social climate in which the Nevels family operates in Detroit.

Harkins (2004) argues that while hillbillies were seen as ignorant, degenerate, and dangerous, they were also simultaneously viewed as wholesome remnants of a simpler, purer time in American society. Northerners in particular found mountain crafts and folkways attractively unique, and Mr. Skyros's appreciation of Gertie's white oak splint basket does not seem unusual.[5] Although Mr. Skyros's reaction to the basket and its producer might make it seem as though he exoticizes Gertie and the Appalachian region, his respect for the craft prevents such oversimplification. Unlike the giggling children loitering in the hallway, who laugh at Gertie's accent, Mr. Skyros shows respect for Gertie.

Through a discussion between Gertie and Mr. Skyros about the basket's beauty, Arnow makes clear that they share an appreciation for natural beauty, and the basket functions as an object that represents the shared language of art. In establishing a dialogue between Mr. Skyros and Gertie, Arnow suggests that we might read the basket as a kind of text. Both Mr. Skyros and Gertie have the literate ability to read that text, allowing them to communicate through an artistic medium. Arnow's rendering of this exchange between city-dwelling Mr. Skyros and Appalachian-born Gertie not only emphasizes Gertie's literate skill set, but it also reveals Gertie's ability to communicate effectively with those outside her home-based discourse community, at least within a limited scope.

Clytie and Enoch, though, express embarrassment over the basket, as when Clytie says, "Mom, I don't think people up here carries baskets" (*TD*, 188), and Enoch begs, "Mom, don't make me carry this old basket no more. Some youngens called us hillbillies and throwed snowballs" (247), revealing feelings of shame connected to their mountain heritage. By depicting Clytie's and Enoch's desire to distance themselves from both the basket and the Appalachian place it represents, Arnow implies that in order for objects to communicate effectively, the bearer of the "text" must present it as worthy of being read. This instance also operates as a representative illustration of the way Arnow dichotomizes her characters' identity choices: even though Gertie is shy in her new environment, she remains proud of the basket, while Clytie and Enoch shun any connection to mountain crafts.

Arnow soon returns to the issue of school-controlled literacy when Mr. Skyros seems concerned that Gertie might not feel comfortable leaving the basket with him. Gertie responds, "I've left four youngens here. I oughtn't to mind leaven a old split basket" (*TD*, 202), as if whatever he might do with the basket could hardly compare to the changes her children will undergo as a result of Detroit schooling. Mr. Skyros tells Gertie that her children will be "all right," but Arnow also makes clear that he understands the transitions necessitated for the children by their relocation to Detroit. He hesitatingly reassures Gertie: "This school has many children from many places, but in the end they all—most—adjust, and so will yours. They're young" (202). By separating the words *all* and *most* with a dash, Arnow tempts literary critics to debate his meaning: if we combine *all* and *most* to mean "almost," his statement could imply that although many of the children appear to have adjusted, none of them have truly forsaken all of their pre-Detroit identities. This notion supports the kind of dialectical negotiation theorized by literacy scholars, yet when read with the eventual decisions of the Nevels children in mind, his statement means that most, but not all, children choose a Detroit-approved identity, just as Clytie and Enoch adjust, while Reuben and Cassie resist identity reformation.

Pondering Mr. Skyros's predictions, Gertie questions him further about the way he uses the word *adjust*, and he tells her, "Yes, adjust, learn to get along, like it—be like the others—learn to want to be like the others" (*TD*, 202). In connecting adjustment with desire, Mr. Skyros signals that in order for such discourse transitioning to be successful, the children must want to change, and here Arnow reveals how the residents of Detroit shape the Nevels family's view of itself. The scene of a boy calling Enoch a hillbilly on his first day of school marks the beginning of Enoch's desire to reshape himself and his identity—what Mr. Skyros calls adjustment—and Arnow portrays Enoch's transition as both voluntary (to maintain some sense of self-esteem and to avoid mockery for his mountain ways) and required (to function in Detroit). Additionally, the adjustment Arnow portrays implies a stark choice between Kentucky and Detroit, between old and new.

While transitioning from a primary to secondary discourse often embodies such difficult decisions, literacy scholars like Paulo Freire argue that the negotiation between discourse communities opens a dialectical space in which critical consciousness can begin to take shape. Such critical awareness of one's place in the world makes communication and growth between two discursive worlds possible. In *Pedagogy of the Oppressed*, Freire calls this process cultural synthesis, and he writes that "in cultural synthesis—and only in cultural synthesis—it is possible to resolve the contradiction between the world view of the leaders and that of the people, to the enrichment of both. Cultural synthesis does not deny the differences between the two views; indeed, it is based on those differences" (1970, 162).

By applying this idea to *The Dollmaker*, we see that Arnow views the city of Detroit as the leader and the Nevels family as "the people." In order for cultural synthesis to occur, each party must be aware of the other's differences and willing to work toward a collective understanding. Arnow, however, does not grant her characters such willingness. As mentioned in the beginning of this chapter, this authorial decision should not be read as a literary flaw, but rather as Arnow's way of commenting on the dire—and all too often overlooked—identity choices literacy requires in a new, unfamiliar environment.

This short but potent scene reveals an additional layer of understanding as Gertie continues to ponder Mr. Skyros's definition. She realizes that "adjusting" would entail far more than learning to get along; it would also mean leaving behind many of the values and perspectives of Kentucky not accepted in Detroit and essentially adopting a homogenized set of middle-class values. Arnow highlights Gertie's resistance to this idea when she describes Gertie's reaction: "'Oh.' [Gertie] pondered, looking down the hall—ugly gray—and at the children laughing in the doorway, then turned to him with a slow headshake. 'I want em to be happy, but I don't know as I want em to—to—'" (*TD*, 202). Mr. Skyros prompts her by asking, "Adjust?," and Gertie replies, "Leastways not too good" (202).

Here Gertie emphasizes that while she wants her children to succeed in school, she does not want them to forsake old literacies tied to their Appalachian home. In this particular scene Arnow portrays Gertie as perfectly capable of reading the requirements demanded by the school system, but as resisting them. Just as the paper-littered snow surrounding the school evokes the collective forsaken identities of the schoolchildren, the gray hall in which Gertie contemplates "adjustment" suggests the liminal space of transition from one discourse community to another (and the drastic shift between black and white). Arnow's characterization of the color gray as "ugly" also describes how Gertie feels about the situation in which she and her children find themselves.

Their conversation concludes with a disclosure between Gertie and Mr. Skyros that suggests a sense of collusion between them. Before she leaves, Mr. Skyros leans in, "like one preparing to share a secret," and hopefully tells her, "Maybe they won't adjust at all. . . . Most of us do, but there's always hope that one—" (*TD*, 202). He stops before finishing, as if the possibility of one of her children remaining unchanged seems unlikely at best. Although Arnow leaves this statement incomplete, its inclusion operates as an important feature: like Gertie, Mr. Skyros shares hope for independence in the face of the school-based pressures of adjustment. It is not only Gertie who resists the drastic transitions necessary for literacy commodification—Mr. Skyros does too. Before Gertie leaves he tells her, "Your children will be all right. They will, I fear, adjust better than their mother" (202). Although we could read his statement as sympathetic toward Gertie and her refusal to adjust, taken within the context of the reading developed thus far, his statement instead credits Gertie for her resistance, and he fears the consequences of her children reshaping their identities.

The conversation that takes place between the two also perfectly captures the dilemma Gee outlines in *Social Linguistics and Literacies: Ideology in Discourses*, in which he explores the inherent conflicts that arise when a person's home-based discourse differs with a school-based discourse. Discussing African American children, Gee argues that "in becoming a full member of school Discourses," these children "run the risk of becoming complicit with values that denigrate and damage their home-based Discourse and identity" (1996, ix), and Gee also acknowledges that this same dilemma exists for many other groups.

Certainly the Nevels children find that to be accepted in school they must alter the way they act, dress, and especially the way they speak. These alterations operate as a particularly damaging form of literacy required by the school system and one that results in a palpable sense of loss for those renouncing their Appalachian identities. Gee points out that "the most striking continuity in the history of literacy is the way in which literacy has been used, in age after age, to solidify the social hierarchy, empower elites, and ensure that people lower on the hierarchy accept the values, norms, and beliefs of the elites, even when it is not in their self-interest or group interest to do so" (1996, 36). In the case of *The Dollmaker*, because most of the Nevels children can already read and write before arriving in Detroit, the literacy that solidifies the social hierarchy present in Detroit is one of forced discourse transition, forsaken Appalachian identity, and "adjustment."

Grounded upon the required literacy of adjustment, the Detroit school system functions as a social institution whose goal is to produce remarkably similar pupils who become commodities, and this process of commodification occurs largely as a result of imposed literacies. In keeping with Harvey Graff's (1979) sociological study about the effects of literacy rates for industrialized workers in nineteenth-century Canada, Gee claims that simply learning the technical skill of reading and writing does not guarantee acceptance or success in the dominant discourse (in the case of the Nevels family, the school-based discourse of urban Detroit). However, as outlined in previous chapters, Gee's definition of literacy as the "mastery of a secondary Discourse" (1996, 143) illustrates that the Nevels children have an important choice to make regarding their discourse community affiliation.[6]

Because they are able to read the requirements for acceptance within the Detroit school system, the most critical literacy demanded of the Nevels children is one of abandonment: Clytie and Enoch find approval in the school community only when they sever ties with their former (mountain) way of dressing, speaking, and conceiving of the world. Once aware that Detroit rejects their mountain heritage, they follow suit and thereby master the secondary discourse of Detroit, which has obvious disdain for all things Appalachian. Conversely, Reuben and Cassie opt for rejection by the city in a desperate attempt to preserve their mountain identities. As these choices are made, readers begin to see that Arnow leaves no room for any sort of negotiation between Appalachia and the new urban environment in which the Nevels family lives. Her presentation of this divide, and the consequences that ensue, sends a rhetorical warning that enjoins readers to embrace a more flexible approach when encountering similar identity dilemmas in their own lives.

In addition to the work of literacy theorists, sociologist Pierre Bourdieu's (1984) concept of cultural capital also proves useful when considering the Nevels children's struggle to gain entrance into the dominant discourse. As Bourdieu points out, economic and social capital are almost always necessary in order to gain cultural capital, and the Nevels family certainly has no economic capital to spare. Moreover, the goal of the Detroit school system in which the Nevels children participate is not entrance into the dominant discourse; rather, the system aims to produce pupils ready to become industrialized (if educated) factory workers. One of the ways the school goes about achieving this goal is through literacy instruction. The Detroit school system has no room for the kind of cultural longing both Reuben and Cassie possess because such loving affiliation with an area and set of values so far removed from urban Detroit will only result in unhappy pupils and, later, unhappy workers. If, however, the school system achieves its goal of adjustment, as it does with Clytie and Enoch, then students will accept the required literacies of the city, leaving school prepared to labor in an effort to meet the ongoing payments that characterize the cycle of debt factory workers face upon entering the industrialized economic system.

Identity Decisions and Their Consequences

Soon after the children begin school, Arnow reveals which of the Nevels children will purposefully and knowingly transition into this new, secondary discourse and which will refuse. Clytie refashions herself and her modes of speaking early on, and when talking to teachers Gertie self-consciously remembers, "Clytie didn't want her to say 'youngens'" (*TD*, 329). Enoch reacts similarly, as when he seems embarrassed to see his mother standing in the school hallway watching him through the door: "[Gertie] saw him sitting up near the front of the room with a book and some papers on his desk. She looked at him, smiling, until he lifted his head. He turned red, looked quickly away, then down, and began a furious scribbling. She stood an instant watching, her smile dying slowly" (331).

Just before Enoch sees her, Gertie remembers that before the family moved to Detroit, she and Clytie had been responsible for educating Enoch, and she was proud to see him working and learning in a "real" school. While he gains the technical ability of literacy in Kentucky, and continues honing those skills in a Detroit school, the contextual situation in which Enoch learns has changed drastically; by consciously avoiding his mother because of embarrassment, he has made a decision to discard his home-based discourse of Kentucky. Such a decision understandably hurts Gertie, but it also fosters Enoch's ability to understand the city of Detroit, and Clytie finds similar results in her strategies of "adjusting." Later in the novel, after the family has lived in Detroit for over a year, Gertie reflects that Clytie "looked like any thousands of other girls Gertie had seen" (*TD*, 519), and Arnow makes Clytie's transformation abundantly clear.

Unlike Enoch and Clytie, Reuben chooses to maintain ties with his home discourse and thus finds himself at odds with Detroit and its classrooms. Gee sheds light on Reuben's dilemma when he explains that the friction between discourse communities can be "particularly acute when they involve tension and conflict between one's primary Discourse and a dominant secondary Discourse, since one's primary Discourse defines one's 'home' identity and that of people with whom one is intimate and intimately connected" (1996, 146). After facing ridicule from his classmates, and even his teacher, Reuben still refuses to sever the kind of intimate home ties he has that Gee describes.

When Gertie tells him that he should not carry a knife, because Detroit is "differ'nt," he responds: "I've allus carried a knife. I ain't a quitten now. I ain't a maken myself over fer Detroit. I ain't a standen a taken nobody's lies—like you done" (*TD*, 316). Still angry with Gertie for moving the family to Detroit to be with Clovis (instead of standing up to her mother and buying their own farm in Kentucky), Reuben takes an accusatory tone with his mother, implying that his decision to rebel outshines Gertie's choice to follow Clovis to Detroit. Finally he secretly borrows money from his father and returns to Kentucky. Here Arnow highlights the difference in acceptable reactions to Detroit based on gender: Gertie praises Reuben's departure, but she feels unable to undertake such an escape for herself, no doubt as a result of her mother's biblically supported preaching to "leave all else an cleave to thy husband" (135). Even though Arnow emphasizes the fluidity of gender roles when Gertie eventually earns the bulk of the family's income in Detroit, typically a masculine role, Gertie rigidly adheres to her perceived womanly role by moving to Detroit, to the detriment of her family.

Reuben never verbally articulates his reason for leaving Detroit. The only line in his letter that explains his decision reads, "I can't stay here no more" (*TD*, 363), signaling that the loss of his Kentucky cultural roots is too much to bear. Arnow's decision to include a double negative in Reuben's message makes an important statement as well: although Reuben's sentence formation is considered grammatically incorrect in terms of Standard American English, readers understand and connect with its painful sentiment. Moreover, Arnow spends several scenes establishing Reuben's literacy skills early in the novel, suggesting that he may have intentionally included the grammatical "mistake" as a form of written resistance to Detroit and its literacies, an emphatic doubled response of "no." As such, the note to his parents serves as a permanent, written record of his ultimate refusal to sever ties with his Appalachian identity, one that Detroit judges as illiterate and nonfunctional.

The Detroit view of Appalachia also mirrors the way many Americans misperceive mountain people and their literate abilities, and Arnow's attention to Reuben's refusal to submit to this view further highlights the situational conflict literacy often introduces to marginalized groups while also subverting stereotypes about mountain illiteracy. No doubt literacy scholars like Gee and Freire would argue that such a portrayal prevents Reuben from gaining potentially positive elements of the secondary discourse of Detroit, working toward critical consciousness, or understanding the differences between home and Detroit that would be necessary for any hope of eventual cultural synthesis. Yet in other ways, the work of those same literacy scholars helps rationalize Arnow's representation of Reuben.

Although Arnow establishes the Nevels children's literate abilities while the family lives in Appalachia, the sudden removal from Kentucky and the ensuing traumatic relocation to Detroit makes Reuben's transition to another discourse unlikely. In *Literacy: Reading the Word and the World*, Freire and Donaldo Macedo discuss the importance of learners' understanding and feeling comfortable within their home discourse before transitioning to another, and their theories shed light on Reuben's resistance in Detroit: "The refusal to read the word chosen by the teacher is the realization on the part of the student that he or she is making a decision not to accept what is perceived as violating his or her world" (1987, 123).

In Kentucky, Reuben willingly takes part in literacy events led by his mother in the safety and security of their mountain cabin, but he refuses to participate in learning situations that take place in a Detroit classroom, where both students and teachers alike mock his speech, dress, and his very being. He maintains, "It ain't like back home. . . . Back home they ain't no youngens to giggle ever time I say somethen" (*TD*, 260). Such situations prove the New Literacy scholars' insistence that literacy operates in a complicated social context; Reuben literally refuses to work toward gaining the cultural capital required of him in Detroit. Arnow frames Reuben's "deviation" as an understandable and potentially admirable form of resistance, even as it fails to alter the dominant discourses in power. Because Reuben refuses to function in Detroit, he must return to Kentucky; his only other alternative would have entailed an attempt at adjusting to Detroit, and Gee warns that such techniques are "almost always socially disastrous" (1996, 143).

Similarly, in her discussion of Amish literacy practices, scholar Andrea Fishman describes how a young boy's (Eli) definitions of literacy align with those found in his classroom, even though those definitions differ from "mainstream" ones. In speculating about what would happen if Eli's value system and beliefs about literacy were at odds with those of his school, she writes,

> I suspect that Eli would have had to make some difficult choices that would have amounted to choosing between what he had learned and learned to value at home and what he seemed expected to learn at school. To conform to his teacher's demands and values, he would have had to devalue or disavow those of his parents—a demand that public schools seem to make frequently of children from cultural or socioeconomic groups differing from those of their teachers or their schools, a demand that seems unfair, uncalled for, and unnecessary, not to mention counterproductive and destructive. (1990, 37–38)

The demands Fishman imagines might be placed on Eli in a non-Amish school are exactly the ones placed on Reuben in Detroit. Freire argues that successful learning situations must "acknowledge men and women as historical beings" and take their "historicity as [the] starting point" (1970, 65). Reuben's school, teachers, classmates, and much of Detroit at large refuse to acknowledge and respect the history and culture of the Nevels family. Clytie and Enoch deal with this reality by forsaking their home-based discourse in favor of a new secondary discourse, but

Reuben chooses to abandon Detroit entirely and instead returns home to a physically laborious life of farming. No negotiation between home and Detroit takes place for any of the Nevels children.

Although Arnow critic Haeja Chung reads Reuben's departure as a "disaster" (1995, 218), Arnow depicts Gertie as proud of Reuben for standing up for himself, suggesting that Gertie, at least, views his leaving as not disastrous but as a liberating act. When Gertie learns that Reuben is safe in Kentucky she says, "I'm glad. Real glad" (*TD*, 363), expressing relief that Reuben no longer has to fight the ongoing battle of adjustment in Detroit. Before Reuben leaves, Gertie visits Reuben's teacher, Mrs. Whittle, to discuss his unhappiness at school. Rachel Lee Rubin has asserted that the significance of Mrs. Whittle's name is its indication "that Gertie's artistic integrity is already outside of her control, located here in the denatured, pseudorational advocate of 'adjustment'" (1998, 183). If we substitute "literacy" for "artistic integrity" in Rubin's statement, it becomes clear that while Mrs. Whittle controls the school-based literacy rejected by Reuben, she also represents the control the city of Detroit—or rather, the financial need it generates—eventually has over Gertie's prized talent of whittling.

Mrs. Whittle treats Gertie as a second-class citizen, saying to her: "You hill—southerners who come here, don't you realize before you come that it will be a great change for your children? For the better, of course, but still a change" (*TD*, 333). Here Mrs. Whittle takes for granted that she knows best for Gertie's children. Gee calls this kind of dogmatic, ideological opinion a tacit theory of language, because people with such beliefs "have not spelled out the generalizations on which their claim rests" (1996, 13). In his introduction, Gee challenges his readers with his claim that "it is a moral obligation to render one's tacit theories overt when they have the potential to hurt people" (x).

Certainly Mrs. Whittle's theory rests on the hurtful assumption that Gertie and her children are lesser, but instead of engaging in the kind of dialogue with Gertie that Gee encourages, Mrs. Whittle simply goes on to bitterly explain that the influx of people from the Appalachian Mountains and elsewhere has resulted in overcrowded schools, making her job more difficult. She almost calls Gertie a hillbilly but manages to stop before saying the term in its entirety, presumably out of some sense of superficial courtesy.

Later in their discussion Mrs. Whittle ridicules Gertie for using the word *recollect* instead of *remember*. She then discusses Gertie's children: "The others have, I understand, adjusted quite well, especially the younger boy

[Enoch] and the older girl [Clytie], but Reuben—I remember him. . . . He has not adjusted" (*TD*, 334). Mrs. Whittle, like other school officials Gertie encounters, insists that adjusting is necessary. In a clever rhetorical strategy Gertie asks her, "You mean . . . that you're a teachen my youngens so's that, no matter what comes, they—they can live with it" (335). Mrs. Whittle agrees, and Gertie furthers the analogy by asking if learning to adjust would cause her children to accept the views of Hitler if they were schooled in Germany or support communists if they lived in Russia.

This line of questioning infuriates Mrs. Whittle, and Gertie explains at the end of their conference that neither she nor Reuben want to "adjust," and that Reuben "cain't hep the way he's made. It's a lot more trouble to roll out steel—an make it like you want it—than it is biscuit dough" (*TD*, 336). Here Gertie explicitly reveals an adherence to her home-based discourse. Even though she knows Reuben would have an easier time at school if he "adjusted" (as Enoch and Clytie do), she supports and understands his refusal to do so, even inadvertently crediting him as being stronger than his siblings. Here it is important to note that "the way Reuben is made" does not prevent learning in a secure environment, like the Kentucky cabin of his childhood. However, when expected to adjust to the requirements of the Detroit classroom—requirements that Arnow makes dependent on losing his sense of Appalachian identity—Reuben stubbornly refuses to be molded.

Like her children, Gertie has the ability to read the city of Detroit, and to some extent, she must read the city in order to provide for her family. Conversely, Reuben harbors no such obligation, and Arnow grants him the freedom to resist the literacy of Mrs. Whittle's classroom. This resistance prevents Reuben from engaging in any sort of dialectical learning process, and Arnow celebrates the preservation of his mountain identity.

The fictional conversation that occurs between Mrs. Whittle and Gertie happens all too often to the "real" people of Appalachia, particularly urban Appalachians who have migrated to cities like Cincinnati. Purcell-Gates (1995) chronicles the story of Jenny and Donny, a mother and son struggling to become literate.[7] In several instances Jenny explains that Donny's teachers are unwilling to help her, even though she tells them she cannot read his assignments or help him with his homework. Purcell-Gates explains, "The teachers felt that the culture [Jenny and Donny's urban Appalachian value system], as a whole, did not value education, that the parents did not know how to parent, and that the parents did not instill a desire for success" (37).

Even worse, when Purcell-Gates contacts one of Donny's teachers to discuss Jenny's difficulties in reading the teacher exclaims, "I *knew* she was ignorant as soon as she opened her mouth!" (164, italics in original). Purcell-Gates goes on to write that "[Jenny and Donny's] mountaineer dialect and accent invite contempt and/or derision from other urban dwellers" (38).

Similarly, in *The Dollmaker* Gertie's use of "recollect" when speaking to Mrs. Whittle, along with her constant struggles not to use unacceptable words like "youngens," betrays her as notably Other, branding her as a nonmember of the school-based discourse in which her children must participate in Detroit. As Gee points out, "In socially situated language use, one must simultaneously *say* the 'right' thing, *do* the 'right' thing, and in saying and doing express the 'right' *beliefs, values,* and *attitudes*" (1996, 124; italics added). Gertie fails to say, do, or express herself in the "right" way; such a deviance creates divisions between Gertie, her children, and her children's teachers.

Factories Here at Home; Factories There at School

As Gertie's children grapple with issues of identity within the Detroit school system, Gertie and Clovis struggle to stabilize the family's finances. The resulting commodification of Gertie's whittling talent parallels the school's commodification of the Nevels children's literacies. As early as the family's journey to the city, Arnow reveals that Gertie's talent carries with it the potential to earn money when a girl aboard the train tells her, "I'll bet yo could make big money whittlen. City people sometimes loves handmade stuff. It's worth mo'n a dollah—way mo'n that if you count the time" (*TD*, 149). Gertie remains skeptical, but when she carves a crucifix for her neighbor Victor, he inadvertently advertises her work when he places it in his window for the entire alley to admire.

Soon people begin offering to purchase hand-carved crucifixes from Gertie, and Clovis realizes the earning potential of such work. Always the supporter of modernization and machinery, he suggests using tools to expedite the process: "You could make a pretty good Christ with a jig saw" (*TD*, 317). Gertie initially resists the idea, but as the family's financial situation becomes dire, she listens to Clovis's counsel that "in this town a body could sell a million a them things if they was cheap enough. I do believe . . . that I can rig up some kind a jig saw, cheap, and that ud do th work in a tenth a th time" (368). Sadly, although carving functions as one of Gertie's only pleasures in Detroit, with Clovis's new machinery she realizes that "now it was money she wasted when she whittled a thorn, a strand of hair, or a fold in the loincloth that didn't have to be there" (369). As Gertie's once favorite pastime becomes commodified, her living space becomes a factory-like space, paralleling the transition into industrial society her children have already encountered in school.

Once Clovis creates a machine that will cut identical pieces of wood for crucifixes, dolls, or anything else Gertie can make to sell, he proudly suggests that the entire family get involved: "Tell you what, we'll start us a factory . . . Yer mom can be th pattern maker; I'll be the toolmaker, tool-an-die man, and repairman; you, Enoch, can be machine operator; Clytie can run th trim department; an Amos—well, on jumpen-jack dolls, fer instance, he can be a 'sembly hand—run the strings through the holes" (*TD*, 477). By assigning specific jobs to each child, the production process mirrors that of a factory's assembly line, and the children participate in the commodification of Gertie's most prized talent—the ability to whittle. Enoch's suggestion to hang a sign over the bedroom door that reads "Nevels' Woodworking Plant" further emphasizes the ways in which a once safe domestic space now functions as a factory. Like his sister Clytie, Enoch anxiously adapts to the drastically new discourse community of Detroit. After suggesting the sign he realizes: "It would be better to put No. 1 after the name so that people passing by would think that there was more than one Nevels plant" (477).

Gertie loathes the idea of factory-produced pieces, and she especially dislikes the machine that allows such production: "It was like a monster from some fairy tale that, instead of grinding salt, spewed ugliness into the world" (*TD*, 485). Here Arnow references the Norwegian folk tale "Why the Sea Is Salt"[8] to dual effect: Gertie's reference once again alludes to her literary awareness, and it also recalls the moral of a tale that depicts the consequences of greedy consumption. In the story a man obtains a device that can grind anything the owner wishes, but the owner must know how to stop the machine when enough of the desired product has been made. Several times in the story characters purchase the grinder without learning how to properly operate it, and they must return it to the original owner so he can make it stop grinding.

In the final scene, a man hastily takes the grinder to the middle of the ocean and tells it to grind salt without knowing how to turn it off. The grinder continues to produce salt until the boat sinks, and the tale declares that the grinder still sits at the bottom of the ocean today, making ocean waters salty. In comparing Clovis's doll-making device with the story's grinder, Arnow suggests that once the Nevels family starts using the contraption to make dolls, they will not be able to stop. Even more disturbing, Arnow's comparison implies that the mass production of dolls will create insatiable consumers as well as prevent Gertie from creating her own original artwork.

Despite Gertie's hatred for the work, the family's need for money overcomes her resistance to factory-produced art. Gertie's production of the dolls replaces Clovis's previous factory work as one of the family's main sources of income, since plant shutdowns, layoffs, and union strikes result in frequent unemployment. By this point in the novel readers understand that in the same way that Gertie loses the enjoyment of slow, careful carving to quick production for profit, so too do the children lose aspects of their mountain selves when choosing to succeed in Detroit.

Gertie's second oldest son, Enoch, offers a notable example of such a change by laughing at a caricature of a hillbilly woman in the newspaper comics. The narrator describes the woman, who in many ways evokes Gertie's journey from the comfort of Kentucky to the discomfort and rejection of Detroit, as "barefooted, sunbonneted, driving a raw-boned mule fastened to a homemade sled. They were going to town, and the woman on the way changed her bonnet for a silly looking hat with a big bird and a little long-stemmed flower; the old mule looked round and bucked and knocked down the woman" (*TD*, 523). The cartoon reminds Gertie of her beloved mother-in-law, Kate, and she feels angry that Enoch finds humor in the illustration. Consequently she lightly slaps him but then immediately regrets it, saying only "It wasn't funny" in her defense (524).

As Joyce Carol Oates notes in the novel's afterword, Enoch has "learned the proper contempt for a 'hillbilly,'" and this episode once again demonstrates the cost of accepting the kind of literacy valued by Detroit (*TD*, 606). Perhaps even more disturbing than his contempt, in this scene Enoch seems to have forgotten his first day of school when other children called him a hillbilly. In having him laugh at the cartoon of a mountain woman, Arnow erases any remaining ties with his Appalachian identity; he has now become literate in prejudice.

Enoch's reading of Detroit also teaches him how to sell things, and he demonstrates the capitalistic tendencies of an effective entrepreneur once Gertie consigns herself to making mass-produced dolls to sell. Near the end of the novel Arnow depicts Enoch's now standardized sales pitch:

"Dolls—genuine hand-carved dolls. Solid maple, safe fer a baby—unbreakable string—safe fer a baby" (*TD*, 503). Although Gertie makes the dolls from cheap scrap lumber, and they are painted in what she considers a cheap and loathsome fashion, Enoch's sales strategies work, bringing in much-needed family income. Enoch's school-induced desire for factory-produced materials echoes his mother's forced doll-production techniques, both signaling "adjustment" to a new factory-like discourse in Detroit.

Too Little, Too Late

Like Reuben, Gertie's youngest daughter, Cassie, refuses Detroit-initiated homogenization, and Gertie struggles to reconcile how she feels about Cassie's resistance. After Reuben's return to Kentucky, Gertie clings to Cassie because "Reuben was lost to her [and] the alley had the others" (*TD*, 380). Although Gertie feels a sense of pride when she thinks of Reuben's refusal to "adjust," she also knows that in order to have a chance at success in Detroit, her children must adjust; she only wishes that they could somehow hold on to their Appalachian selves while doing so. In not allowing negotiation between their Appalachian and Detroit identities, Arnow limits the cultural exchange process literacy scholars have identified in literacy acquisition and discourse community transition, but, as mentioned earlier, this limitation further highlights the dilemmas her characters face. Likewise, her focus on Gertie's desire once again proves rhetorically strategic when readers pause to consider its futility, given her stubborn refusal to consider any kind of negotiation between home and Detroit. Clovis even tells Gertie that she too needs to adjust: "That's one a yer big troubles, Gert . . . you won't give in to bein' like other people. But it's somethen millions an millions a people has got to do, an the sooner a person learns it, th better" (368).

Gertie feels guilty "killing" Cassie's imaginary playmate, Callie Lou, since it is the last significant remnant of Cassie's mountain identity, but she follows through with her decision because Clovis warns that if she does not, "th other youngens'ull git to thinken she's quair, an you'll have another Reuben" (*TD*, 368). Mrs. Anderson, a neighbor, makes a similar admonition: "You'll have to help [Cassie] grow out of that dream world. . . . The other children think them queer, and it gets harder and harder for them to adjust" (379). Just as Gertie feels torn about Reuben's departure, it is with great difficulty that she "kills" Callie Lou. The narrator reveals: "[Gertie] was breathing hard, choked up inside, fighting down a great hunger to seize and hug and kiss the child, and cry; 'Keep her, Cassie. Keep Callie Lou. A body's got to have something all their own'" (380). Eventually Gertie decides that Cassie can "have Callie Lou at home," but Gertie's first real attempt at negotiation comes too late, since all along Cassie has kept Callie Lou alive outside, which later results in a tragic train accident.

Even Gertie recognizes that although Callie Lou does not fare well in Detroit due to other children's taunts, Callie Lou would be safe in Kentucky, and Gertie wishes "the war [was] over and they [were] home, a family whole again with Reuben, and only the trees and Gyp to hear the talk with Callie Lou" (*TD*, 372). Perhaps Cassie could have kept Callie Lou in Kentucky, but had she attended school (as the children did when one was available), it seems likely that her classmates would have mocked her imaginary friend, just as they do in Detroit. In presenting Gertie's longing in a romanticized way, Arnow fails to acknowledge that the death of an imaginary friend might be part of Cassie's maturation regardless of whether she lived in Kentucky or Detroit.

Instead, Gertie blames Detroit for the death of Callie Lou and consequently of Cassie as well: Cassie's insistence on keeping Callie Lou causes her to stray farther and farther away from the apartment so Gertie won't hear their conversation, and she eventually retreats to the railroad tracks to play with Callie Lou. Tragically, a train kills both girls, literally and figuratively. Cassie's refusal to banish Callie Lou results in death, a symbolic representation of the destruction Detroit inflicts on those who refuse to remake themselves in its image. Cassie's death by train proclaims that for Arnow's characters, the choice between life and death, Kentucky and Detroit, is an "either-or" decision: the Nevels family must acquiesce to the city's requirements or return home.

In Cassie's gruesome death scene and the events that follow, Arnow explicitly illustrates the consequences resulting from forced discourse transitioning. Notably, the two characters that suffer most are female. Reuben refuses to participate in the Detroit classroom and community, and as a young male he succeeds in returning home. However, when Cassie exerts what little agency she has as a young girl by keeping the symbolic representation of her mountain self alive, her insistence kills them both, resulting in an almost unbearable loss for Gertie.

In an interview with Chung, Arnow says that when writing the novel, she "kept thinking of Gertie, who couldn't learn [to function in Detroit], partly because she didn't really want to" (Chung 1995, 213). However, as the person responsible for the family's financial survival, Gertie has little choice but to function in Detroit, while Reuben has the option of escape. Even as Gertie assumes the traditionally male role of provider for her family, her devotion to her family leaves her with a fatalistic outlook that prevents any further attempts at the negotiation she timidly began when she decided Cassie could keep Callie Lou at home.

Unions: Another Missed Negotiation Opportunity

In the same way that the Nevels children must read the Detroit school system, Clovis quickly learns that in order to keep his factory job, he must read and understand the written, social, and cultural rules of the city, including the nature of factory work. Before leaving Kentucky, Gertie listens to a post office conversation about factory work in Oak Ridge. The following comment foreshadows Clovis's Detroit job, as well as the predicament of the Nevels children in the Detroit school system: "People worked without knowing what they did, and never asked" (*TD*, 114).

Gertie overhears a similar remark when her neighbor Sophronie explains to a group of women how she fell from the factory "merry-go-round," a large piece of assembly machinery on which she works: "On a merry-go-round they ain't no fallen back—no gitten ahead. You go jist as fast as it goes" (*TD*, 296). This term presents new information for Gertie, and in reading its meaning she slowly begins to realize that industrial work does not guarantee financial success for the family, nor does it ensure safe working conditions for Clovis and his coworkers. The symbolism in Sophronie's words illustrates the entrapment of factory work—once families purchase items on payment plans, they must continue to work in order to meet payments, and low wages and unsafe conditions prevent workers from ever moving ahead economically. Arnow's choice to reference a piece of machinery as a "merry-go-round" also evokes images of children and playgrounds, yet once readers realize, with Gertie, that the merry-go-round is anything but safe, they are again encouraged to see the parallels Arnow draws between industrial work and Detroit schooling.

In a book set in industrial Detroit, unions understandably play a significant role, yet they fail to provide any real sense of agency—or negotiation between competing discourse communities—for Arnow's characters. When Gertie registers her children for school and does not have a family physician to list on the necessary forms, the secretary tells Gertie to list hers since "it don't make no difference, nohow ... Them doctors, they've got a strong union, stronger than u CIO. They'll come if they wanta an yu ain't got seven dollars, an if they don't wanta come yu seven dollars don't do yu no good" (*TD*, 199).

Arnow portrays Clovis's factory union in a similar way, yet he participates in it because he feels obligated to do so. He even tells Gertie, "Gert, time an agin I've told ye I don't know nothen about the union's business" (*TD*, 511). Despite a purposeful distancing from union politics, Clovis gets hurt guarding another union man, and he seeks revenge by presumably murdering his attacker. Instead of portraying unions as a space for negotiation and dialectical learning between two different discursive worlds, Arnow presents union membership as another troublesome—and even violent—requirement of living in an urban environment. Such a depiction sentimentalizes the family's existence in Kentucky (the home of vast resource exploitation by coal and timber companies during the time in which the novel is set), and Clovis's participation in union activity emerges as yet another aspect of leaving behind his Appalachian identity.

A Grim Ending with a Lesson for Readers

Near the novel's close Gertie continues to produce dolls in a factory-like manner in hopes of supporting the family financially, but excepting the time she spends carving her treasured block of wild cherry wood, her carving brings little pleasure. She often laments her former life in Kentucky, as when the narrator provides a snapshot of Gertie's regret:

> To have Dock [the family mule] in a barn, even a rented barn, and around her food for the winter, and then be able to stand in the barn hall and listen to the rain while she held the night's milk . . . and above her on the hill would be the house with her children, all her children, safe. To live that way, without debts, unions, boys in cars, foremen, traffic; to be free from the fears, forever at her back—. (*TD*, 524)

Gertie can only dream of her past life, since she never achieves it in reality. In a wrenchingly sad effort to earn more money for the family, Gertie chops her prized block of wood into pieces—the project she has painstakingly worked on for years—so she can use the lumber to make wooden figures to sell. In the novel's afterword, Joyce Carol Oates writes that "Gertie is an 'artist,' but a primitive, untheorizing, inarticulate artist" (*TD*, 608). Oates's commentary obfuscates the crucial fact that Gertie's ability to whittle speaks for her in a way that she cannot, and that her carving skills allow her a creative erudition that she never enjoys by any other means. Even so, the financial survival of her family trumps any desire Gertie has for creative expression, and her decision to destroy the last remnant of pleasurable carving illustrates that she reads, comprehends, and acquiesces to the ultimate requirement of the city—total submission.

When considering the novel's end, William Schafer calls Gertie "the most imprisoned of [the novel's] prisoners" (1986, 50), an accurate description since with Reuben living in Kentucky and Cassie buried in a nearby cemetery, Gertie functions as the only remaining character who longs for her Appalachian home—and the literacies it values—but must stay in Detroit. Tragically, Arnow provides no viable avenue for Gertie to pursue in negotiating her longing for home with her necessary existence in Detroit. Gertie's destruction of the block of cherrywood signals her sadness and frustration at accepting the fact that she will probably never return to Kentucky—and perhaps most disturbing of all—the children she has who remain in Detroit have completely forsaken their Appalachian identities in favor of city-approved ways of being.

Although Arnow expands notions of literacy to encompass more than the technical ability of reading and writing, she does not allow her characters to experience the flexibility that her definition seems to encourage. In forcing her characters to choose totally and completely between Kentucky and Detroit, Arnow leaves no space for the emergence of understanding between these vastly different discursive worlds. As a consequence of this rigidity, both in terms of literacy and gender identity, her characters suffer immeasurably. Yet Arnow's portrayal serves a rhetorical purpose by repeatedly illuminating the missed opportunity of negotiation, and this lesson resonates with readers. By providing her characters with the polarized choices of leaving or staying, home or city, abandoning or adjusting, Arnow highlights the importance of recognizing the full range of strategies available for negotiation between primary and secondary discourses, between female and male.

CHAPTER 3

Narrating Socialization: Linda Scott DeRosier's Memoirs

As discussed in chapter 1, critics generally agree that the Local Color movement, as well as travel writing from the late nineteenth century, was largely responsible for beginning negative written portrayals of Appalachia, and throughout the remainder of the twentieth century, literary portrayals of the region continued (and still continue) to shape national perceptions of the mountain South. Equally important to shaping those perceptions are the sociological studies and reports often conducted and written by non-Appalachians. John F. Kennedy's presidential campaign focus on West Virginia and Lyndon B. Johnson's subsequent War on Poverty resulted in unprecedented media attention, and anthropological and sociological reports about the region soon followed. Generally such portraits highlighted the most pitifully destitute situations camera crews and researchers could find, and studies conducted by academics—no matter how small or skewed—were often upheld as unquestionably true.

Perhaps the most damaging media portrayal began with Charles Kuralt's 1964 CBS special, *Christmas in Appalachia*, which was followed years later by the 1989 CBS *48 Hours* episode "Another America," with Dan Rather. A decade after "Another America" aired, Rory Kennedy's 1999 documentary, *American Hollow*, appeared; and ten years later viewers saw Diane Sawyer's *20/20* special, *A Hidden America: Children of the Mountains*. Also discussed in chapter 1, such depictions of Appalachia often highlight a devastating poverty that plagues parts of the region while simultaneously ignoring the presence of middle-class and upper-class mountain residents.

Eastern Kentucky–born author Linda Scott DeRosier takes issue with these unbalanced representations of Appalachia in her (1999) memoir, *Creeker: A Woman's Journey,* and her (2003) follow-up work of creative nonfiction, *Songs of Life and Grace*. In both works DeRosier emphasizes traditional literacy events, which literacy scholar Shirley Brice Heath defines as "any occasion in which a piece of writing is integral to the nature of the participants' interactions and their interpretive processes" (2001, 445). In her depiction of these events, DeRosier reflects on instances in which reading and writing operate as the catalyst for gaining new cultural literacies. As with other authors and characters considered in this project, the process of becoming literate, in a technical as well as a discursive sense, introduces significant benefits and also significant conflicts to DeRosier's life and to her conception of the world. By writing about those gains and dilemmas, DeRosier speaks both to Appalachians and to non-Appalachians.

The rhetorical decision to write a memoir situates DeRosier's work so that someone from her home community of Two-Mile Creek (or any other Appalachian person) would likely be interested in reading it, but her explanation of Appalachianisms, like the intricacies of Appalachian vernacular speech patterns, also makes clear that she envisions a non-Appalachian audience as well. A professor of psychology, DeRosier has the training and skills to write an "academic" account of Appalachia, but in our interview she lamented that in many cases, academic writing is "couched in such a way that if a normal person read it, they'd never understand it" (2007). Although DeRosier could have crafted a fictional account of Appalachia, she instead sets down her own story of the region, and her work has the potential to resonate with readers as the story of one Appalachian woman's life. Even though DeRosier's academic colleagues declared that *Creeker* did not "count" toward her scholarly record because "it was not a professional book" (DeRosier 2007), its memoir form spans the gap between the two discursive worlds DeRosier struggles to negotiate in her own life through literate activity: her Appalachian home and the discourse community of academia.

The creative nonfiction genre of *Songs of Life and Grace* similarly transcends the divide between home and academia that DeRosier faces. As in *Creeker*, her subject matter centers largely around a personal family history, but she uses those experiences to speak out against the image of illiteracy that has been projected onto the Appalachian region since the turn of the century, and through her writing she reveals how she was able to accomplish the kind of negotiation that Arnow's characters never achieve.

In 2003 University of Kentucky (UK) students taking UK 101, the first-year orientation course, were required to read *Creeker* as part of the course's curriculum, a venue and situational context that reflects the book's capacity to reshape and realign what DeRosier deems misperceptions of the Appalachian region. UK professor and literacy scholar Janet Carey Eldred led a training workshop for faculty on how to integrate *Creeker* into their UK 101 courses, and mid-semester DeRosier visited the UK campus to speak with approximately five hundred students about her memoir. According to the UK associate dean of students, Rebecca Jordan, students responded more positively to the book after DeRosier's visit, explaining that some of them first had trouble relating to a story about "a woman's journey" (Jordan 2010). Even so, the effect for students from Appalachia seemed positive, at least in part since one student from eastern Kentucky told Jordan that "she was afraid to speak in her other classes, because she was worried that students would make fun of her accent," but "DeRosier's book helped give her confidence" (2010).

Based on statistics gathered at the University of Kentucky, professor emeritus Herbert Reid estimates that in the last twenty years, Appalachian students comprised somewhere between 15 and 30 percent of the UK student body; and in 2002, 14.2 percent of the UK student body hailed from Appalachian Kentucky (Reid 2003, 2007). By choosing DeRosier's memoir as required reading for one of its courses, UK ensured that Appalachian students, as well as students and professors from other regions, read DeRosier's account of Appalachia. Consequently, a diverse audience learned about the centrality of literacy in DeRosier's life, and through reading, they also began to understand that in writing *Creeker*, DeRosier works to overturn stereotypes of mountain illiteracy while also depicting the costs associated with literacy acquisition. In many ways her works also illuminate one of the central arguments of this study: the price that DeRosier pays for entrance into the academic community—a tangible sense of loss with her home community—remains necessary in order for her to share the strategies she uses for negotiating two different discursive worlds.

Hybridizing Literacy Narratives and Narratives of Socialization

Both of DeRosier's works depict her socialization into secondary discourse communities, and literacy scholar Janet Carey Eldred contends that "all fiction historicizes problems of socialization, including literacy" (1991, 686). Certainly literacy—and knowledge accumulated through literate activity— often functions as the catalyst for socialization and a realization that one's home discourse community differs, sometimes drastically, from other such communities. In subsequent work with Peter Mortensen, Eldred goes on to write that narratives of socialization "chronicle a character's attempt to enter a new social (and discursive) arena. Many texts, especially coming-of-age stories that show characters negotiating the world around them, often contain detailed and insightful investigations of how language is acquired and how it creates particular regional and private identities. In these narratives, literacy is a necessary component, although it is not emphasized" (1992, 513). Whereas Mortensen and Eldred use the emphasis or de-emphasis of literacy tropes to distinguish between narratives of socialization and literacy narratives, DeRosier's work functions as a hybrid of the two.

Like literacy narratives that "foreground issues of language acquisition and literacy," DeRosier's works also operate as narratives of socialization since they "chronicle [her] attempt to enter a new social (and discursive) arena" (Eldred and Mortensen 1992, 513). This sort of genre hybridity allows DeRosier to employ particularly effective rhetorical strategies in both texts that reveal how she moves between her Appalachian primary discourse community and the secondary discourse community of academia, as when she refuses to change her mountain accent. In describing how she moves physically and emotionally away from her home community of Two-Mile Creek, Kentucky, DeRosier illustrates the need for self-monitoring in both her home and academic discourse communities, and although DeRosier frequently narrates activities centered on traditional literacy throughout each work, she focuses most of her depictions on the losses and gains incurred as a result of gaining the new literacy of entrance into a secondary discourse community.

As she continues her formalized education, she increasingly learns that her Appalachian way of being contrasts with accepted ways of being in the academic community, and these realizations cause identity struggles that manifest in several ways, including her name change from Linda Sue Preston to Lee Preston after entering college. Through writing both *Creeker* and *Songs of Life and Grace*, DeRosier identifies misconceptions of Appalachia and its people (both written and otherwise) and works to overturn inaccurate assumptions that inevitably portray mountain people as ignorant, socially inept, and lesser.

Situating DeRosier's Shifting Identity

Stereotypical assumptions about substandard mountain education are so pervasive that they even make their way into the preface to *Creeker*, when history professor Margaret Ripley Wolfe writes that the memoir "tells the story of an educated and cultured American woman who came of age in Appalachia" (*CAWJ*, xi).[1] Although Wolfe writes a complimentary introduction, calling *Creeker* "a remarkable alternative to much of what has been published about the Appalachian region and its women" (xii), Wolfe also suggests that DeRosier's story operates as an unusual one. By placing education, culture, and America along the same trajectory, Wolfe hints that some greater entity of nation, not region, produced DeRosier, who just happened to come of age in an Appalachian place, an area not historically known for its education or high culture. Both *Creeker* and *Songs of Life and Grace* provide a narrative response to this suggestion, and DeRosier consistently adds to what she considers an incomplete representation of Appalachia and its people.

Although DeRosier acknowledges the existence of "the everlasting cycle of poverty and hardship in the hills and hollows," she also adamantly asserts that although the story of mountain poverty "is most certainly a part of Appalachia . . . it is not the whole story, not by a long shot" (*SLG*, 205).[2] In publishing *Creeker* and *Songs of Life and Grace*, DeRosier makes a significant contribution to the written representation of Appalachia, especially through her focus on mountain literacies. When asked in our interview if people sometimes assume that DeRosier or someone in her family is illiterate because she grew up in Appalachia, she responds: "Did I? Do I? Everybody assumes that" (2007).

In *Creeker* and *Songs of Life and Grace*, DeRosier consistently returns to stories in which literacy plays a central and oftentimes gendered role, yet she generally does so without narrating specific literacy events. Although she writes of her grandmother teaching her to read, and she repeatedly mentions her mother's love for reading and writing letters, usually DeRosier does not describe scenes in which she learns literacy skills; instead, literate activity operates as a backdrop for the stage on which DeRosier lives her life. Always present, multiple literacies usher drastic changes into DeRosier's life from early childhood to present-day learning activities.

The emphasis DeRosier's mother (Grace) and maternal grandmother (Emma) place on the centrality of traditional literate activity in a productive life influences DeRosier during her adolescent years, fostering a lifelong affinity for books that later culminates in DeRosier's earning a doctorate in psychology. Yet despite the ways in which DeRosier's mother and grandmother emphasize the practice of reading and writing, neither Emma nor

Grace could prepare DeRosier for the vastly different discursive world she encounters after leaving Two-Mile Creek to attend Pikeville College and later graduate school at the University of Kentucky. For Emma and Grace, pleasurable reading fostered avenues for private contemplation not granted by their laborious duties as wives and mothers. DeRosier also derives great pleasure from reading, but unlike her mother and grandmother, the education she gains through literate activity necessitates and ultimately helps her navigate the two different discourse communities of her Appalachian home and the academic environment in which she works.

Throughout her life DeRosier forges new paths not previously taken by other women in her family, since such freedom was not granted to her mother or grandmother. Despite their sometimes outspoken attention to literate practices, both Grace and Emma functioned within sexist societal limitations that prevented them from pursuing many of their individual dreams, as evidenced when DeRosier states, "My poor old momma was a freight train that never could get to the station. She had a formidable intelligence and absolutely nowhere to focus it that would have been considered appropriate in that time and place" (*CAWJ*, 17). Even so, Grace and Emma resist these gendered constraints in various ways, and much of their resistance revolves around literate activity, as when Emma finds a way to provide a high school education for all of her daughters, an unusual practice in the Kentucky mountains during the 1930s and 1940s.

Not surprisingly, Grace and Emma pass this strain of resistance connected to literacy on to Linda Sue, who later enters a completely different discursive world of university life at Pikeville College and remakes herself, morphing from "Linda Sue Preston, social misfit [to] Lee Preston, everybody's sweetheart" (*CAWJ*, 127). Lee's college years during the 1960s, a time when more opportunities were slowly becoming available to women, allowed her to explore options not easily available for her mother or grandmother, and such investigations resulted in a constant obsession over passing for "normal . . . not hillbilly" (179). Reflecting on these memories, DeRosier writes: "*Technically*, I left Appalachia when I was thirty-nine years old. But I submit to you that I really left Appalachia and the comfort and pain of shared values that early September Sunday when my daddy loaded up our black-and-yellow '57 Chevrolet and hauled all bad-haired ninety-four pounds—not counting my three new sweater sets—of Linda Sue to Pikeville College. That was the end of Linda Sue Preston right there, and I think my daddy knew it" (123).

For many years DeRosier clings to her non-Appalachian identity of Lee, but when she begins work as a professor at Kentucky State University, a historically black college, she writes that because of her "hillbilly" background, she understands the marginalized position of many of her students. This realization results in a return to her Appalachian roots, and when she accepts a job as director of the new Institute for Appalachian Affairs at East Tennessee State University, she reflects, "After two decades of having leaned on my creation [Lee Preston] for strength, I finally felt ready to let her go; I went to my new job as *Linda* Preston Scott" (*CAWJ*, 189).

In a cyclical turn of events, we see that DeRosier's familial (and often feminine) exposure to literacy practices prepares her academically (but not socially) for the journey to college, where she reshapes her identity and denies some connections to Appalachia. Yet her educational endeavors culminate in a job as an academic, where she returns in spirit to her mountain heritage, and it is this return via highly skilled literate practices that allows her to create *Creeker* and *Songs of Life and Grace*. Both works provide moving accounts of Appalachia that resist the stereotypical mountain portrayals so long perpetuated by nonnative scholars and documentary directors.

Although he writes from a different situational context than DeRosier, Richard Rodriguez notes a steady tension between home and academia in his memoir, *Hunger of Memory*. Highlighting the connection between Appalachian literacy narratives and working-class narratives previously discussed in the introductory chapter, he writes that "education requires radical self-reformation," yet he also contemplates, "If, because of my schooling, I had grown culturally separated from my parents, my education finally had given me ways of speaking and caring about that fact" (1983, 67, 72). Rodriquez identifies both the gains and the losses associated with a shift in discursive affiliation, but he seems to assign more value to his education than to the values and lessons learned in his home community.

Literacy theorists like James Paul Gee and Paulo Freire identify the impetus for remaking oneself as a desire to fit into dominant ideological practices, no matter the cost to one's own discourse community affiliation. In some aspects, DeRosier's journey aligns with theirs, but with one important addition—she reflectively reidentifies with her mountain heritage from the perspective of a grown woman comfortable identifying with her Appalachian roots, and in this way she adds a positive dimension to the generally painful transition literacy theorists describe, ultimately revising the path Rodriguez writes about.

Literacy on Two-Mile Creek

From the beginning of *Creeker*, DeRosier establishes her literary authority by referencing William Faulkner's famous allusion to Yoknapatawpha County as his fictional postage stamp of native soil: "This is my postcard from Appalachia written from the beginning of the 'Big War' through the 'Age of Aquarius' and running headlong, as quickly as all my baggage will allow, into the twenty-first century" (*CAWJ*, 1). In evoking Faulkner, DeRosier immediately connects one of the most respected writers of the American South with her account of Appalachia. Doing so signals an awareness of past Southern literary traditions, and it also foregrounds the connection she has to the Appalachian region and its people. Not only do *Creeker* and *Songs of Life and Grace* tell the story of Southern mountain people, but they also relate DeRosier's personal story, and her account of the region consistently returns to a theme of storytelling through both oral and literate forms as major forces that shape the course of her life.

In describing the cultural significance of Decoration Day (in DeRosier's home community of Two-Mile Creek, a celebration that occurs on Memorial Day in which family members gather to place flowers on the graves of loved ones),[3] she explains that her family and neighbors maintained an important relationship with the dead, "an attachment that often played itself out in frequent trips to the burial ground and the repeating of stories— perhaps apocryphal—about those who rested therein. It may be because my people never saw themselves in books, history, or fiction that makes it so important for us to tell and retell who was who and what was what in the graveyard" (*CAWJ*, 69). As readers we are tempted to take issue with DeRosier's claim that Appalachian people seldom find representation in books, history, or fiction, since literary depictions of mountain people have been popular since the Local Color movement. However, DeRosier soon elaborates, proving her declaration accurate.

Although the ability to read functions as an important skill for many of her immediate family members (namely her mother and maternal grandmother), the same cannot necessarily be said for the rest of her community. To illustrate, DeRosier writes about an instance that occurred with her neighbor and uncle, Keenis Holbrook. After Keenis returned from a trip to Baltimore, DeRosier recalls, "several of us were sitting around on his front porch listening as he regaled us with descriptions of his adventures in the big city" (*CAWJ*, 25). Here again she emphasizes the importance of oral traditions, especially when shared with others in the community. During the story, Keenis cites Baltimore as the capital of Maryland, and ten-year-old DeRosier corrects him by stating Annapolis as the capital. Keenis nonchalantly tells her she is wrong, but not to be swayed, DeRosier retrieves her geography book from her house and displays its contents for everyone to see. Remarkably, DeRosier remembers: "Uncle Keenis glanced at my book, said, 'No, it's Baltimore,' and continued with his tale. Everybody accepted his declaration as the final word, and that was the end of the story. Book-learning was not very credible on Two-Mile Creek" (25).

Considering this scene alongside DeRosier's claim that her people seldom saw themselves portrayed in literature, this perceived lack of representation may be because some members of the community, like Keenis, put little stock in literary depictions. Even so, in creating and participating within this oral tradition, the members of DeRosier's home community of Two-Mile insist on a type of recognition through storytelling, at least within their home space. The inherent problem with this form of sharing is that it circulates only within the Two-Mile community, seldom reaching outside regional boundaries, except for the occasional retelling of a story for an absent family member. DeRosier's literary rendering of such events reaches beyond these limitations, ensuring that her Appalachian experience finds printed representation. And although not stated explicitly, DeRosier goes on to suggest that community aversion to written texts may be attributed to what she considers an inadequate written portrayal of Appalachia.

Continuing a theme she establishes in *Creeker*, in *Songs of Life and Grace* DeRosier emphasizes the lack of balanced representation of mountain people. When explaining that her parents' "story is not bound by blood but by community," she goes on to assert, "We are of a kind, we rural, hill-country Appalachians. We are common folk, misunderstood by scholars, thus not often seen in books. We are family" (*SLG*, 117). Here DeRosier carefully distinguishes between scholarly portrayals of Appalachian people (which she oftentimes deems inaccurate) and more truthful representations in which she describes the presence of both literacy and illiteracy. Ironically, it is DeRosier's scholarly training that enables her to write accounts of her people, and her career as an academic as depicted in her writing sheds light on the divide between scholarly analysis and the kind of truth DeRosier feels she can reveal about her home-based discourse community.

Later in *Songs of Life and Grace*, she describes the family friends (Bob and Jane Allen) who agreed to help with DeRosier's primary research, as "my people. They are consummate Appalachians, the kind of folks never seen in the documentaries of gaunt, sad-eyed hill folk standing before ramshackle cabins. Nor are they represented by portrayals of Appalachia inhabited by the weary disadvantaged and the fat cats who've taken advantage of them" (*SLG*, 205). In writing both *Creeker* and *Songs of Life and Grace* DeRosier works to fill this gap in representation, and she reflects:

> I don't come from the kind of people who pass-along by setting words to paper, so my heritage has been largely ignored by folks who come from the East reaching down to help us. Those folks dropped in on us, then returned to their offices in universities or federal agencies and wrote of the everlasting cycle of poverty and hardship in the hills and hollows. It's hard to find a smile in the entire recorded history of rural Appalachian people. . . . If there is one point I want to make here, it is to separate my rural Appalachian people—we of the creeks and hollows—from those rural Appalachians we have so long seen reflected in pictures of sad-eyed hill-country folk on ramshackle porches. This rural Appalachian story—the one I inhabited growing up and the one that is with me every single day, whatever my zip code of the moment may be—is one of hard work and hope. (*SLG*, 205)

In the above passage DeRosier comments on the damaging effects of unbalanced written (and media) accounts of Appalachia. Although DeRosier pays special attention to her mother and grandmother's inclinations for reading and private letter writing throughout her memoirs, as readers we do not get a sense that public writing played a central role in either woman's life. Conversely, university scholars and federal agents recorded their perceptions of Appalachia, and DeRosier asserts that they do not capture a well-rounded vision of mountain life. DeRosier makes clear that she takes great pride in depicting what she feels is a more comprehensive view of eastern Kentucky, and in creating her own written account of Appalachia, she also explores vast identity changes wrought by literacy acquisition.

Depicting Resistance through Speech

In part, DeRosier discusses the rich vernacular traditions of her childhood to establish the differences between her Appalachian community and other groups she later encounters. In depicting Appalachian orality as unique in relation to Standard American English, DeRosier prepares readers to understand the disparities she later encounters when she leaves home. One such difference worth noting is the pronunciation of the word "Appalachia." Natives of the region (at least in southern and central Appalachia), as well as the majority of Appalachian scholars, pronounce the word with a short ă, sounding like "Appalatcha," whereas non-Appalachians generally use a long ā, sounding like "Appalaysha." In his history of Appalachia, John Alexander Williams quotes anthropological linguist Anita Puckett's observation that "people who said *Appal āchia* were perceived as outsiders who didn't know what they were talking about but were more than willing to tell people from the mountains what to do and how they should do it" (2002, 14).

Along a similar vein, early in *Creeker* DeRosier highlights the divide between Appalachian and "formal" names for various geographic locales: "Between Paintsville and Inez, you will find Meally, which is Buffalo; Williamsport, which is Two-Mile; and Boons Camp, which is Greasy. I could go on and tell you about Thelma, which is Bob's Branch; Thealka, which is Muddy Branch; and Whitehouse, which is Bee Branch, but no need. All the places have two names" (*CAWJ*, 5). She then explains that government officials came through the area giving names they deemed appropriate, "since the residents of those communities were mostly illiterate" (5). As in her retelling of the Keenis Holbrook incident, DeRosier does not deny the presence of illiteracy in Appalachia; rather, she criticizes the rest of America's response to it, particularly those of government officials since they placed so little value on local naming conventions.

While discussing the unique nature of mountain expressions in our interview, DeRosier says, "Let me tell you, the vocabulary is not limited in my community" (2007). Horace Kephart documented this wide range of expressions as early as 1913 in *Our Southern Highlanders*, and even though he appears to compliment the mountain people by claiming that the mountaineers he observed were not "simple characters that can be gauged at a glance," he writes from a smug, observational perspective, and in other areas he calls many of his mountain companions illiterate without declaring any evidence for his judgment (203, 83). Just as the officials DeRosier cites disregard the rich oral ability of Appalachian residents and fail to ascribe much significance to it, Kephart's compliment about the complexity of mountain speech patterns does not function free of negative judgments, especially when he deems certain mountain people illiterate. Conversely, DeRosier highlights such complexity to emphasize the literate abilities of people in her community, and she similarly depicts literacy as an expected occurrence in her adolescent household.

In describing her father's resistance to speaking standard forms of English, DeRosier makes clear that he, as well as some (though not all) other members of the community, knew the difference between "proper" speech and mountain speech, yet preferred to use Appalachian dialect. To illustrate, DeRosier recalls that her father would often say, "'[Eastern Kentucky] is the prettiest place they is.' And that's the way he said it, too, using 'they' for 'there,' though he knew the difference" (*SLF*, 159). She goes on to explain, "During my lifetime, my father always used 'they' for 'there,' 'h[y]erd' for 'heard,' 'hoss-peetal' for 'hospital,' and 'see-gretts' for 'cigarettes'" (159).

In *Creeker* DeRosier writes that she "plain worshipped [her] daddy," and his resistance to conforming to standard pronunciations no doubt influenced DeRosier as a child and later as an adult when she learned—often via literate practices—that these ways of speaking were "wrong" (*CAWJ*, 8). Her father's decision to keep his mountain accent mirrors DeRosier's future decision to reclaim hers, and her respect and love for him intensify the dilemmas she faces as she learns that much of the academic world negatively views many elements of her home culture. Even so, she always tries to keep her Appalachian accent, because "it would have been a rejection for [her] to sound any other way" (2007).

Literacy scholar James Paul Gee notes that in some cases, such adherence to a primary discourse can be advantageous: "When we come across a situation where we are unable to accommodate or adapt . . . we become consciously aware of what we are trying to do or are being called upon to do, and often gain deep insight into the matter. This insight (meta-knowledge) can actually make one better able to manipulate the society in which the Discourse is dominant, provided it is coupled with the right sort of liberating literacy" (1996, 146–47). DeRosier's statement that sounding any other way would be equivalent to rejecting her home community demonstrates the kind of deep insight that Gee references, and in acknowledging the choices at hand, DeRosier gains some sense of power over the identity struggle that literacy introduces to her life.

Moreover, as the author of her own Appalachian memoir—one that was selected by a large research university (UK) as required reading for first-year students enrolled in the university orientation course—DeRosier's telling of her decision to keep her accent helps audiences understand why someone might consciously refuse to adopt a homogeneous way of speaking. In some sense, maintaining mountain speech patterns allows DeRosier to navigate the space between her primary discourse of Appalachia and the secondary discourse of academia. By writing about her decision to keep her accent as a cultural marker, her memoir has the capacity to realign audience ideas about mountain speech and people's sometimes stubborn allegiance to regional identities.

Despite the sense of power that DeRosier gains, she notes that officials believed only the technical ability to read and write should grant authority to name a place: "This [insistence on government-sanctioned names] appears to me to be indicative of the power and credibility given my Appalachian forebears by all those well-meaning, philanthropic folk who came from Washington and the northeast to reach down and protect us from our own ignorance" (*CAWJ*, 5). Rich with sarcastic overtones, DeRosier's statements point to one of the foundational problems of the discourse transition she encounters when leaving home—much of the nation conceives of Appalachia as illiterate, and because systems of power are tied to literacy, assumptions of mountain illiteracy result in almost automatic marginalization for mountain people.

Considering such marginalization, literacy scholars James Collins and Richard Blot continue the vein of critical inquiry begun by New Literacy Scholars by thinking about literacy as a strong-text skill set and as something that occurs in a social arena, but the theme of their work most pertinent to DeRosier's comments is their consideration of the systemic control over conceptions of literacy by those in power. In the foreword to *Literacy and Literacies: Texts, Power and Identity*, Brian Street comments: "If agencies and educational institutions could convince others that the only model of literacy was theirs—for instance, that literacy was an autonomous, neutral, and universal set of skills—then the particular cultural values that underpinned this surface neutrality could be sustained whilst not appearing to be so" (Collins and Blot 2003, xiii).

In DeRosier's example of acceptable and unacceptable naming of geographic places, she reveals that government officials judge the Appalachian people's naming system as inferior. As Street notes in his introduction, when agencies in power succeed in convincing others that their form of literacy operates as the only acceptable form, they have succeeded in two ways: government officials have claimed the "official" definition of literacy, and they have also brought their cultural belief system to the forefront while appearing to remain unbiased. This kind of transmission of cultural values tied to literacy greatly affects those considered illiterate, as DeRosier later reveals when discussing the dilemmas she encounters at Pikeville College and again during graduate school at the University of Kentucky.

DeRosier also explains that just as mountain locales have two names (one given by Appalachian people and one handed down by government officials), the mountain people DeRosier writes about also use English in ways that vary, sometimes drastically, from official Standard American English. She notes in *Creeker* that "for most of us from Appalachian rural areas, *English* is a second language. It is not just the accent or dialect problem; there is a difference in the ways words are used" (*CAWJ*, 58; italics in original). DeRosier's renaming of English recalls Brian Street's discussion about the definition of literacy and its relationship to power structures previously noted: just as certain definitions of literacy serve those in power, so too do specific definitions of what "counts" as proper English. Throughout both *Creeker* and *Songs of Life and Grace*, she defines these terms where they might cause confusion for a non-Appalachian reader, explaining, for example, that "'whipporwill' is a term used in the hills for one who is so 'pore' or thin as to look unhealthy," and "drinking and sworping" means going on an alcohol binge (*CAWJ*, 19, 44, 63–66).

Of course these terms are often specific to eastern Kentucky, while other parts of Appalachia have their own set of linguistic particularities, but in setting apart Appalachian speech as its own distinctive language, DeRosier implies that the cultural differences between mountain people and "outsiders" are just as great as those introduced by language divides. Yet she notes that she does not feel disadvantaged by this fact: "Although much of what I have read about language and culture suggests that working-class speakers are disadvantaged because they speak in restricted code, I doubt that such is true of native Appalachians. If restricted means the code is restricted to members of that culture, this is true of my people also. But if restricted means lacking in range, I do not think this is true for us" (*CAWJ*, 63). Even so, mountain speech does set her and her community apart from mainstream discourses, like the "townspeople" Shirley Brice Heath identifies in *Ways with Words*.

Not only does DeRosier overtly address these differences, as in the above passage, but she also illustrates these disparities rhetorically through the genre of memoir and creative nonfiction. She bridges the space between "academic" and fictive writing by freely using Appalachian phrases and sayings, but she also makes clear that other, more dominant discourse communities generally interpret Appalachian speech as substandard. Her works consequently encourage us to understand that the choice to transition from a mountain home-based discourse community to a university-sponsored one requires a shift in affiliation.

Reading Matriarchal Literacy Trends

DeRosier repeatedly returns to the theme of literacy as the ability that allowed such a transition, and in doing so, she reveals the central role her mother and maternal grandmother played in her literacy attainment. Like her grandmother Emma, DeRosier's mother, Grace, also finds avenues for self-expression through the acts of both reading and writing. When distinguishing between her mother and other women of the community, DeRosier writes, "Still another difference between my mother and the other mothers on the creek was that my momma never sat down in front of the fire or on the porch and just rested. There was always a magazine, book, or crossword puzzle in Momma's lap (*CAWJ*, 15).

Multiple literacy researchers, including Shirley Brice Heath, note that children exposed to "mainstream" literacy practices early in childhood often fare better when faced with literacy tasks in the classroom. The frequency with which Grace engages in literate acts (both reading and letter writing) influences Linda, and during our interview DeRosier commented, "The best thing for me in terms of identity was that from the beginning, I knew that there's nothing I couldn't do if the first step was pencil and paper" (2007). Grace's steady reading habits encourage Linda in her own literate endeavors, and even though she enters college "absolutely unprepared socially [and] completely unprepared emotionally" (2007), she fulfills all academic requirements with little trouble.

In *Songs of Life and Grace*, DeRosier continues her emphasis on the frequency of Grace's reading habits, and after moving to a coal camp in McDowell County, West Virginia, DeRosier's mother also began writing letters home. These letters often detail activities Grace completed throughout the day, including descriptions of her latest cleaning or cooking tasks, as well as reports on family members and the weather. By including excerpts from many of these letters in *Songs of Life and Grace*, DeRosier showcases not only the writing ability of her mother, but also the important connection these letters provide to loved ones at home in Kentucky. After presenting a segment from one such letter, DeRosier reflects: "Both my parents would have been content to live in a mining camp, and I doubt they would have tried to move out of it if Daddy's work had not been so far from their parents" (*SLG*, 61). While DeRosier's family stays in West Virginia, Grace continually writes to her mother (Linda's grandmother), Emma, and in this way the letters provide an important connection to home.

Even though Emma (or as DeRosier refers to her, Emmy) took care of her disabled husband and eight children, she still carved out time for solitary reading, despite the fact that "pure drudgery was the standard for country women in those days—a life filled with birthing, nursing, and bringing up as many babies as the Lord sent, while continually laboring in both house and field" (*SLG*, 42). Yet similar to Linda's memories of her mother, DeRosier highlights the central role of literate activity in her grandmother's life: "I do not recall [Emmy] ever sitting without something to read or something to work on in her lap . . . When alone, she always had something to read" (*CAWJ*, 35).

Just as Emmy encourages her daughter Grace to read, she does the same with Linda, as when Linda remembers, "My Grandma Emmy Mollette had taught me to read two years before I began school, so I was never required to read the little blue soft-cover primer but proceeded directly to the excitement of 'Jerry saw toys and toys and toys!'" (*CAWJ*, 10). In several scenes we understand that Emmy teaches Grace, Grace teaches Linda, and Emmy also teaches Linda, creating a maternal legacy of literacy instruction that spans three generations. Additionally, letter correspondence between Emmy and Grace comprises an important part of their relationship, especially when distance separates them during Grace's time at the coal camp in West Virginia.

Despite the practicality of letter writing as a viable means of communication, DeRosier makes clear that her grandmother Emmy's views about both reading and writing aligned with the rest of the community's—literate activity might bring pleasure, and developing literate skills takes time and devotion, but these activities could never qualify as work, since "reading was a waste of time when there were chores to be done, an indication that the reader was not doing his or her share of the work necessary for survival" (*CAWJ*, 16). DeRosier writes that Emmy viewed the act of reading as "something that brought infinite pleasure [and] it was important for her to get the real work—the incessant house and field work—out of the way so that the pleasures of the day could be enjoyed in one book or another" (*SLG*, 126).

Emmy passes this attitude about pleasurable reading on to DeRosier, as evidenced when DeRosier admits, "[Growing up] I was just dead lazy, because all I wanted to do was read" (2007).

Although DeRosier draws connections between time spent reading and laziness, she also makes clear that Emmy's affinity for books functions as a type of resistance to the oppressively patriarchal system in which she lives her life. In order to help support her mother and siblings after her father's departure, Emmy dropped out of school after the sixth grade, and DeRosier recalls: "To hear her tell it, she loved school but had no other choice but to quit and care for the younger children and help her mother do the necessaries around the place. That marked her, though, for she was very proud that despite being put in practically the same position as her mother [because of Emmy's disabled husband], she was able to see every one of her children through high school" (*SLG*, 126).

In one case, despite a lack of cash funds, Emmy arranged to pay the administrator at the Mayo Vocational School in Paintsville, Kentucky, with fresh vegetables, canned goods, and hog meat so that her daughter, Amanda, could attend classes (*SLG*, 125). DeRosier notes that while many neighbors encouraged Emmy to force her daughters to drop out of school and help around the farm, she proudly refused, since "while she insisted her boys get a high school diploma before they went to the mines, WPA, or some other job of work, her intent was that all her children be able to figure well enough to keep folks from cheating them and that they learn to read for the pure fun of it" (127). Here DeRosier pays careful attention to the distinction that for Emmy, education played an important practical and leisurely role for both her sons and daughters.

Reflecting on her grandmother's beliefs, DeRosier writes, "In my view, degrees and diplomas may well prepare me to make a living, but the information and habits attendant to an education add immeasurably to the making of a life" (*SLG*, 127). Literacy functions as the foundational core of those educational habits, and Emmy valued literate ability for its assumed connections to a better economic life, as well as a more intellectually fulfilled existence, but what makes these beliefs admirable is that DeRosier emphasizes that she acted upon them in a time when education for women was often not a priority.

DeRosier repeatedly stresses that as an adolescent she too subscribed to expected gender roles: "It never occurred to me that I would ever do anything other than [cooking, straightening, 'nussing' as wife and mother] or live anywhere other than on Two-Mile Creek. I was female; that was my future" (*CAWJ*, 21). In *Creeker* DeRosier explains that marriage was a crucial step in beginning a "real" life, and she writes, "When I say I wanted to get married, I mean that I truly thought of nothing else" (117); and in an interview she says, "I wasn't just marrying Brett Dorse. I was marrying what I wanted to be" (2007). In *Songs of Life and Grace* she details the identity submersion that women underwent upon marriage in her Appalachian community:

> Traditionally, boys "married on" and girls "married off," so the process was a little different for a female. Taking a man's name was just the beginning of a woman's commitment to her husband; indeed, she became part of his family, his community, and his work. Though, on occasion, folks in her new environs might remind each other that some wife or another had been perhaps "a Barnett from over on Hammond," the woman's identity was expected to be completely submerged. Even in speaking of the woman, folks would use past tense: "Elmer Jackson's wife *was* [not *is*] a Barnett from over on Hammond." (*SLG*, 56)

In many ways, the change that DeRosier outlines here mirrors the same identity shift that occurs as a result of literacy-initiated changes. Once DeRosier leaves Two-Mile Creek and eventually establishes her career as an academic, she discovers that the new discourse in which she operates has little room for the distinctive (and cherished) cultural markers that identify her as Appalachian, particularly her mountain speech patterns. DeRosier recalls one instance when after presenting a paper at a scholarly conference in Boston a professor in the audience tells her, "I don't think I have ever heard an intelligent person talk the way you do," and to further illustrate the ludicrous—and yet common—nature of his comment she remembers, "and he thought he was paying me a compliment" (*CAWJ*, 67). When asked whether the change in female identity necessitated by marriage parallels that of an Appalachian person encountering a wholly different discourse community within the university setting, DeRosier responded, "Of course" (2007).

Although DeRosier attends college after high school graduation instead of marrying, she spends several pages explaining this unexpected turn of events that leads to a drastic shift in identity. At sixteen she falls in love with Johnny McCoy, but his eventual rejection of their relationship leaves her devastated. A subsequent relationship with Billy Daniel fails to fulfill her in the same way that her time spent with Johnny McCoy did, yet she still hopes for a marriage proposal. When one does not come, she decides to attend college and reflects: "While that looks like a good decision from where I'm sitting now, I want to make it clear that going to college was not even on the B, C, D, or E list of routes I wanted to take with my life. College was a detour, at best, and I detoured by way of Pikeville College" (*CAWJ*, 117). She goes on to explain that although she had multiple scholarship offers from other, larger schools farther away from home, she "tossed all those offers of free education in the nearest trash can in hopes that Billy—who was studying drafting at Mayo State Vocational School in Paintsville—would decide to marry me if I stayed close to home and continued to see him" (117).

Although the relationship with Billy ends, DeRosier's journey to Pikeville College results in identity changes that she could have hardly imagined upon first climbing the college's "ninety-nine steps to success," and as she makes the transformation from Linda Sue Preston to Lee Preston, she remembers, "I didn't want anybody to know that I was sort of looking forward to college for fear they'd think I was getting above my raisin'" (*CAWJ*, 127). The fear she describes here aligns with trends noted in literacy scholar Katherine Sohn's work: As mentioned in earlier chapters, Sohn chronicles the educational histories of three Appalachian women who attend college as nontraditional students, and she finds that these women worry about how their home communities will respond to their continued education. One of Sohn's interviewees (Mary) admits concern over losing her common sense as a result of college, and Sohn explains that some of her Appalachian students resist the homogenization of their native dialect, fearing "getting above their raisings" (2006, 24, 35).

DeRosier's fears echo those of the women in Sohn's study, yet while DeRosier repeatedly describes the constant need for self-monitoring, Sohn does not report that the women in her study experience this sort of self-inflicted censorship. Important to note, however, is the fact that the women in Sohn's study all remain in their native Appalachian communities, whereas DeRosier leaves hers to pursue her education. While literacy events no doubt introduce identity dilemmas to both DeRosier and the women in Sohn's study, DeRosier expresses the greatest amount of pressure to act out those changes.

Setting the Stage for Literacy-Induced Change

Although college provides the first series of incidents that illuminate the differences between DeRosier's home-based discourse community and the academic community, she chronicles several experiences on Two-Mile Creek that foreground the discursive divide she experiences upon beginning college, and all of these incidents happen in a place focused on literacy instruction—the classroom. DeRosier recounts that during her fifth-grade year at Meade Memorial, no less than seven teachers taught her class, since the children "wore 'em out one after the other" (*CAWJ*, 52). Her least favorite teacher, Janis Carroll, "was [at the school] long enough to get across the message that civilized behavior ended once you left the city limits of Paintsville" (52).

Like many fictional teachers discussed in this project,[4] Miss Carroll devalues the language practices of her students and takes pains to introduce them to a more "cultured" lifestyle, oftentimes through music. DeRosier remembers that Miss Carroll generally had trouble controlling the classroom, and during these times she would "burst into song, which might have been effective at calming us if she had sung something that was recognizable. In a class full of kids who could have sung every lyric to 'I Saw the Light,' 'Sugar in the Gourd,' or 'Fair and Tender Ladies,' Miss Carroll was given to bringing us light opera selections" (*CAWJ*, 52–53).

Cultural theorist Pierre Bourdieu claims that because of its spiritual properties, "music represents the most radical and most absolute form of the negation of the world, and especially the social world, which the bourgeois ethos tends to demand of all forms of art" (1984, 19). Yet in DeRosier's case, nothing could be further from the truth: instead of singing songs familiar to Appalachian children, Miss Carroll chooses foreign opera selections, which consequently sends a message of cultural judgment: their songs are not worth singing. In this way DeRosier's process of socialization (as Janet Carey Eldred defines it) begins, and literacy instruction provides the impetus for classroom gatherings and subsequent singing.

Not surprisingly, Miss Carroll also makes value judgments about the children's dialect and verbal expressions. DeRosier remembers, "Whenever one of us said we were *done* with a task, she would counter with 'Nothing is *done* but a chicken.' She encouraged us to respond to anyone using the term that way by asking, 'Are you a chicken?'" (*CAWJ*, 53). Here Miss Carroll not only judges the mountain expressions of her students, but she also indoctrinates her pupils with her own value system by actively encouraging them to mock other students who do not speak "properly." Sadly, this practice echoes the strategies Cora Wilson Stewart employed in the Moonlight School program when trying to "restore" English to "its proper dignity" (Stewart 1922, 27). Literacy narrative author Sharon Jean Hamilton laments this sort of instruction, asserting that "historically, we have placed such a low value on some regional or cultural dialects that we have often blinded ourselves to the human insight articulated through them; conversely, we place such a strong value on so-called standard English dialect that we often assume wisdom in banality" (1995, 110).

Likewise, Mikhail Bakhtin's concept of speech genres proves useful in analyzing the consequences of Miss Carroll's teaching methods, particularly his idea that verbal utterances are not simply uttered by the speaker and then interpreted by a passive listener, as some linguists once believed. Instead, Bakhtin argues, "the fact is that when the listener perceives and understands the meaning (the language meaning) of speech, he [or she] simultaneously takes an active, responsive attitude toward it" (1986, 68). The active response Miss Carroll encourages is one that supports her cultural value system, and regardless of whether her pupils respond in the intended way, her pedagogical direction leaves a lasting impact, especially for DeRosier: "Miss Janis Carroll and her city ways were soon gone, but not before she taught us the difference between who she was and who we were" (*CAWJ*, 53).

When discussing a similar relationship between Eliza Doolittle and Henry Higgins in George Bernard Shaw's *Pygmalion*, Peter Mortensen and Janet Carey Eldred argue that as an author, Shaw "begins to understand that region and speech are closely aligned with identity, and that attempts to change a person's language are, in effect, attempts to fabricate a new person" (1992, 523). Miss Carroll attempts such a fabrication in DeRosier's classroom, and as DeRosier continues with her educational endeavors, she encounters more of these attempts. Fostering a shift in identity, these encounters result in amplified self-monitoring, especially when returning to her Appalachian community.

Similarly, when DeRosier describes the Christmas presents sent to her elementary school from "big cities in the East," she highlights an awareness that the gifts were meant to "help" her and her classmates (*CAWJ*, 87). Significantly, the transmission of this message occurs in the classroom (as do Miss Carroll's lessons on dialect), and DeRosier only later reflects, after many more years spent in classrooms and libraries, that the toys were "sent by somebody who wanted to buy his way into Heaven or to pay us back for the coal rights we sat on. No doubt his astute grandpa had come into our hills and bought those coal rights from our illiterate granddaddies for ten cents per acre, and they were mined by our daddies for a dollar a load until so much of the coal dust filled their lungs that they choked on it" (87). Notably, DeRosier receives these gifts in an environment designed to prevent technical illiteracy.

Through her commentary DeRosier highlights the injustice of profit divisions, and she implies the irony of big-city residents sending Christmas presents to presumably poor mountain children: she remembers receiving a red, green, and yellow macaroni bracelet in the third grade as her present, and even though it "fell apart before Christmas Eve, [she has] never forgotten it" (*CAWJ*, 87). When asked in an e-mail why she remembers the bracelet, DeRosier agrees that as a cheap gift it represented outsiders' reaching down (not out) to mountain people, a pivotal example of a classroom incident that foregrounds what later happens when she leaves Two-Mile Creek.

However, she also agrees that this realization took years—and the acquisition of many new literacies—to materialize, and for a long time she thought of the bracelet as simply a special gift. Either way, the shoddy Christmas present symbolizes the opinion many city dwellers have of rural areas like Two-Mile Creek, and DeRosier interprets their continued Christmas presents as a type of penance. Perhaps even more importantly, this experience, along with the teachings of Miss Carroll, makes DeRosier aware of the discursive differences between Two-Mile Creek and other areas, particularly more urbanized places, and these differences become even more apparent once she leaves home to pursue a postsecondary education.

Remaking an Identity during the College Years

When narrating this transition from Two-Mile Creek to Pikeville College, DeRosier stresses the difference in these two communities, foregrounding the dilemma in discourse community affiliation that she later experiences: "While it may well have been close to home in distance, Pikeville College was light years away in all the things that nobody talks about but are critical to know—such as how to pass for normal, how to fit in, and most of all, how to keep folks from knowing that I had no idea what I was doing while I figured out how to do it" (*CAWJ*, 123). Literacy lies at the foundation of this process of socialization, and just as Janet Carey Eldred describes

"Barn Burning" as a story that "chronicles [the main character's] developing awareness of social power structures, of class distinctions, and of conflicting family and communal values," DeRosier's memoirs also tell "a story of conflicting discursive worlds" (Eldred 1991, 689).

Even so, it would be misleading to assert that all of the changes DeRosier underwent resulted from a one-sided imposition of these discursive conflicts. In part, DeRosier purposely reshaped and revised her image in hopes of better conforming to expected gender roles and thus having a more productive social life at Pikeville. Thanks to the socialization that began in high school, she knew that being a bookish, thin mountain girl would probably not increase her popularity in college any more than it had in high school. Consequently, she changes her name and reflects, "Probably the first step toward changing my life began when I changed my name.... As I pictured it, the birth of a whole new character would begin with the creation of 'Lee' Preston.... Lee sounded to my ears like someone who was popular, beautiful, sexy, and fun—everything Linda Sue wanted to be but was not" (*CAWJ*, 126). She finds success with her new identity, and after gaining a few highly sought-after pounds, Linda becomes a more popular version of herself, but this time as Lee. As DeRosier continues to identify with this new persona, it begins to take on elements of her new university discourse community, resulting in a split with the former Appalachian identity embodied by the name Linda.

Unlike Linda, Lee remains silent much of the time, especially when asked about her classroom performance: "I received four A's and a B at midterm, but I told everybody that I had 'done okay' because it was the highest set of grades I had heard about in the dorm. I had learned in high school that admitting I made good grades created a barrier to the kind of popularity I was aiming for" (*CAWJ*, 128).⁵ DeRosier learns to disguise her academic prowess in order to achieve popularity, and this masking technique is no doubt a gendered one. A quietly demure girl, Lee Preston "knew when to keep her mouth shut," while "Linda Sue Preston had been just full of ideas and opinions, and that had gotten her exactly nowhere socially" (128).

Although it seems that DeRosier's new creation of Lee aligns with the identity submersion DeRosier describes in typical mountain marriages throughout her childhood, when asked in our interview whether Lee was more in line with gender norms than Linda Sue, DeRosier responded, "No, actually, I think it'd be just the opposite." She goes on to explain that while "Linda Sue wanted more than anything in the world to be married... Lee

[was] a lot freer spirit" (2007), but in some cases DeRosier's descriptions of a subdued Lee suggest otherwise. Most notably, Lee downplays her literate ability and success in the classroom, while Linda Sue openly read books, but she also remembers, "However much I loved to read, I would have given up reading in a flash if I had found a girlfriend to talk with or a boyfriend to pay attention to me" (*CAWJ*, 109).

During her first weeks at Pikeville College, DeRosier meets Brett Scott, and the couple marries before she graduates, which results in yet another identity dilemma. Instead of ending her education, her marriage has the opposite effect: although DeRosier remembers that she "saw no point in continuing" school after her marriage, Brett strongly encourages her to finish college, and she does (*CAWJ*, 137). A few months before graduation her husband tentatively secures a position as an English teacher for her at a nearby high school, and plans to build a house on land given by Brett's father begin to take shape.

Since DeRosier has hopes that her husband (not herself) will go on to earn a doctorate, the thought of settling down in a house of their own causes her to question whether Brett has serious intentions to attend graduate school. In an effort to increase the couple's mobility, and thereby increase the chance that Brett will move to another city to attend graduate school, DeRosier takes the Federal Service Entrance Examination and acquires a job with Social Security. Consequently, she must attend training in Asheville, North Carolina, and while she does not relish the thought of being away from her husband for several months, she reflects, "I recall thinking that I was not exactly sure what I wanted to do with my life, but I was dead certain that I did *not* want to spend it eight miles out of town with a couple of kids, a full-time job, and a husband on the golf course all the time" (*CAWJ*, 141; italics in original).

In this instance DeRosier's resistance mirrors that of her grandmother Emmy (in insisting that all of her daughters graduate from high school), even though her mother, Grace, warns her that if she continues with her independent behavior, her marriage will fall apart. In many ways, this warning echoes the one issued to the teachers in Lucy Furman's novels and also the advice Gertie's mother gives her in *The Dollmaker*. Unlike Gertie, though, DeRosier ignores her mother and pursues her own goals separate of her husband, ultimately fostering the sort of discursive negotiation Gertie never achieves. But at this point in the narrative, DeRosier does not know how to drive a car, and "both [her husband's] family and [hers] were appalled at the idea of [DeRosier] moving away," but she remembers, "I had figured out by then that there was more of the world out there, and I desperately wanted to be part of it" (*CAWJ*, 141–42). Her love for reading contributes significantly to her learning about a larger world, and once she learns about different places, people, and ways of being through books, she soon longs to experience those things firsthand.

A Growing Independence Fueled by Literacy

Once DeRosier begins Social Security training in Asheville, she discovers that her nights and weekends are completely free, giving her more time for reading and more opportunity to investigate different discursive worlds through literary media. Unattached from her husband and her role as wife, she remembers, "I was pretty much free to do whatever caught my fancy. Thus, I did what I had always done when left to my own devices: I read from the time I got home from work until I turned out my light" (*CAWJ*, 144). Although DeRosier reads to learn new information while in college, and again in graduate school, during her time in Asheville reading serves two purposes: it allows DeRosier to escape into in an alternate literary world, and the process also helps further define her identity and sense of self. She writes:

> Since I learned to read, I have never been bound by this body, not for a minute. I discovered in Asheville the meaning of freedom, which for me is time to read whatever I find interesting whenever I want to slop around in my own aloneness. I say aloneness rather than loneliness because I think the Asheville experience set a precedent for me. If there is a book at hand, I am never alone. My leisure during the three months in Asheville was spent primarily in the lives of the characters I read about, and I reveled in it.... The only preparation I had for being in the world on my own was what I had read. (*CAWJ*, 145)

During her school-age years on Two-Mile, DeRosier remembers, "I never saw anyone even remotely like myself in anything I read—even the contemporary stuff," and this trend continues even when she reads voraciously in Asheville (*CAWJ*, 58). DeRosier consequently becomes aware of a literary void that she sets out to fill in *Creeker* by writing what she deems the authentic story of an Appalachian woman's journey to multiple literacies. Her literacy-based exposure to different places, people, and ways of being also simultaneously prepares her for a larger world, as she indicates in the above passage.

Although DeRosier learns much about herself and others through the process of reading, her time spent in Asheville introduces her to a different discourse community through her relationship with the only other female in her class: Marie Claire Lentini. DeRosier admits that similar to the time in which she began her studies at Pikeville College, now she also "had to figure out how to pass for normal, how to fit into this new context," but because of her experiences at Pikeville College, she "now felt confident in venturing into new social situations" (*CAWJ*, 145). This confidence serves DeRosier well in her work environment and even in her friendship with Mary Claire, at least while the two women are in Asheville.

Two years after DeRosier and Mary Claire leave Asheville to begin their jobs in other cities, DeRosier travels to Baltimore to visit Mary Claire, and during this visit the literacy skills that DeRosier had previously relied upon for success fail her. In preparation for the trip, DeRosier remembers that she "[read] up for weeks on Washington [DC] and environs," so when Mary Claire's brother asked what city sights DeRosier would like to see, she said she wanted to visit the zoo, since she had never seen a giraffe. DeRosier remembers, "Mary Claire's brother slowly shook his head, looked at her, and said, 'Where do you *find* these people?' We all laughed" (*CAWJ*, 151). Quite obviously, the discourse community in which Mary Claire grew up expected its members to be familiar with "common" attractions, such as a zoo. To put the idea in Pierre Bourdieu's terms, visitors of such a place had the economic capital to gain admission, as well as the cultural capital necessary to appreciate what the zoo had to offer.

Conversely, although DeRosier had read about the sights in Washington, DC, she had never lived near a zoo, nor had the opportunity to visit one. Similar to Janis Carroll's expectation that the children of DeRosier's elementary school classroom would appreciate opera, Mary Claire's brother can hardly believe that DeRosier has never seen a giraffe. Even so, she carefully points out that she made up for that lack of experience later in life: "A decade or so later, however, when I frequently flew into Dulles from London or Bangkok, I never failed to wish I had Mary Claire's number so that I could call her and report that I had indeed been to the zoo and seen the giraffe—on four continents" (*CAWJ*, 151).

DeRosier makes clear that her time spent training in Asheville exposed her to different discursive worlds in a positive way, but that exposure also came at a cost: as she learned about Catholicism, different foods, and independent women from Mary Claire, she also subjected herself and her home community to ridicule from Mary Claire's brother. Just as DeRosier later encounters multiple situations in which literacy is integral in introducing new discourse communities, immersion into those communities also results in a palpable sense of loss and results in what DeRosier calls "self-monitoring" (2007). Despite this new need to monitor herself, DeRosier also reflects, "If I had learned one thing during my sojourn in Asheville, it was that I could take care of myself. Although I wanted Brett Dorse to join me in Louisville, I no longer needed his presence to prop me up every moment of my day. For me, this was one giant step" (*CAWJ*, 151). The acquisition of new literacies no doubt fosters this step, and with it DeRosier assumes the position of a more independent woman.

Gaining Acceptance

The next step in DeRosier's life tests this newfound independence when she encounters a host of identity conflicts as a graduate student. DeRosier moves to Corbin, Kentucky, with her husband and son, and she continues to work for Social Security until the long, required driving distances and a subsequent car accident cause her to seek work elsewhere. She acquires a job teaching at Sue Bennett, a Methodist junior college, and the requirement that she earn her master's degree marks the beginning of a major transition in DeRosier's life. Her entry as a student at Pikeville College results in the creation of Lee Preston (from Linda Sue Preston) and a distancing from her Appalachian self, and the start of life as a graduate student—along with all of its required literacies—furthers this discourse community distancing from Two-Mile Creek.

DeRosier's gender also plays a major role in her decision to teach: "Although I still believed that money was the reason for my not quitting work and being forced back to school, I think a good part of my decision had to do with my assessment of the difference between my life and the lives of other women my age" (*CAWJ*, 165). She goes on to explain that like many other wives she knew, she followed her husband's golfing schedule by faithfully attending tournaments, adjusting her activities to fit his, and she remembers that she "spent just about every weekend for eight summers of [her] life engaged in this waiting game [waiting for her husband to finish playing]" (167).

She goes on to remember that while she dreaded the thought of attending summer school, "one positive aspect was that I had assignments to complete, books to read, and papers to write. . . . I was not looking forward to teaching either, but, by this time, I could see that, for all my thinking that I did not want to be working, my life just seemed more interesting than the lives of those nonworking golf-groupie wives" (*CAWJ*, 167). As in the past, DeRosier succeeds in her academic endeavors, but when she begins work on her doctorate in psychology at the University of Kentucky, while also teaching as an instructor, she enters the new discursive arena of "advanced" academia. Different from her experiences as an undergraduate at Pikeville College, where her literacy skills met her academic (if not social) needs adequately, she encounters a new situation as a PhD student.

DeRosier's transformation to Lee at Pikeville College, and her continued revising of herself after her marriage to Brett Dorse, friendship with Mary Claire, and training in Asheville, reaches its pinnacle as she begins her studies at the University of Kentucky. In this new environment, DeRosier realizes that her colleagues are wholly immersed in intellectual thought processes: "The thing that impressed me, however, was not that they took classes, read books, and wrote papers, but that they never shut up about what they were doing" (*CAWJ*, 172).

Unlike DeRosier's home community of Two-Mile Creek, where her childhood textbook-supported declaration about a state's capital goes ignored, in the university setting DeRosier finds that she did not have one "inkling of what [her office mates] were talking about," and consequently could not enter into their philosophical and theoretical conversations (*CAWJ*, 173). She goes on to remember, "For the first time in my twenty-seven years, I was in constant contact with folks talking over my head, and I was not amused. Here I was having a veritable salon in my office, and I could not even participate. I mean, to hell with that business!" (173). To remedy the situation, DeRosier checks out forty books from the university library and reads them during her winter break in 1968. In this instance an important shift occurs: whereas DeRosier's constant reading at home on Two-Mile sometimes (though not always, especially with her mother and grandmother) isolated her from her community, in the university setting this penchant for reading operates as a necessary component for admission into the university discourse.

Although DeRosier writes that reading those forty books did not qualify her to participate in the discussions held by her colleagues, reading them allowed her to know "enough to phrase a question," and she reflects, "And with that, my former life, my marriage, and everything I had ever thought I knew and believed changed forever. One more time: *Education, if it takes, changes the inside of our heads so that we do not see the same world we previously saw*" (*CAWJ*, 173). Here DeRosier italicizes her statement about education, as she repeats it for the third time in *Creeker*. Several years earlier DeRosier thought that her happiness hinged on marriage, but now she reflects: "Thus it was that my own education was able to give me exactly what I had been looking for all along: love, and through that love, salvation. I read those books and truly fell in love for the first time in my life. I fell in love with ideas and with a world where such thoughts appeared to be in infinite supply—the university" (173).

A Shifting Identity

Primarily, DeRosier relies on a skill set grounded in literate ability to gain entrance into this community, and although entrance brings great pleasure to DeRosier's life, it also distances her from another community she loves dearly—her home on Two-Mile Creek: "Graduate school also seemingly rooted out the last vestiges of my Appalachian essence, though I did not know it at the time. Passing for normal—not hillbilly—was a journey I had embarked upon when I entered Pikeville College, and each year thereafter I had moved a bit closer to my goal" (*CAWJ*, 179). In this instance DeRosier discusses "passing for normal" in academic circles, but she also later realizes that this transformation causes her to appear rather abnormal to her home community. In this way her relationship with those on Two-Mile Creek changes by requiring more self-monitoring and consequently, a loss of spontaneous expression. Even so, during our interview DeRosier pointed out that in her opinion, she has also made substantial gains as a result of this self-monitoring: "I have a range of friends from a lot of different kinds of life, and it's the sort of thing that it's hard sometimes to mix people, but you know, I still live both of those lives" (2007).

In a chapter aptly named "Finding My Voice," DeRosier narrates one particular scene that illustrates how her shift in identity—from Linda Sue, to Lee, to Lee with a PhD—changes her interactions with homefolk:

> Some years back, I was at a dinner-on-the-ground with about forty members of my extended family—folks who love me. We were

sitting in the grass, eating Hazel Lee Johnson's cabbage rolls, when I used the word "atrocity." I don't even remember the context, but I do recall that it practically stopped the meal, mid-bite. Nobody said anything: there was just this pregnant pause where everybody stopped what they were doing to take note of what had been said. That one slip was as offensive as would have been bringing up the fact that I had returned from Japan the Friday before, which I would *never* have mentioned in that setting. That sort of glaring lapse has not happened often and never quite so blatantly. Usually, I am more careful, but it does require some degree of self-monitoring. (*CAWJ*, 61, italics in original)

What DeRosier deems "offensive" here is not the notion of "atrocity" but the fact that she has spoken a word outside of "normal," everyday Appalachian speech. DeRosier interprets the word's utterance as an intrusion on the mountain assembly, and she understands that using a word like "atrocity" represents entrance into a larger, much different discourse community, a community to which no one else at the gathering has access. Working Class Studies scholar Carolyn Leste Law helps explain DeRosier's dilemma when writing about the divide between home and academia: "To talk about my studies seemed ridiculous and stuck-up at best in a context that appeared to be as mistrustful of academia as academia was condescending to it" (Dews and Law 1995, 4).

Although DeRosier writes that inclusion into the university setting provides her salvation, it also molds and shapes her into a much different person than the Linda Sue Preston who left Two-Mile Creek to attend college (*CAWJ*, 173). In learning a new set of university-accepted speech customs, and by using those new customs while at home, DeRosier risks alienating those in her home community. For this reason, she strives to mask certain elements of her university life, but as DeRosier notes, this requires self-monitoring.

Even though DeRosier writes that "home is largely an idea, a place where we go and know that whatever changes we have made in our lives, we will still always belong right there," her recollection about the dinner-on-the-ground illustrates that some changes made to a life should not be emphasized in the home context (*CAWJ*, 34). Despite the fact that DeRosier kept (and still keeps) close ties with home, she says that after graduate school, "when I was home, I always acted as if I had not changed, but they knew

I'd changed. . . . I didn't recognize [it] until I wrote it down, [but] I don't think I much liked myself during those days" (2007). Although successful in school, DeRosier recognizes that her relationship with her home community has changed, and even now, she says that she is "probably much more of a self-monitor[er] at home" (2007).

In addition to masking certain elements of her literacy-initiated academic identity, DeRosier also finds that she must render certain aspects of the university discourse community into something more acceptable to her Appalachian home discourse community. In *Creeker* DeRosier comments on the gendered split in acceptable behavior on Two-Mile Creek: men can occasionally drink alcohol, "but no decent woman takes even one alcoholic drink" (*CAWJ*, 60). Such divisions generally do not exist in academic communities, and DeRosier writes, "Champagne brunches, cocktail parties, and wine-and-cheese functions come immediately to mind as events that must be translated into something acceptable to homefolks" (60). Not only does this statement reveal a difference in acceptable behaviors according to gender, but it also illustrates the shift in socioeconomic class that can accompany new literacies. This reflection makes clear that the academic community of which DeRosier is a part, as well as her home community, each has their own tacit understandings that govern behavior according to class and gender, but as her comment illustrates, in certain instances those understandings are at odds. Consequently, the responsibility of mediating those differences falls on DeRosier, making her the hinge point between two opposing views.

As with her usage of the term "atrocity," DeRosier must again consider which parts of her university life to share with people in her home community, and which parts to exclude. She reflects, "I have found it easier to supervise the content of my speech, however, than to monitor the form—the way I phrase my comments, the words I use, and those terms that are common in my everyday life" (*CAWJ*, 61). The fact that DeRosier dearly cherishes both communities only exacerbates her desire to make members of each community comfortable, often resulting in the constant negotiation of her own identity.

For example, as a result of the literacy-initiated identity changes DeRosier experienced, she must choose between two very different rhetorical approaches when discussing the relative safety of air travel. While visiting with her friend Bonnie Sue Ratliff on Two-Mile Creek, Bonnie's ten-year-old grandson (Jacob) eagerly asks DeRosier about the various places she has traveled.

Thanks to his incessant questions, DeRosier admits visiting a long list of foreign countries, and when another neighbor (Vidie) asks if DeRosier travels to these places on an airplane. When she says yes, Vidie asks if DeRosier worries about plane crashes, and DeRosier describes how she responded to Vidie's concerns: "Fearing all was lost anyway, I launched into lecture number 347, the old song complete with statistics about how much safer it is to ride on an airplane than it is to ride in a car, when suddenly I knew exactly what to do. Abruptly, I said, 'You know, Vidie, I figure if the Lord's gonna take me, he's gonna take me wherever I am, whatever I may be doing. So, I just don't worry about it" (*CAWJ*, 62). This response satisfies Vidie, but only because DeRosier successfully shifts her rhetoric midexplanation, something DeRosier says she does "routinely" and "everywhere" (2007).

In first answering Vidie's questions using statistics to back up her argument, DeRosier initiates a type of syllogistic reasoning popular in academic communities, but before she finishes this explanation, she tries a different approach. In evoking the Christian fundamentalist reasoning of the churches so widely accepted in her home community, DeRosier leaves the worrying up to God, and this strategy aligns with the belief system of her audience members. The fact that DeRosier first cites statistics in her argument and only later takes a different, more audience-appropriate approach reveals that in some situations, years of schooling have caused DeRosier to first rely on academic forms of reasoning and only later on those she first learned as a child in her home community. She has become what literacy scholar Lillian Bridwell-Bowles calls a rhetorical shape-shifter, "moving cautiously from one form and medium to another, changing perspectives as necessary to understand multiple points of view, while at the same time staying in touch with [her] 'self'" (1997, 2).

Finally Jacob names a country that DeRosier has not visited (India), and she feels relieved that the conversation moves in another direction, as when she writes: "I know the rules. It's those sudden shifts I have to watch out for" (*CAWJ*, 63). In constantly monitoring herself and her responses, DeRosier loses a sense of freedom of expression in her home community, especially during those times when she would normally respond in academic terms but refrains from doing so in the company of those on Two-Mile Creek. When asked if this common shift in rhetoric saddened her she responded, "No, it's been so long now that, you know, it's just a natural thing . . . it's not a conscious decision," and later she says that she automatically molds her responses for one particular group or another (2007).

Reconnecting with an Appalachian Sense of Self

During this time, although DeRosier stays physically connected to her Appalachian home through frequent visits, she focuses her academic energies on teaching and continuing work on her dissertation in the field of psychology, neither of which focuses on Appalachia. These academic pursuits consequently continue to distance her emotionally and physically from home. After receiving her doctorate in 1972, she secured a tenure-track teaching job at Kentucky State University, but she notes, "There was, however, one difference between Kentucky State University and the other universities where I had taught before: KSU was a traditionally African American university, and I was the only white female Ph.D. on campus" (*CAWJ*, 181).

In this role DeRosier faces numerous challenges in overcoming her own assumptions about African Americans while also working to overturn her students' misconceptions of white women. Despite the many differences between DeRosier and her students, she reflects, "Teaching at Kentucky State taught me about making connections with students whose culture was different from my own while letting me see just how similar my background was to theirs" (*CAWJ*, 182). Her reflections help further illustrate the connections that the introduction to this book draws between marginalized groups for whom literacy introduces conflict as well as positive change: "If you did not see the difference in our skin color, we were remarkably similar. Many of them were, as I had been, first-generation college students; they too had never planned to go to college; they believed income was the only marker of success; they didn't much trust anybody outside their own families; and, where higher education was concerned, they also wanted to 'get in, get over, and get out'" (182). At this point in her life, DeRosier can identify elements reminiscent of a young Linda Sue Preston in her students, and she understands the difficulties these students encounter as they struggle to master the university discourse. In an unexpected turn of events, DeRosier purposefully sheds her identity as Lee, reverting back to Linda:

> All of this took me by surprise. By 1972, prior to going to KSU, I had become so thoroughly assimilated into the culture of academe that with the exception of my still-distinctive speech patterns, I was well-nigh close to passing for normal—as in non-hillbilly. As a result of my six years at Kentucky State University, I rediscovered the hillbilly girl sequestered since my early days in Pikeville and found

that I could use cultural insight, long repressed, as a bridge to understanding more about ways my students came to know. (*CAWJ*, 183)

Almost ironically, the discursive divide that prompts avid self-monitoring at home also allows DeRosier to recognize that many of her students cope with a similar divide. In reclaiming the cultural literacy of her Appalachian home, she successfully connects her experiences with those of her students.

Also during her time at KSU, DeRosier begins conducting research on the effects of culture on cognition, particularly in her home county in eastern Kentucky (*CAWJ*, 184). Thanks to a series of speaking engagements about this research, Mars Hill College in Western North Carolina invites her to speak about Appalachian culture, and she reflects, "Consequently, by the time I spoke at Mars Hill College, I was in full hillbilly mode. I had rediscovered my roots completely, and by that time I was taking another look at the twists and turns my life had taken in light of this new knowledge" (186–87). Her speech leads to a job offer (and acceptance) to be director of the Institute for Appalachian Affairs at East Tennessee State University. Thus her realization about the similarities between her students and herself acts as a catalyst for a return to her Appalachian identity, and while she still engages in a great deal of self-monitoring while at home, she can more easily incorporate aspects of her home discourse into her academic life, particularly her research.

When explicating narratives of socialization, Janet Carey Eldred notes that Toni Cade Bambara and Geneva Smitherman "both assume a 'double-edged' voice that appropriates the values of education without erasing the language of African-American identity and, more importantly, that dramatizes the tensions between these coexisting discursive worlds" (1991, 695). If we replace "African American" with "Appalachian" in this quote, Eldred's observation applies to DeRosier as well: both of DeRosier's memoirs operate as powerful narratives of socialization for which literacy initiates substantial identity conflict and change.

During our interview DeRosier reflected, "It is very hard to maintain your value system . . . in a world where that value system is not the one most wanted" (2007), a fact of which she no doubt became increasingly aware as she acquired new literacies through years of schooling. Near the end of *Creeker* DeRosier writes, "One thing I know: The hills of eastern Kentucky and the values and customs of that place and those people remain a central part of me today. It is left to me, then, to recognize that fact and draw strength from it or attempt to deny the connection, thereby cutting myself off from it. In either case, it exists" (*CAWJ*, 219).

The literacy skills passed to DeRosier from her mother and grandmother, as well as those skills learned in a classroom, cause DeRosier to "deny the connection" for a time, but she later decides to "draw strength" from her Appalachian identity, and those same skills enable her to narrate her journey of socialization through literacy attainment. In *Creeker* she reflects, "I also believe I have been able to achieve full membership in both Appalachian and academic speech communities, although it has taken some time and a sense of watchfulness" (*CAWJ*, 66). When asked in an interview if this required watchfulness saddened her, DeRosier replied, "Actually, it probably makes me angry more so than it saddens me" (2007), a feeling no doubt stemming from past inaccurate representations of Appalachia. Near the conclusion of *Creeker* DeRosier writes, "Appalachia haunts both of us [her and her sister], albeit in somewhat different ways, and we speak to each other of regaining possession of what we have lost upon leaving" (*CAWJ*, 227); but in our interview she conceded that "it could not be regained by going back" (2007).

Consequently, DeRosier channels her response into her memoir writing, and through depicting scenes that explain the difficult identity choices she made as a result of literacy acquisition, she illuminates both the gains and the losses that can result from entrance into a new discursive arena via literate practices. Her memoir and work of creative nonfiction both operate as hybrids of the literacy narrative and narrative of socialization, rhetorically negotiating a divide between the two genres. This strategy reflects a similar negotiation between home and away, Appalachian and non-Appalachian, since DeRosier writes about her mountain experiences in a way that speaks to a wide variety of readers: in some instances she explains Appalachian speech patterns, while in others she refers to elements of mountain life that assume a certain knowledge about Appalachian lore. The seamless literary blending of these two worlds encourages her audience—whether Appalachian or not—to learn new social, cultural, and possibly even technical literacies as she tells the tale of her own literacy-initiated entrance into new discourse communities. In this way, DeRosier's texts serve a purpose similar to *The Dollmaker*, but instead of warning readers away from "either-or" situations, DeRosier illustrates how to navigate the spaces between an Appalachian primary discourse and a non-Appalachian secondary community, all the while working to overturn century-old stereotypes of mountain illiteracy.

Interview with Linda Scott DeRosier

EAL: Near the beginning of *Creeker* you emphasize the importance of literacy in your family by writing about how your mother was always reading a magazine or book. Do you recall any instances of assumed illiteracy as you grew up? Did you encounter people, then or in later years, who assumed that you or someone in your family must be illiterate, since you're from Appalachia? Also, how have stereotypes connecting Appalachia with illiteracy affected your work?

LSD: I have two or three things to say about that. First of all, reading was such a priority. For me, for my grandmother, for my mother, and for me, reading was not work. Reading was leisure, and what that means is that it becomes something you get away to, rather than something you get away from. Homework was considered onerous; that wasn't reading to us, it was doing homework. And you know, there are two reasons to read: one is escapism and that kind of pleasure, the other is for information; and the trick to getting a good education is when you can get those two to be the same thing. It's like when you get your *APA* journal every month it's just like reading *McCall's* magazine or *Cosmo*, or whatever magazine it is that you like. Journals, if you're really into what you do and really love what you do, the journal becomes that.

Now in terms of whether I encountered people who assumed that I or someone in my family was illiterate, Did I? Do I? Everybody assumes that.

EAL: Yes. I want to hear all about that.

LSD: I mean, everybody assumes that. It's the sort of thing that people are absolutely certain, and again, I think this is one of the reasons that I held on to my accent and the dialect for so long. Because people simply assume that if you look the way I do, and you sound the way I do, you can't find the restroom door and read the Ladies sign on it. And that being the case, as I said, I am certain that a number of the things that I have done have been fueled by the anger that comes from that. You know, we have these emotions, and emotion carries energy, and if you lash out at anybody who says anything or who treats you as if you don't have walking-around sense, if you tell them what you really think about what they think, what you know they think, you always lose. You just look small, and the person will of course deny it, and so you become accustomed to people talking down to you and not trying to prove anything to them. You know, so I think the belief is widespread. When *Creeker* came out and it did so well, a lot of people, you know back home, they think I'm John Grisham, they think I'm just making it big-time.

EAL: You're Margaret Mitchell!

LSD: Oh, exactly! And the thing about it is, I have a former colleague, a guy with a PhD, bright guy, worked with me, he obviously respected me, or whatever. He said, "You know, Lee," this was, he knew me in those days when some people still called me Lee, and he called after he had read *Creeker*, and he said, and he knew enough people back there to know how well the book was doing, and he said, "You know, Lee, I can't believe that that book is doing as well as it is. You know, I didn't think anybody from east of Winchester could read."

EAL: Oh boy.

LSD: Yeah, I mean, again, it's so like the guy who said, "I've never heard an intelligent person talk the way you do." They think they're giving you a compliment. What happens, very often, and this is true of race, ethnicity, class, and whatever, if people meet you and even get to know you, and if they come to respect your intelligence or your work or whatever, they think you're an exception. And if there is anything I'm about, it's about saying, "Hey look, you know, anybody can do anything. You just have to put your shoulder to the wheel and do it." And so I've been obviously teaching that for thirty years.

EAL: I was just looking at your website before you called; what did your daddy used to say, "You gotta get in there and grind"?

LSD: "Gotta get in there and grind." There were a couple, Daddy had many sayings, and a couple that my sister and I are very fond of. I never associated that "Get in there and grind" until I was writing about that picture that's on the front of *Songs* and all the sudden I thought "Well, of course!" You know, his granddaddy was a miller, you know, get in there and grind.

EAL: Oh, literally! You gotta grind.

LSD: Exactly, and I never associated that until I was writing some copy for *Songs*. Another thing my daddy used to tell me that I think about at least fourteen times a day when I won't tell people what I think—any time we'd get ready to go out somewhere, like if we were going to the movies or we were going to a ball game, or even after we were all married we'd go out somewhere, and especially if I was going somewhere to do a paper or speech, my daddy'd say, "Now don't show your ass." [Laughs] And so that's with me all the time. He thought people who spoke out were ridiculous.

EAL: I understand.

LSD: Showing their asses. And let me just say that if I am taking a class, I encourage my students, I put them in groups, and I encourage them to talk a lot. But when I went away on sabbatical twelve years ago and went back to school [to Harvard], let me just say, I sat in the back of the class, and I never said a word. Because again, first of all, I didn't want to show my ass [laughs]; and secondly, it's the sort of thing if you, you know, if you listen to other people, you'll learn a lot about their point of view. And if you thought they cared about yours, you might give it to them. Because if I'm in front of the classroom, or if I'm invited to go speak, or on a panel or whatever, I always contribute. But if I'm out there, I certainly, I just am not the sort to say, "What did you just read that's not a gloss on what Wittgenstein said earlier?" I mean, my feeling is that, Daddy didn't approve of people who, back home they'd say, "show out."

EAL: My parents say that too, "Just showin' out."

LSD: Yeah, and let's face it, some of us were just flat-ass born to show out. It's in our nature. [Laughs]

EAL: We've got the streak.

LSD: Exactly. I'm not sure which chromosome that is, but we've got it. Anyway, again, I expect people to assume that I'm illiterate and that my kind are illiterate, and if they come to know me and respect what I do, that's one of the reasons that I sound the way I do. I try in every way I can to prove that I'm not an exception, because you know it's easy to say, "You were so smart" or "You were so rich" or "You were so . . ." you know, when it comes down to knowing things and understanding things, it's between you and you. Did I tell you about that new history book for the state of Kentucky?

EAL: I looked at that on your website—*The Faces of Kentucky* for fourth graders.

LSD: Let me tell you that my picture is not in the thing about writing, it's in the thing about work. Quoted from *Creeker* about work, and that's just the best thing that could happen to me. If you show that you can work hard and not be exceptionally talented, or brilliant, or whatever, but if you work hard at whatever it is you choose to do, then you'll get better at it, and you'll do well at it. And I want kids to, real kids, to see that.

EAL: My dad has sayings too. Two of his favorites are: "Don't forget whose holding all the cards" and "The harder you work, the luckier you get."

LSD: It's worth remembering that. About how stereotypes connecting Appalachia with illiteracy have affected my work: there are people who maybe couldn't read very well or didn't read very much, but in my chapter on language, when I talked about the colorful language, how Daddy'd say "I'll knock a fart out of you," or "long as a rake handle," let me tell you, the vocabulary is not limited in my community. There is a vast range of ways to use very few words, and there's a creativity in those sayings; sometimes you wish some of the people who had bored you to death trying to teach you things would recognize that kind of thing.

But back to those notions of illiteracy: a few weeks before my father died, he was in a little service station store, picking up a package of cigarettes. And he said, I'll never forget it—we happened to be home at the time, and he came home and said, "You know, I went in to get my cigarettes, and I'm paying for my gas, and getting my cigarettes, and this young man said to me, 'Can you read?' and I said, 'Well, a little, I reckon' and he pointed at something, and he couldn't read, he couldn't even read the things that were on the candy bars or something, or whatever it was that he wanted. He said, "I can't." Daddy was not the kind to say, "What is wrong with our educational system?" He said he just shook his head and said, "You think about that. You think about that. There's that young feller can't even read."

EAL: When writing about Appalachian dialect in *Creeker*, you write, "I also believe I have been able to achieve full membership in both Appalachian and academic speech communities, although it certainly has taken some time and a sense of watchfulness" (1999, 66). Does this sense of watchfulness sadden you at all? Is there also a sense of loss here?

LSD: Actually, it probably makes me angry more so than it saddens me, because you know when you're in academe, as I wrote in one of the books, they can only admit to watching television if it's certain shows.

EAL: Oh, you can't admit that you watch *The Simpsons*. That's not acceptable.

LSD: Oh, absolutely not. Especially, and so, that's a part of culture. In my opinion, culture is so interwoven with literacy that you really can't even look at one without the other.

EAL: I agree completely.

LSD: And it is so integrated. Is there a sense of loss here? As a matter of fact, I think I'm damn near bilingual, and I mean I'm not talking about the French exam for getting the degrees. I think that when you're able to speak with a whole range of people and make yourself understood, when that whole range of people speaks to you, and you can understand them, you are so far ahead of the game. And in terms of a sense of loss, for me it's more of a sense of gain. I have a range of friends from a lot of different kinds of life, and it's the sort of thing that it's hard sometimes to mix people, but you know, I still live both those lives. You know, I still am the person who is the professor and the person who is Linda Sue Preston, Lifie Jay Preston's little girl.

EAL: One of my favorite scenes in *Creeker* depicts you explaining your travels to Bonnie Sue Ratliff's overly inquisitive grandson. I think your shift in rhetoric when explaining the necessity of flying to Vidie was brilliant ("You know, Vidie, I figure if the Lord's gonna take me, he's gonna take me wherever I am, whatever I may be doing. So, I just don't worry about it").

LSD: I do that routinely. I do that routinely everywhere. I have all those Appalachianisms that I use in the classroom.

EAL: Well, in that particular instance, the divide between your academic self (in which you'd explain the relative safety of flying using statistics) and your "Appalachian" self (in which you rely on an explanation supported by a belief system) seems obvious, and I wondered: Do you feel as though you're constantly molding yourself, and your responses, for one audience or another? If so, what's lost (or gained) in those transitions?

LSD: I try to do what seems to be asked of me with everybody, and so, I've done that for so long that it's to a point of automaticity, and a lot of times I don't even have to think about it. The thing is, academic writing is couched in such a way that if a normal person read it, they'd never understand it. And so I've always kind of considered it my mission to tell the kids in my class: here's the deal, here's what's going on. Does that sense of watchfulness sadden me? No, it's been so long now that, you know, it's just a natural thing.

EAL: Related to my previous question, you write that "in order to maintain a sense of wholeness and of loyalty to the community that I was brought up in, I have held on to an accent that is too often mistakenly seen as an indication of lower intelligence than many other accents in the United States" (1999, 66–67). I wondered if you could tell me a bit about how you maintain your accent: Is it a conscious decision? In other words, do you purposely consider various pronunciations and then choose one before speaking?

LSD: It is not a conscious decision. At some point I think it might have been, but at this point, as I said to you before [in a previous conversation], there are some words, that when I hear myself talk—the only reason that I know that I've changed "shurf" to "sheriff" and "chur" to "chair" is because, you know, I've been on TV some, and I've given interviews some, and I've seen me, and my accent sounds just the way we talked when I was growing up, except for a few notable exceptions, like "sheriff" and "chair." So I've not tried to keep it.

EAL: You also write, "Outsiders use our dialect to peg or recognize us, while we use it to figure out and establish who we are" (1999, 58). Could you tell me a bit more about the connections you see between dialect and identity formation?

LSD: I think that because I grew up as a part of a closed community, it would have been a rejection for me to sound another way. Now, if I'd gone away, to Ohio, for example, and then come home, they would have allowed me to change, because you know, people did that. As a matter of fact, the whole business is about nuance. People would grow up saying "Edny and Leony" instead of "Edna and Leona" and go off to Ohio for fifteen minutes, and they'd come back and no longer are they saying "Edny and Leony"— they're saying "Edna and Leona." But they also said "spaghetta" and "Cincinnata." It's the nuance people don't get. And if, you know, there are many, many words, even now, after all this time and such, there are many words that I know but I will not say because I'm not sure how to pronounce them. And, you know, I know that if I use them, I'll show my ass [laughs].

Now, let's see: the connections between dialect and identity formation. I think you only know about your identity if somebody wakes you at three in the morning and says, "Who are you?" and you give your name; then they say, "Who are you? Who are you?" and keep pushing that "Who are you?" Well, I'm Daddy's daughter, and I'm Brett Preston's mother, and I'm Arthur's wife, and you know, I'm the basketball player, I'm a golfer, and so on. I grew up in a place where I didn't always feel that I fit in, but I knew I had a place. I knew I had a place, and I might have been wrong in what I was believing and the way I was acting and such, but I knew I had a place. And, the best thing for me in terms of identity was that from the beginning, I knew that there's nothing I couldn't do if the first step was pencil and paper. And having that meant that I went to college absolutely unprepared socially, completely unprepared emotionally, *but* because I could do the silly work, you know, but I could do that stuff, I've never questioned my ability to learn anything, and that enables you if you know that in your head. You don't have to tell anybody, but if you know that about yourself, you'll try any damn thing. And just power right through it, and so part of the whole self-confidence in terms of dialect and identity formation, I think that is at the core of mine, because usually people went off to Ohio and began to say "spaghetta" and "Cincinnata," and I didn't. Because that would have been embarrassing to me. It would have been embarrassing to me, and I don't ever want anybody to take me for other than who I am, and so as a result, there are people who find me very attractive until I open my mouth, and then you can see it's bimbo city, and as I get older that's probably not the case, but it certainly was.

EAL: Have you read *Saving Grace*, the Lee Smith book?

LSD: Yes.

EAL: That just flashed through my mind, you know, when she goes to Gatlinburg and she's got the heels, and the lipstick, and she's with Randy Newhouse, bless her heart [laughs]. Anyway, that was just a tangent, but . . .

LSD: But no, again that's another thing too. I think there are no tangents. I think everything fits together. Part of the way we shape our own identity is allowing ourselves to say, by damn what comes, and we'll go back and work on that later. Because identity is not firm. I think that my identity at the core is definitely Appalachian.

EAL: In *Creeker* you admit that Arthur regularly does housework, but you "would be embarrassed if he discussed doing so with my family or members of [your] home community" (1999, 60). I understand the different gender norms in Appalachian communities and "mainstream" society, but could you comment a bit more about your statement? Would such an admission create strife in your relationship with your home community?

LSD: I tell you, not strife, just a reassessment of my ability. In order to do the other things I do outside the home, the housework has to be done, first. The house has to look good first, because, otherwise, I'm a bad wife. That's not the case in my husband's head—he grew up in Connecticut—but it's the case in mine, and part of what I brought from the mountains with me is a sense of my purpose, my purpose in life is to marry and have grandchildren and love 'em all, and be very happy with that. And I think I still try to pretend that I've got some of that.

EAL: Related to that, concerning your creation of Lee Preston, would you say that Lee was more in line with gender norms than Linda Sue?

LSD: No, actually, I think it'd be just the opposite.

EAL: Really? How so?

LSD: Well, because I think Linda Sue wanted more than anything in the world to be married; Linda Sue was a much safer person. Lee was a lot freer spirit.

EAL: That's really interesting, because I had read it the opposite way.

LSD: Yeah, by the time I became Linda again, I had both of them. By the time I became Linda again, I felt very powerful. Actually, Lee Preston had a great time and thought well of herself. Lee Scott was where I accomplished everything. I mean, I owe Brett Scott everything, the world. He made me go back to school. He made me get a job. He didn't make me, but by the time I went back to school we needed the money, and so he didn't mind my working. And he supported me in my work, even after I had a child, when nobody thought I ought to work. And so everything I accomplished by the time I was thirty, thirty-five, thirty-eight, or something like that, was as Lee Scott, and I felt that name fit me better than anything. So I married Arthur, and I kept the name Linda Scott, Linda Preston Scott, but eventually changed it to Linda Scott DeRosier.

Well, as a matter of fact, one of my defining moments was in Idaho. It was a speaking engagement in Boise. They had a Lenten luncheon thing they did every Wednesday during Lent, and they would ask somebody there who was especially competent or whatever, somebody who was well known, to come and give a lecture on "my best thought." You had to do thirty minutes on "my best thought" and you could take it any way you wanted to and any degree you wanted to.

At that point in my career my vita was I think twenty-two pages. The guy who introduced me was a very powerful Presbyterian minister in the area. He introduced me and he stood there with my twenty-two-page vita in his hand, which he'd had for, like, you know, six weeks or something, from the time he asked me to do it. He stood there with that in his hand, and he said, "Today we are fortunate to hear from Dr. Linda Scott DeRosier, wife of the president of the college of Idaho."

EAL: He did not.

LSD: He did, and you know, there's no easy recovery from that. And that has happened so many times, so many times. And so it's the sort of thing that until you get to where you can laugh about it and tell people how stupid those other people are, there's nothing you can do with that. At one point during our time in Idaho, Arthur got a call from this principal about a commencement address, and he said, "We want to ask your wife to speak at our commencement, but we wanted to get your permission first."

EAL: As if he would say, "Let me check her calendar. I'm not sure she's allowed to leave the house on that day."

LSD: [Laughs] Exactly! It's just astonishing.

EAL: Along those same lines, when explaining how you decided to accept the Social Security job, with resulting training in Asheville, you write, "For the first time in my life [I] refused to go along. I recall thinking that I was not exactly sure what I wanted to do with my life, but I was dead certain that I did *not* want to spend it eight miles out of town with a couple of kids, a full-time job, and a husband on the golf course all the time" (1999, 141). Would you say that your experiences at Pikeville College were responsible for this shift and this newfound ability to stand up for yourself?

LSD: I think there are times when you don't know what you're doing, and you can't even rationalize what you're doing, because you could not explain what you're doing, even to yourself. But where you have some sort of preliminary insight, where you think, "Okay, if I make this choice right now, here's how it's going to be." And that's spoken as one who didn't learn to drive until she was twenty-two years old. I've been forced into a corner to do practically everything that's of value in my life. I think it was only upon reflection that I saw that for what it was. I said in one of the books, I said: Thank God I married the smartest boy I ever went out with. At the time I didn't marry him because he was smart, and I didn't marry him because I thought he was going to make a fortune and so forth. I married him because I was in love with him. I wasn't just marrying Brett Dorse. I was marrying what I wanted to be.

EAL: I was very interested in your graduate school experience, especially when you wrote that "graduate school also seemingly rooted out the last vestiges of my Appalachian essence, though I did not know it at the time. Passing for normal—not hillbilly—was a journey I had embarked upon when I entered Pikeville College, and each year thereafter I had moved a bit closer to my goal" (1999, 179). While it's clear from these quotes that continued education brought a sense of belonging within the academic community, would you say that it further distanced you from your home community? I wondered if you could tell me a bit more about how people at home reacted to this new Linda Sue, whose last vestiges of Appalachian essence were gone.

LSD: When I was home I always acted as if I had not changed, but they knew I'd changed. And frankly, as I think about it, that's another thing I didn't recognize until I wrote it down: I don't think I much liked myself during those days, but you know, I always went home. You know, a lot of people go away and they just don't come back, or they come back once a year or whatever. As long as I lived within half a day's driving distance, I was home every two weeks.

EAL: Did they accept you just as much as before, when you were fifteen years old, or was there any tension? I mean, obviously if you're going to pop out with words like "atrocity" [laughs].

LSD: Yeah, that's the thing. I tried very hard not to do that, but, but I also never made much of the whole degree thing. Because my mother kept warning me that if I kept on, I was going to lose a good husband.

EAL: Oh.

LSD: And I did of course, but for very different reasons. Mother and Daddy came to my graduation for my master's and for the doctorate. And so they were there, and they supported me, and I think at some level they appreciated it. I don't think people outside academe know much about what it means and the work involved, and you know, I don't think they recognize what that's about. It's interesting too, the way that *Creeker* has been received back home.

EAL: Yes. I am really interested about that. How have people reacted? Do they come up to you and just shower you with praise, or is it like with Thomas Wolfe; are they mad?

LSD: All of the above, actually. I have been amazed at how many people like the book and have said so and have contacted me and such. At the same time, there are those who, when I was researching *Life and Grace*, didn't want to talk to me. This is the thing about memoir. It's not only your writing that's being criticized, it's your life! [Laughs]

But back to your question about how education has changed my relationship with home, from the beginning I have tried really hard to not change that much. But people who don't do a good bit of self-monitoring are either foolish, or sooner or later they'll pay for it. You know, it is very hard to maintain your value system in a world where that value system is not one most wanted. Generally we speak about people who are high self-monitors or low self-monitors. I used to be a pretty high self-monitor, and I think as I've gotten older, I may be a lower self-monitor. In the areas of expressing myself, I think I have become far more comfortable with my home ground here in academe, because as I've gotten older and had a success here or there, they can like it or not. [Laughs] And so I think I'm probably much more of a self-monitor at home, or it may just be that I've integrated all of those things, and again, that whole business of saying "atrocity," generally, and I am not as guilty as that.

EAL: Why do you think that you did more self-monitoring when you were younger?

LSD: I think I did more self-monitoring in academe when I was younger. I mean, in my husband's graduate program, in the doctoral program, in those days, there were several professors who would not accept women in their classes, because they didn't believe they could think that deeply. The people who are the most biased, prejudiced are the people who do not know it because they're going out of their way to help us up. That's the difference between reaching down and reaching out. I know my students can teach me things, not because they've covered the material I have, but because as we drag each other through this material one more time, I'll be able to see—if I make myself—it through their eyes. And that's a one-to-one kind of thing, and once you figure that out, you really can make some tremendous strides on your own, in terms of metacognition, standing outside your own thinking and figuring it out. And so none of this, in terms of self-monitoring, none of this was I aware of on the front end, even though I teach this stuff. [Laughs] On the back end, I can look back and see it.

You know, I've had people who work with me, say to me, after *Creeker* came out and it was such a hit, they'll say to me, "You know, that doesn't count. Your book doesn't count." And I'd say, "What do you mean?" "I mean it doesn't count; I mean it's not a professional book." And in that respect, they're absolutely correct, and you know, it doesn't even make me mad for them to say it. I find it kind of funny, because I don't think any of them could write *Creeker*; in order to do that, you've just got to sit down and think nobody in the world is going to read this, and I'm going to write it so that my kids know stuff that I have forgotten to tell them. My son read it, and he said, "Mom! I can't believe that! What about this?," and "What about that?" Because you know, you don't talk about those things.

EAL: I am fascinated by the incident you describe when Keenis Holbrook denied that Annapolis was the capital of Maryland, saying instead that it was Baltimore. You go on to write that "book-learning was not very credible on Two-Mile Creek" (1999, 25). Since leaving for the ninety-nine steps to success at Pikeville, you've endured a lot of bock learning: How do people on Two-Mile view your current profession, as well as your long list of advanced degrees?

LSD: I would suggest to you that most of them, especially since *Creeker* and *Songs* came out, have some knowledge that I've got you know, a degree or two, but I don't think they have any idea what that means. I think increasingly, nobody knows what that means, with all the online and Saturday classes, and low-residency things, where you go and stay two weeks and leave, which for some people can be really, really good. I think they are all surprised; they were all surprised with *Creeker*, but since *Creeker* came out, several people back there have either self-published or pulled together a book and managed to get it privately published, and those are in their view just as good and sometimes better than *Creeker*, because *Creeker* is just a personal story, and that's fine with me. You know, anytime anybody wants to write, I've encouraged them to. I believe self-expression is really good.

EAL: At the end of *Songs of Life and Grace* you write, "I wish I could say that we had as much faith [as in the ability to work] in using education as a means of gaining some control over an unpredictable world, but that would be a lie" (2003, 207). Can you talk a little more about that?

LSD: My grandma Emmy wanted a high school diploma, because she could see that a person who went to high school probably wouldn't have to work as hard. And furthermore, if my ancestors, those people who worked in the hot sun and never got what they wanted to eat, much less decent medical care and such, if they see me sitting at this desk, on any given day and calling it work, putting on my high-heel shoes, and going into class in my mauve suit, they'd know that I'd run the biggest scam that ever there was. You know, I've made my bones over theirs, and the difference maybe between me and other people is that I so appreciate it. I appreciate every hill of potatoes that they hoed, and I see that as a step in the direction of this line going forward. My children are all better off than I am, my grandchildren are better off still; it's the kind of thing that man, I can look back or forward and just feel wonderful about it.

You know, education is a means of gaining some control over an unpredictable world. It won't make your life easier, but it'll make your life more understandable.

EAL: At the conclusion of *Creeker* you reflect, "However painful or pleasant those insights and visions may have been, I never . . . ever . . . lost my feel for home" (1999, 220). Earlier you also write that for you and your sister, "Appalachia haunts the both of us, albeit in somewhat different ways, and we speak to each other of regaining possession of what we have lost upon leaving and of building us a cabin up the holler where the pigs used to be" (227). Could you tell me more about what you feel you've lost in leaving, and whether you think it could be regained by going back?

LSD: No, it couldn't. First of all, it could not be regained by going back. And secondly, part of it is what I wrote three times in *Creeker*: "Education, if it takes, changes the inside of our heads so that we do not see the same world we previously saw" (1999, 124, 125, 173). Everything you learn, you will lose your innocence about that thing. And you will lose your ability to feel that. I think I told you already that the day I married Brett Scott, the day I walked down the aisle, I felt the most successful I'd ever felt. I would love to feel that again, but what I'd have to give up to feel that is not something I'm willing to give up, and it's the same way with home.

If I had never left, first of all, I can't imagine what kind of life I would have had. And I would not have known that; it's just like, do people on Two-Mile appreciate my degrees? Not necessarily, and they probably appreciate the degrees and maybe even the lifestyle that comes with those degrees, my ability to go places, the traveling and the this and the that; different people would define it probably different ways. But the thing that I have, that's worth more to me than anything else in the world, is my own understanding of things. And I don't think I could have gotten that any other way.

EAL: In *Songs of Life and Grace* you write about the identity submersion women underwent upon marriage, and it seems as though the change necessitated there mirrors that of an Appalachian person encountering a wholly different discourse community within the university (2003, 56). Would you say that's accurate?

LSD: Of course it is. It is the sort of thing that you give up some things and you get some things. On every occasion, what you give up for most people has to do with choices. And sometimes it's worth that, and sometimes it isn't. And that's the case, you know when you go to university, you give up one set of choices, in my view a fairly limited set of choices to get another set of choices which are broader, we hope.

EAL: To change the subject a little, I'm interested in your portrayal of your mother. Since she was the fierce fighter of the "hillbilly necklace" (a dirty or suntanned ring around your neck), is it fair to say that was she always resisting media-supported stereotypes associated with Appalachia?

LSD: Good Lord yes. There are places in *Creeker* that my mother would have died. Because she was very concerned about the way people perceived her and us. If I put on something that she didn't think looked particularly sophisticated, she'd say it looked "creeky."

EAL: Creeky.

LSD: As in "on the creek." I don't think I've said that in either book. It's one of those things that, "That looks creeky," she'd say.

EAL: That makes sense. I wondered the same thing about your idea of being poor, which "meant having to sweep the yard instead of mow the grass" (1999, 113). Where do you think this idea came from?

LSD: It was the difference between poverty and trash. You know? Trash is you've got so damn many kids that they run around barefoot and then they wear down the grass, and you don't have any grass in the yard; then you have to sweep it so it won't get dusty all the time. And the idea, the difference between having to sweep the yard and mow the grass, is the difference between poverty and trash. Once Daddy put me up a swing in a big ol' apple tree in the front yard, and I started wearing out the grass, so Mama made me take it down.

EAL: We've talked about your mother some, and I'd like to hear more about your father. I was interested to read about his forms of literacy, especially the running list of figures he kept. Where and how did you discover his diary?

LSD: No, he didn't have a diary. He had one of those little lined three-by-five kind of notebooks with lines on it. And on there he just had figures. Dates and figures, and that was it. And we found it in his desk after he died, and none of us knew that he had it.

EAL: How far back did it go back? When did he start recording? Are there dates?

LSD: Yeah, there are dates, and you know, I don't remember. I let Sister have that, because you know she's in business, and she does more with figures than I do. And I might be able to find out. I know it was at least ten years between; there were probably others. I don't think he started it when he was working in the mines, because you know he did construction, and I think he probably started it when he'd figure for his construction things. You know, he built a spec house, and I think he probably started it then.

EAL: It's also clear that your father was quite the storyteller, and I wanted to know if he read books and magazines as avidly as your mother and grandmother.

LSD: Yes and no. And again, all of us considered reading to be pleasure, not a form of work.

And if that didn't come through in *Creeker*, it should have. I was just dead lazy, because all I wanted to do was read. And still, I have to resist that every moment of my life.

EAL: In the chapter about your father you explain that he knew the difference between "they" and "there," yet he always used "they" (instead of "there") in his speech. Why do you think he choose to repeatedly use nonstandard forms of English? I'm tempted to argue that this was a form of resistance; do you agree?

LSD: I say yes, because let me tell you, I think that his hanging on to his accent was very much the same as my hanging on to mine. I think that probably if I hadn't gone away to school, I would have sounded very differently if I had stayed back on Two-Mile. I think I would have been influenced by television, but as it was, I was put on notice fairly early; nobody at Pikeville College told me that I sounded dumb, because most of the people at Pikeville College sounded the same way. And I had teachers from away who came there to teach [and] believed they could teach us stuff without our changing the way we expressed it, and so I think that worked. And the moment I got out of there and went to Asheville I was told that they appreciated my work, but I was not going to be able to do anything unless I changed the way I expressed myself.

EAL: Did that hurt your feelings? How did you react to that at that time?

LSD: Well, at the time I thought he was probably right. And I intended to do something about it, but clearly I didn't.

EAL: [Laughs]

LSD: I was only there for thirteen weeks, and so it's the kind of thing that then I went to Louisville, and they sounded a lot fancier than I did too, because you know, once you get that much past Winchester in Kentucky, if you get west of Winchester, they sure don't sound the way we sound.

EAL: Well, there was the colleague that said he didn't think anybody east of Winchester could read, right?

LSD: Exactly.

EAL: That wraps up the questions I had for you. Thank you so very much for spending this time with me, answering these questions.

LSD: It was my pleasure.

CHAPTER 4

"Overcoming" Backgrounds: Competing Discourses in *The Unquiet Earth*

> When I was in school [in the 1950s and '60s] . . . we were never told there were Appalachian writers. We didn't read stories set in the mountains. And Appalachian people were not in the history books. So I assumed that we had no history; we had no literature. Those subjects happened someplace else; and we were just dead. Other places were where things happened. I had no idea I could be a writer.
>
> (T. Douglass 2006, 246)

In the above interview excerpt, West Virginia author Denise Giardina makes clear that the absence of Appalachian writers in her school-based curriculum directly impacted her (in)ability to conceive of herself as an author. During our (2007) interview conducted through e-mail she also remembered, "I don't think I read one single book about my place when I was a child. The closest I came was a book by Lois [Lenski 1959] called *Coal Camp Girl*." Lenski's regional series for children depicted life in various places across the country including Louisiana bayous, Arkansas cotton fields, and West Virginia coal camps. Although Lenski conducted primary research for each of her books, sometimes living in the areas she wrote about for several months, Giardina also remembers that in *Coal Camp Girl*, "the terms were different" (2007).

While Lenski's story depicts the hardships endured by mining families, including mine accidents, unsafe slate heaps, toxic refuse pools, and constant financial worry, as with most children's literature, each perilous circumstance ends in a happy resolution. Such endings rarely happened in Giardina's childhood home of Black Wolf coal camp near Bluefield, West

Virginia, especially when her family had little choice but to leave the camp when she was thirteen years old and move to the state capital of Charleston to find work. Giardina reflects, "I think losing my whole community, and not only leaving but having it torn down, really marked me, and so maybe I felt a need to re-create what had been lost" (T. Douglass 2006, 244).

The realization that she could write about her home did not occur until Giardina encountered Lee Smith's *Blackmountain Breakdown* as an adult, a novel that takes place near Giardina's coal camp home (T. Douglass 1993, 388). Throughout her childhood and early adolescent years Giardina remembers, "I just assumed no one would write about where I was from because it wasn't worthwhile" (2007). When asked about where that notion came from, Giardina responded, "I think the instances that reinforced negative cultural value judgments were on TV—*The Real McCoys*, *The Beverly Hillbillies*" (2007). In addition to these damaging media portrayals of ignorant hillbillies, the literature Giardina read while growing up also taught her that with the exception of Lenski's magically happy endings, seemingly no one wrote about Appalachia.

After becoming more familiar with Appalachian writers like Mary Lee Settle and Lee Smith in her adult years, Giardina began writing about her home and its political struggles. Although her first book (*Good King Harry*) takes place in England and focuses on Henry V, Giardina's next two novels portray the plights of miners in Appalachia. Her 1987 novel, *Storming Heaven*, re-creates the Battle of Blair Mountain; and her 1992 novel, *The Unquiet Earth*, weaves a fictional story around the Buffalo Creek disaster.[1] As in Giardina's own life, the characters in *The Unquiet Earth* encounter messages in both literary and oral forms that announce Appalachian inferiority. The transmission of these messages spans several maternal generations beginning with Flora Honaker, continuing with her daughter Rachel, and ending with Rachel's daughter Jackie. Jackie's character functions as an autobiographical representation of Giardina, and as a child Jackie believes that the only kind of stories that exist in her hometown are "dumb old hillbilly stor[ies]," since "real writers live in New York apartments or sit at sidewalk cafes in Paris" (*TUE*, 106, 108),[2] not in West Virginia coal camps.

In both Giardina's real life and in *The Unquiet Earth*, the technical act of reading initially discourages writing, creating self-doubt and a lack of confidence in writing about personal experiences. More poignantly than any other text considered in this project, *The Unquiet Earth* illustrates how the specific literary omission of Appalachia combined with negative media portrayals of the region affects the perceived (in)ability to write. Giardina repeatedly focuses readers' attention on how one facet of technical literacy (reading) can be potentially detrimental to the other (writing).

Like Giardina, as Jackie matures she learns to value her home and recognize the possibility that she can write about it, yet, similar to other works considered in this project, that knowledge comes at a cost. When Jackie leaves West Virginia to work in Washington, D.C., she loses a geographic and emotional connection with her home, and Giardina recounts a similar experience when she reflects, "I'm not the same person who was the ten-year-old kid in Black Wolf, West Virginia. Now I eat sushi and curry. I feel I have lost something, in a sense, as much as I have gained" (T. Douglass 2006, 248).

In "Reading Literacy Narratives" Janet Carey Eldred and Peter Mortensen ask, "What happens if speaking a new language means cultural displacement? What happens if speaking a new language means losing self?" (1992, 515). The language that both Giardina and Jackie learn through reading is one that demeans their experiences, and it is only through enduring further loss, by leaving Appalachia and entering into other discourse communities, that either woman is able to give voice to her experiences. Their paths once again highlight how literacy attainment can function as simultaneously perilous and empowering for mountain women.

Despite the painful loss Giardina experiences, she gains the insight necessary to believe in the value of Appalachian literature. Consequently, she pursues a career as an author in which she reveals the sometimes devastating consequences of literacy acquisition, as well as the capitalist exploitation that occurs daily in the coal fields, to reading audiences. Drawing from the loss of her home community that marked her as a child, Giardina marks audiences in her own way by creating fiction that urges readers to rethink their preconceived notions of Appalachia while also questioning the pedagogical approaches of non-Appalachian teachers, as well as harmful coal mining practices.

As discussed in the first chapter, American audiences have been schooled by literary and popular media to imagine Appalachia as a repository for socially undesirable hillbillies, those who are among other things drunken, ignorant, and illiterate. Giardina works from within and out of this long-established tradition, and the biographical story of her journey away from and back to Appalachia combines with the fictional strategies she uses in her novel to reveal that writing—whether for literary audiences, political audiences, or a combination of both—ameliorates some of the divide between discursive worlds introduced by multiple literacies. Speaking to this point, Giardina declares, "I have achieved a measure of contentment through conjuring lost places and writing about them" (1998, 131). Jackie finds similar resolution working as the editor of a newspaper in her hometown, a venue in which she can write about the politically charged issue of strip-mining and mountaintop removal in Appalachia. Through her fictionalization of Jackie's struggle to negotiate varying discursive worlds, Giardina demonstrates how writing fiction allows her to write about both the personal loss she has incurred from gaining new literacies and the destruction and devastation caused by unethical coal mining practices.

Media Effects

Throughout *The Unquiet Earth* Giardina uses multiple narrators to tell various sections, and through these different perspectives she reveals how print-based texts send potent cultural messages to her characters that affect how they perceive their Appalachian home and their place within it. Rachel Honaker's mother, Flora, spends countless hours poring over mail-order catalogs and magazines to see the latest fashions, and she models her daughter's dresses after advice given in these articles. Most of the material for the dresses comes from secondhand charity donations, yet Flora believes that the knowledge she gains from *Ladies' Home Journal*, *McCall's*, and the *Pictorial Review* makes her able to render the clothes acceptable and even fashionable. Rachel remembers, "I wore the white dress and red coat on Class Day to impress the teacher, who was young and fresh from Transylvania College and in the mountains for some kind of adventure" (*TUE*, 7). Like many of the readers Giardina addresses in her fiction, Rachel's teacher has been schooled through literary and media images to imagine Appalachia as a wildly exotic place, ripe for the kind of adventurous cultural tourism she seeks upon going there to teach students.

Similar to many of the fictional and real Appalachian students considered in this project, including the Nevels children and Linda Scott DeRosier, Rachel defers to her teacher's cultural authority and assumes a kind of automatic inferiority. In one instance Rachel walks her usual two-mile route to school, and on Class Day it rains, so she arrives at school in a water-soaked outfit. When she takes off the coat she sees that it "wept and left red splotches all over my white dress. It was like I'd been shot, like I'd been through bloody battle" (*TUE*, 7). Rachel understandably feels embarrassed, but what most mortifies her is that she feels ashamed in front of her teacher, a Bennett from Louisville that her mother has read about in the society pages of the newspaper. Her mother tells her that the Bennetts are "quality people," and Rachel had hoped to impress her teacher with her clothing (7).

Conversely, when Rachel's first cousin, Dillon Freeman, narrates the event, he neglects to mention the stains on her dress, instead commenting that "when she stood up to recite, she looked like a queen" (*TUE*, 7). Later we learn that despite their familial relationship, Dillon and Rachel become lovers, and we realize that Dillon has always admired Rachel.[3] Dillon's admiration does not depend on Rachel's clothing, primarily because he sees no reason for Rachel to feel embarrassed. Dillon's mother, Carrie Freeman, works as a nurse in the mountains and has little time or patience for frivolous superficialities such as style, and she passes this nonchalance about social codes on to Dillon.[4] Gender roles also figure into how Rachel and Dillon view the stained dress, and Rachel's notion of appropriate feminine behavior combined with Flora's literacy-supported teachings leaves her humiliated over her ruined clothing. In this scene Giardina begins setting up Rachel's and Dillon's views of the same Appalachian place as very different, and those differences remained largely tied to knowledge about social class, gender, and notions of "high" culture gained through literate activity.

Giardina further emphasizes Rachel's exposure to mainstream notions of cultural capital when Rachel remembers: "At night, when we listened to Lum and Abner on the radio, [Flora] sat beside a lamp turning the pages [of her magazine] slowly, her head bent reverently over the glowing photographs" (*TUE*, 8–9). Through her reading Flora experiences a kind of social edification that sets her and her family apart from many rural West Virginia families, including Dillon's. As she bends her head "reverently," Giardina makes clear that Flora values the cultural habits perpetuated in her magazines above that of her own mountain culture, and she wants to distinguish her family from "trash from the head of the hollow" (9). Rachel even remembers that her mother "learned out of her magazines how to fold a napkin, how to set out the silverware just so and lay the knife so the curved side faces the plate" (9), and she trains Rachel to follow these dining etiquette rules as well.

Ironically, while Flora reads her magazines in what she perceives to be a necessary step in rising above her mountain culture, the rest of the family listens to the Lum and Abner radio show. The program aired nationally from

1931 until 1954, depicting the comedic antics of Columbus "Lum" Edwards and Abner Peabody from the then fictional town of Pine Ridge, Arkansas, based on the real town of Waters, Arkansas. Although not geographically part of the Appalachian region, the leading actors' hillbilly characterizations closely relate to those of Appalachian mountaineers, and entertainers frequently made connections between Arkansas and Missouri mountain people and those from Appalachia.[5]

For producers in the business of making profit from hillbilly caricatures, geographic details mattered little, and lines distinguishing the two groups were rarely clear. As such, when Rachel listens to these broadcasts with her family, the hillbilly stories she hears send the cultural message that mountain people are different and largely ignorant. Episode titles like "Abner Hates Being in High Society" reinforced perceived disparities between mountain and mainstream culture, and by fictionalizing the radio show in her novel, Giardina draws from this tradition to highlight the dichotomy between Flora's societal aspirations and the popular media image of the hillbilly.

Scholar Anthony Harkins theorizes that in some cases these hillbilly depictions were forms of "protective self-mockery" that "removed some of the word's stigma and defined their own identity. Playing 'the hillbilly' helped performers and audiences alike come to terms with the ambiguities in their own lives, simultaneously separating themselves from and connecting themselves to a rural ethnic and cultural tradition" (2004, 94–95). This positive spin on a frequently derogatory art form may apply to other radio and television shows, but Lum and Abner originally began performing in blackface and only later switched to their more popular hillbilly act when auditioning; it seems unlikely that their performance was akin to any kind of cultural reappropriation.

Since the pair began their act in blackface but soon decided that audience members might be interested in a move away from the minstrelsy tradition, their decision to act out the comic mountain fool did not operate as any kind of self-protective strategy for the actors, but it did reassure the social status of a listening public eager to distinguish themselves from raucously ignorant hillbillies. This tactic proved especially useful during the Depression, when the line between economic security and potential barbarism (as imagined in Appalachia) seemed precariously close for a large number of mainstream listeners, many of whom were on the verge of bankruptcy. Literary critic Nancy Parrish notes a similar trend when writing about Al Capp's 1934 cartoon creation, "Lil' Abner," and Billy DeBeck's "Snuffy Smith." She argues,

"These were comic images projected upon mountain people—images that, in essence, acted to relieve a prevailing sense of economic anxiety about the Depression by placing at comical distance the poverty that the middle class feared for itself" (1994, 39).

J. W. Williamson (1995) sets forth a similar theory in *Hillbillyland: What the Movies Did to the Mountains and What the Mountains Did to the Movies*. Listening to the Lum and Abner show and observing Flora's almost spiritual devotion to her magazines, Rachel begins to understand her home through these oral and literate forms as negatively apart from much of mainstream America.

Resisting Literacies, Again

Unlike Rachel, who strives to make good grades and please her teachers, Giardina illustrates Dillon's resistance to literacy-based instruction almost immediately. The novel opens with his narration, and he explains that he dislikes school because "you learn spelling rules and grammar rules and that the way you talked all your life is ignorant even though it seems to suit most people fine, and when Teacher goes on and says we live in a free country it's just a little hard to believe" (*TUE*, 6). His description of Teacher in this passage sounds remarkably similar to DeRosier's account of Janis Carroll, and in both instances teachers operate as gatekeepers to the kind of higher society for which Flora longs. Dillon's resistance also echoes Reuben Nevels's actions in *The Dollmaker*, and by contrasting Dillon's resistance with Rachel's acceptance of instruction by teachers that assume mountain inferiority, Giardina's text encourages readers to ponder whether Dillon's gender grants him a greater (or perhaps more expected) ability to resist literacy-sanctioned modes of behavior.

Anthropologist Anita Puckett's research reveals that in some mountain communities, residents expect women to participate in literate activity, but with the exception of preachers, they do not sanction such behavior in men. If the same belief system holds true for Giardina's fictional community of the Number Thirteen coal camp, then Dillon does not face the same reading expectations as Flora or Rachel, and consequently is not exposed to the repeated absence or degradation of Appalachia in literary portrayals. When Dillon begins writing his own book about his family's history near the end of the novel, Giardina portrays this artistic endeavor as an expected event.

Unlike Jackie, who believes for years that she cannot be a writer because she comes from West Virginia, Dillon seems to automatically assume the possibility of becoming an author, though he does "meekly" seek editing advice from Jackie (*TUE*, 297). In this way, Dillon's resistance to literacy-based instruction results in an aversion to reading (as Puckett documented in her research), and this aversion ironically supports the belief that he can write about Appalachia, highlighting how his path to authorship functions as the opposite of Jackie's.

Raised to Leave

Unlike Dillon's mother, Carrie, who remains proud of her Appalachian home, Flora attempts to indoctrinate Rachel with views that denigrate mountain culture. Flora insists that Rachel call her Mother, since Mom "sounded country," and Rachel also explains, "Mother longed for me to go to Berea, where she hoped the offending hillbilly would be whipped out of me and I would marry a future doctor or lawyer and live in Lexington or Louisville" (*TUE*, 8, 9). Flora's mainstream literacy-supported notions about progress and a move away from traditional mountain culture make it nearly impossible for Rachel to avoid the kind of identity conflict this project interrogates, and Rachel reflects:

> So I grew up with the understanding that I would leave the mountains, and as I got older the idea seemed more pleasing. But my ideas about leaving were different than my mother's. I listened to the radio and twice I had been to the movies in Shelby. I knew the way people in other places talked and I practiced sounding like them. I wanted to drink chocolate malteds when I was in one mood and martinis when I was in another, and wear silk hose with seams down the back and pierce my ears and smear the world's reddest lipstick on my mouth. I wanted to be a stewardess. A stewardess was the most glamorous thing a woman could be, next to an actress. (*TUE*, 10)

Here we see that Rachel considers her exposure to mainstream America exciting, and she longs to experience things outside her mountain community. Her dreams of becoming a stewardess, as well as her admiration for acting, also illustrate a future closely bound with gender expectations of appropriate occupations for women. Yet when Rachel leaves home, much to her mother's dismay, she pursues her aunt Carrie's profession of nursing, and as with the Nevels family, she encounters an unfriendly situation that judges her and her home as inferior.

Similar to DeRosier's leaving her home community of Two-Mile Creek, when Rachel leaves Number Thirteen to attend nursing school she encounters drastic differences between her home discourse community and the new discursive world she enters at school. Echoing the disappointment Gertie experiences when she sees her children's new school in Detroit, Rachel feels disheartened when she sees Grace Hospital, the place where she will learn to become a nurse: "The building was yellow brick with small dark windows and the look of the warehouses that lined Back Street along the Levisa. An alley that stank of garbage bins separated the hospital from the Nurses' Home, where the students lived" (*TUE*, 16).

As in *The Dollmaker*, imagery reminiscent of factories and warehouses peppers Giardina's description of the school, and her description of student housing resonates as particularly powerful. Rachel describes many of the students as "frightened country girls from West Virginia and Kentucky away from home for the first time" (*TUE*, 16), and the fact that they live behind the hospital near an alley that reeks of garbage is suggestive of how many of the faculty at the school view their pupils. After hearing her mother, Flora, constantly reference "trash from the head of the hollow," the spatial placement of student housing at Grace Hospital only reinforces what Rachel understands about her mountain culture, making negotiation between home and school fraught with difficult identity choices.

Once classes begin, Rachel's new teacher, Miss Kurtz, further confirms Rachel's suspicions about the school's view of Appalachia. Rachel remembers that her teacher "introduced herself by saying she was from Pittsburgh and had come to the mountains to do her mission work. She held a heavy book against her chest" (*TUE*, 16). Miss Kurtz's ideas about mountain people no doubt align with those perpetuated by the American Missionary Association, and the heavy book she clutches to her chest represents the knowledge she believes she can bring to these supposedly ignorant, backwoods girls. Like other missionary teachers from the North discussed in this project, Miss Kurtz also supports the idea that Appalachians comprise their own separate race, and she uses Arnold Toynbee's 1934 *A Study of History* as proof of mountain inferiority.

She first describes Toynbee to Rachel's class as a British historian, as if his non-American nationality grants him special authority, and she proceeds to read from his book: "The Scotch-Irish immigrants who have forced their way into these natural fastnesses have come to be isolated from the rest of the World. The Appalachian Mountain People are at this day not better than barbarians. They are the American counterparts of the latter-day White barbarians of the Old World, the Kurds, and the Pathans, and the Hairy Ainu" (*TUE*, 16). Giardina's fictionalization follows Toynbee's text almost verbatim, and considering a lengthy portion of his original text further illustrates the sort of ideological framework from which Toynbee and Miss Kurtz operate:

> The Scotch-Irish immigrants who have forced their way into these natural fastnesses have come to be isolated and segregated here from the rest of the World to a much greater extent than their ancestors [in Ireland] ever were... The Ulsterman has retained the traditional Protestant standard of education, whereas the Appalachian has relapsed into illiteracy and into all the superstitions for which illiteracy opens the door. His agricultural calendar is governed by the phases of the Moon; his personal life is darkened by the fear, and by the practice, of witchcraft. He lives in poverty and squalor and ill-health... In fact, the Appalachian "Mountain People" at this day are no better than barbarians. They are the American counterparts of the latter-day White barbarians of the Old World: the Rifis and Kabyles and Tuareg, the Albanians and Caucasians, the Kurds and the Pathans and the Hairy Ainu. These White barbarians of America, however, differ in one respect from those of Europe and Asia... in being not a survival but a reversion. (*TUE*, 310–12)

Toynbee's remarks about geographic isolation support those of earlier historians, and his comment about reversion sends an especially potent message about the degradation of mountain people. That such rhetoric not only makes its way into Rachel's classroom, but actually finds center stage in one of the first lectures given by her teacher, illustrates the sort of stark identity decision Miss Kurtz expects of her students. After quoting from Toynbee she tells her pupils, "If you are to make nurses, you must overcome your backgrounds. You must rise above the handicaps of inbreeding and the filthy living conditions you are used to. At his hospital, we expect you to keep yourselves clean" (*TUE*, 16). Notably, Miss Kurtz does not ask her students to incorporate their backgrounds in this new situation, but rather she demands that they "overcome" everything they have learned in their home-based discourse community in favor of what she has to teach them.

Certainly textbook selections factor as important components of learning experiences, and as literacy scholar Yvonne Honeycutt Baldwin points out, "Textbooks in any classroom . . . are important in and of themselves, for they signify through their content and form particular constructions of reality or particular ways of selecting and organizing the world of potential knowledge. They embody the 'selective tradition' of legitimate knowledge and culture, one that in the process of enfranchising one group's cultural capital sometimes disenfranchises that of another" (2006, 88). Miss Kurtz's decision to recite selections from Toynbee's work undoubtedly disenfranchises her classroom of mountain students, and Rachel's exposure to textbook-supported "proof" of mountain inferiority further emphasizes what she had already learned at home from her mother's reading.

Not surprisingly, Toynbee's derogatory inscriptions about Appalachian people elicit strong reactions from authors and scholars writing about the region. Giardina discusses the excerpt twice by including it in *The Unquiet Earth* and again in her (1999) essay titled "Appalachian Images: A Personal History." She opens the piece with the most offensive excerpt of Toynbee's Appalachian commentary, later noting, "Arnold Toynbee never visited the place he called 'Appalachia'" (164). To illustrate the ridiculous nature of his unfounded comments, Giardina spends several pages chronicling her own Appalachian family history, and she cites two relatives who wrote their own poems and were familiar with poetic conventions popular during the Victorian age. She takes a sarcastic tone in comparing her ancestors to the people Toynbee describes, as when she comments, "I examine old photographs of these kin, looking for signs of encroaching barbarism," and she later concludes, "It seems mountain people in 1900 knew what a camera was. It seems mountain people looked normal" (163).

Giardina's definition of normalcy encompasses the technical ability to read and write for both her ancestors and fictional characters, and she extends this portrayal of Appalachian literacy as an expected part of life when Rachel recites John Keats's "Ode to a Grecian Urn" on Class Day and Dillon's mother Carrie compares his face with a description by Charles Dickens (*TUE*, 8, 31). By juxtaposing intelligent, literate characters (including Flora, Rachel, and Jackie) with notions of an illiterate Appalachia introduced by a non-Appalachian teacher relying on faulty scholarship, Giardina encourages her readers to rethink their own notions of mountain illiteracy. Conversely, Giardina's fictional characters are not made privy to the same insights until they undergo painful discourse transitioning. As such, later in the novel we see how Rachel passes this understanding down to Jackie, who struggles with authorship for years before realizing that she can write stories about home.

Negotiating a New Divide

Similar to the way Giardina presents Appalachian literacy as a typical skill, she also portrays characters capable of standing up to Miss Kurtz and openly questioning her authority. One of Rachel's classmates, Tommie Justice, uses Toynbee's description to embarrass Miss Kurtz by asking for details about Hairy Ainus. When Miss Kurtz hesitates and finally says, "I'm not sure I know or want to know," Tommie fires back, "I just wondered because my cousins over on Greasy Creek, they're all inbred like you said, and they're cross-eyed and they got hair all over their bodies, even on their penises. I just wondered if they might be part Hairy Ainu?" (*TUE*, 16). Tommie's mischievous comment redirects the conversation, and Miss Kurtz enters an uncomfortable discussion about appropriate medical terms. Although Miss Kurtz never responds to Tommie's initial question, she becomes flustered and Rachel remembers, "We knew her then for a coward" (17). The rhetoric Tommie employs when questioning Miss Kurtz recalls the strategy Gertie Nevels uses in a conversation with Miss Whittle, and in both cases those in assumed lower positions manipulate the conversation to disempower the teacher representing power and authority, evoking a positive response from many readers.

Despite this display of resistance, many of the other pupils in the class find Miss Kurtz and the new discursive world she represents unacceptable, and like *The Dollmaker*'s Reuben, they return home. Although Rachel becomes homesick, she stays at Grace Hospital, but she also remembers, "I did lose The Homeplace when I went to school, and it had nothing to do with banks or coal companies. It was the inevitable loss known by those who are not tied to the same patch of earth for all their days" (*TUE*, 15). For the first time in her life, Rachel leaves home for an extended period of time, and she explains that some of her classmates departed because they believe "as strong as any religion, that home can be preserved forever and life made everlasting if we only stay put. And school was not like home. The teachers, even those kinder than Miss Kurtz, were there to goad us on, to judge and criticize, where many of us had known only petting and praise" (17).

Rachel's explanation of why some of her classmates choose to go home recalls the predicament of Arnow's characters, particularly Reuben's abandonment of Detroit and his ultimate refusal to participate in the required dialectical negotiation process that comprises an integral part of literacy attainment. For some of Rachel's peers, Giardina sets up a situation that echoes the "abandon or adjust" options Arnow makes available to her characters, and Rachel explains the attraction of such resistance, since those refusing to participate in a new discursive world believe that in doing so, "home can be preserved forever" (*TUE*, 17).

One of the major themes of *The Unquiet Earth* revolves around the coal mining industry, particularly the way mining companies cheat mountain people out of their land by buying mineral rights or claiming senior patents on the land. Many of the girls that Rachel goes to school with have lost their physical homes, as she does, and adhering to the language practices and belief systems of their home-based Appalachian discourse community helps preserve what has been taken from them. Even so, Rachel chooses to remain at school and weather Miss Kurtz's teaching.

Rachel's Appalachian-related humiliation only increases when she joins the army after finishing nursing school and goes to Manila to work as a nurse during the Second World War. When narrating about her experiences overseas, Rachel remembers, "Every place we went—Fort Jackson, Camp Anzio, Corregidor, Leyte, Manila—we were the only nurses from the mountains. People kept saying, How funny your accents are, Does your father make moonshine? Are those the first shoes you ever had on? At first we laid it on good. I said our family mule slept in the living room, and Tommie told one GI that she never saw a pair of panties until she joined the army. It was fun for a while but then it got old" (*TUE*, 47). Giardina's placement of Appalachian characters, as well as the stereotypes that follow them, in a global context highlights the pervasiveness of negative assumptions about mountain people. Although the soldiers that tease Rachel and Tommie are American, their prejudices about Appalachians follow them outside national boundaries.

Such stereotypes resonate just as strongly today, as when Appalachian scholar Ronald Eller notes in the introduction to *Back Talk from Appalachia* that "it is ironic that in spell checking a draft of this document, my word processing software (Microsoft Word Version 6.0) could not locate the word 'moonshiners' in its dictionary and recommended that I substitute the word 'mountaineers'" (Billings, Norman, and Ledford 2000, xi). When Rachel meets and begins dating Fred, another soldier with similarly stubborn stereotypical views of mountain people, she remembers, "Fred said I was dainty and trim and had delicate hands like a lady should have, which he didn't expect to find in a girl from the mountains" (*TUE*, 48). Rachel does not continue to narrate what Fred would expect to find in an Appalachian woman, but as readers we understand that Fred does not expect that someone as beautiful as Rachel would come from Appalachia.

Resisting Gendered Expectations

For decades gendered stereotypes about mountaineers have portrayed mountain men as lazy, violent, and patriarchal rulers; while women were generally depicted as either sexually wanton or defeminized, thanks to their constant toiling in field and home. Appalachian scholar Elizabeth Engelhardt refers to the Granny and Elly May characters from *The Beverly Hillbillies* to illustrate these two disparate yet related roles, explaining that Elly May generally precedes Granny as "the one with illusory sexual power who married early, had too many children, got old before her time, and turned into Granny" (2005, 3).

After constant farming outside and work in the home, these mountain women were presumed to lose all signs of femininity, and Fred assumes something similar about Rachel. Rachel also remembers how she felt about Fred's comment about her hands and body when she narrates, "This last comment made me mad, but I feared to argue for I had written to my mother about him. She wrote back, 'Your new friend sounds so nice. I know you have been taught to behave properly and I'm sure he appreciates that. I'm very proud of you'" (*TUE*, 48). Unlike Dillon, who we predict would stand up to Fred, Rachel silently accepts his comment, largely in an effort to please her mother.

As discussed earlier, Flora relies on magazines and other printed sources for lessons about how women should behave, and she passes this information on to Rachel, who tries to appease her mother's literacy-supported notions of proper womanhood. Rachel's silence also echoes Gertie Nevels's acquiescence to her mother, who relies on biblical scripture to prescribe a woman's role, particularly within marriage. Both Flora's and Gertie's mothers' print-supported beliefs align with submissive roles expected of women, and they pass them on to their daughters, who in turn internalize the silent submission their mothers demand. In not speaking out against Fred's comment, Rachel grants him a power over her and the home she represents.

Rachel also tries to mold herself to fit Fred's expectations of a proper woman because owning up to other people's reactions to her mountain heritage leaves her exhausted. Rachel's friend Tommie Justice dislikes Fred and asks Rachel if she is "getting above her raising" (*TUE*, 49). Rachel explains, "I get tired of being different. . . . I get tired of people thinking I'm stupid just because of the sound of my voice" (49). As with the Nevels children in *The Dollmaker*, Rachel soon learns that those outside her primary discourse community consider a mountain accent an indicator of lower intelligence, and to avoid such judgment she consciously alters the way she speaks. As with the students James Paul Gee studies, this tactic fosters successful entry into the secondary discourse of army life in Manila, but this decision causes Rachel to mask certain elements of her identity, and this too leaves her tired and confused.

Although Fred promises to marry Rachel, once the war ends and she returns to West Virginia she never hears from him again. Rachel knows that sharp class lines separate them, since Fred "grew up rich in New Orleans where his family owned a jewelry store" (*TUE*, 48), but she seems hopeful that their love for one another will cross class boundaries. When it does not, she begins seeing Tony Angelelli again, an Italian immigrant who keeps books for the coal company. Despite their lack of emotional connection, she marries him, seemingly out of desperation and fear of remaining single. Unlike Dillon, who appears perfectly content to remain single, Rachel feels pressured to marry, no doubt a gendered constraint placed upon her by mountain conventions of womanhood that generally favor marriage over singlehood.

Her days spent at home are long, and she remembers, "I didn't take a job because everyone said it was time for women to settle down and rebuild the home. I sewed curtains and cleaned and learned to cook Italian food, to measure out oregano and basil, pour olive oil in the boiling pasta, slit a squid and remove the thin clear backbone," but Tony does not appreciate her efforts and only demeans her when "the spaghetti stuck together or the bread was too hard" (*TUE*, 63–64). When Tony's friend and superintendent of Jenkinjones mine, Arthur Lee Sizemore, offers Rachel a job with the county as a nurse, she accepts, especially since, as Arthur points out, "Tony won't dare fuss if the offer comes from me" (67). Although her path to employment operates as a patriarchal one, the job still provides her with an opportunity for independence, and she seizes it. As with Linda Scott DeRosier, staying home and assuming the singular role of wife does not fulfill Rachel, and she seeks employment to enrich her life. Also parallel to DeRosier's experiences, Rachel's career choice results in a return to her mountain roots.

When Rachel begins nursing in 1950, she recalls, "It is a different world on Trace Mountain" (*TUE*, 68), and she is able to distinguish this world as different thanks to the new perspectives she gained in school and abroad. One of her main duties involves visiting tuberculosis patients, including Granny Combs. Rachel explains that her "supervisor thought [she] should talk Granny into a nursing home," but Rachel knows that "if you took Granny off that mountain she would have collapsed and vanished like a long-buried body that is dug up and disintegrates when it is exposed to the air" (70).[6] Similar to Rachel's classmates from nursing school who choose to return home, Granny remains tied to the land, as well as the natural remedies she learned there. Granny tells Rachel that she cured her own cold with "honey and corn liquor and chamomile tea," and Rachel remembers, "I drank a cup of her chamomile tea myself. It is still the best thing for a cold, so soothing for a cough and clears the sinuses too. They will not teach that at nursing school and call you a hillbilly if you recommend it, but they will suffer the colds" (70).

After enduring the teachings of Miss Kurtz and other teachers at Grace Hospital, as well as comments from army soldiers in Manila, Rachel knows the difference between standard medical practices and the homeopathic remedies favored by some mountain people like Granny Combs, as well as the value judgments that go along with them. Even though she views some elements of her mountain culture negatively, thanks in part to her mother's literacy-supported beliefs, Rachel also recognizes the value of her cultural heritage, as when she adheres to Granny Combs's medical advice. For Rachel, going away to school further emphasizes the differences between Appalachia and mainstream America that her mother seems so obsessed with, but that distancing also allows her to view home from a new perspective that her mother never experiences.

When Rachel travels overseas, becomes involved with Fred, and then returns home she becomes even more aware of the derogatory beliefs others (and her own mother) hold about Appalachia. Yet at the same time, Rachel's departure and return render her able to recognize and value certain aspects of her mountain culture, like Granny Combs's remedies. Consequently, although Rachel still works to "overcome" her background, she seems less intent on doing so than her mother, Flora. Near the novel's end Giardina also makes clear that Rachel's daughter Jackie finally overcomes the need to "overcome" her Appalachian heritage, thus granting her the ability to write.

Reading That Discourages Writing

In the same way that both Flora and Rachel learn negative messages about Appalachia, so too does Rachel's daughter, Jackie. Jackie's narration begins in 1959, when Jackie is eight years old, aligning with Giardina's birth year of 1951. Almost as soon as Jackie begins narrating sections of the novel, readers recognize her penchant for reading. When Dillon gives Jackie a copy of *Charlotte's Web* as a present, she explains, "I have never had a book belong to me" (*TUE*, 88), but she goes on discuss how her mother takes her to the library on a regular basis, and like Rachel, who quotes Keats, and Carrie, who makes comparisons to Dickens, Giardina figures Jackie's literacy as a normal part of her life. Jackie also makes clear that media inform her conception of the world, and she describes *The Wizard of Oz* as "the only movie I know where a girl is the main character and does most everything right" (90). Like her mother's ideas about movie stars and stewardesses, many of Jackie's ideas about proper gender roles come from media depictions, and her comment about *The Wizard of Oz* demonstrates her attention to feminine representations of independent, successful women.

Despite Jackie's attention to these portrayals, she still seems unable to conceive of herself in such a way, especially in the realm of authorship. When Rachel divorces Tony, she and Jackie move into a new home in the Number Thirteen coal camp. Jackie feels excited that their new house has bookcases conveniently built into the wall, and she remembers, "When we first moved into our new house at Number Thirteen, I figured I would be a writer" (*TUE*, 105), but this declaration does not last long. In the new neighborhood Jackie also becomes friends with Toejam Day. She admits that "Toejam isn't real smart, and his family is poor," but despite their intellectual and class-based differences, Jackie befriends Toejam and often helps him deliver newspapers on his bicycle route. Jackie explains that "while Toejam pedals I tell him stories I made up about the people who live in the houses. They aren't good stories because you can't tell good stories about people around here, but it is what Toejam likes. His favorites are about the people who live on Hunkie Hill. They are Hungarians, Russians, and Czechoslovakians. Toejam can't even say 'Czechoslovakians'" (106).

While Jackie wants to become a writer, and even practices telling stories to Toejam, she remains convinced that "you can't tell good stories about people around here." This judgment no doubt stems from the books she has read, which either omit Appalachia altogether or depict it in a derogatory way. Like Jackie, an adolescent Giardina creates her own stories about people who live in the apartment buildings near her house because at that time she also believes that Appalachian people are not worth telling stories about. Giardina remembers that as a child most of her stories did not contain endings, and she recalls, "I learned about endings later, when I was taught quotation marks and spelling. Learning to spell ended any illusions I may have had that we are totally free and independent creatures. No, there was a higher authority that molded us all to its will and ordered our lives for us, an authority as inexorable in its own way as the booger man. Spelling and grammar are benevolent dictators perhaps, subjugating one raw culture that a broader one may be experienced" (1998, 131). In this passage Giardina explicitly discusses the consequences of becoming literate in a technical as well as discursive sense.

Once aware of standard literary genre conventions that traditionally require a beginning and ending, the spelling and grammar rules that go along with such genre guidelines become dictators, although Giarinda speculates that they are perhaps benevolent ones. She also highlights the subjugation of a "raw" culture so that another larger one may be experienced, paralleling the subjugation of the semiotic to the symbolic noted by French feminist Julia Kristeva (1984). According to Kristeva's theories, intuition guides the semiotic realm of emotion, which can be deciphered only when it breaks through the symbolic representations that govern our language systems. The acquiescence of original story forms to more conventional literary standards that Giardina notes echoes the same submission Kristeva discusses, both of which apply when considering Gee's notions of discourse transition. When authors like Giardina and characters like Jackie enter into a secondary discourse, more often than not they must mask certain elements of their home community, particularly as they relate to language, speech patterns, and dialect. Through writing about Appalachian literacies in fictional form, Giardina provides a space in which such "raw" cultures may break through to reach literary audiences.

Considering a Historical Example

Giardina discusses such subjugation, and the inherent identity conflicts that consequently ensue, again later in the essay when she discusses her experience working as a substitute teacher in Kanawha County shortly after college graduation. In 1974 a controversy over textbook selection erupted in the area when the Kanawha County school board—which was comprised of no native Appalachians—adopted *Interaction* schoolbooks, a set of multicultural books and supplemental teaching materials. Many of the Appalachian residents of Kanawha County, particularly staunch churchgoers, felt that the books were inappropriate, and they protested their inclusion in the schools.

James Moffett, one of the authors of the *Interaction* textbooks, wrote a book about the controversy titled *Storm in the Mountains*. In his introduction he claims, "I have done the Appalachian fundamentalists the honor of not patronizing them," yet later on he declares that the mountain people suffer from agnosis, stating: "What the textbook rebellion exemplified is the not-wanting-to-know that I have called agnosis. Far from being peculiar to fundamentalists, or mountaineers or the uneducated, agnosis limits the thought and action of virtually everyone everywhere" (1988, 187). As could be predicted, his argument angered many Appalachians, including literacy scholar Kimberly Donehower.[7] Giardina also explains her feelings about the case; like Rachel's praise for mountain remedies and her simultaneous efforts to mask her Appalachian heritage in *The Unquiet Earth*, Giardina felt torn between the opposing sides, reflecting,

> I shared the anger of a powerless people at the erosion of traditional mountain values, yet I could not join in the protest against multicultural school textbooks. I still lived up a holler, but I fled each Sunday to a local Episcopal church to worship with people who disdained the ways of "crickers." The innocence I had lost when I obtained my education was irretrievable, and I had become as alien as the mythical Hapsburgs in my Welch apartment building [that echo Jackie's stories told to Toejam]. On the other hand, I felt equally estranged from mainstream America. Who the hell was I? (1998, 130)

In the above quote Giardina describes personal conflict akin to that of her fictional characters, and her biographical struggle to negotiate various discursive worlds mirrors the same dilemmas Linda Scott DeRosier faces, as well as other groups and characters discussed in this project.

Preserving Tradition through Orality

Despite the identity conflict that resulted from her education, one of the elements of her Appalachian culture that remains with Giardina is Appalachian orality and storytelling. As with DeRosier, storytelling operates as an important part of both Giardina's and Jackie's lives. Giardina's showcasing of the importance of oral traditions highlights one way in which Giardina and Jackie negotiate the split between their primary Appalachian discourse and secondary discourse communities they later enter. Similar to Gaynelle and Virgie Cline from Lee Smith's *Fair and Tender Ladies*, who seem to "live on storeys [sic]" (L. Smith 1988, 33), figures in Giardina's early childhood also thrive on storytelling, and she recalls that she "heard the stories first while perched upon the bony old knees of men" (Giardina 1998, 130), including her grandfather and neighbor, Uncle Brigham.

One common mountain story, "Big Toe," figures prominently in both Giardina's essay "No Scapin the Booger Man" and in her novel, *The Unquiet Earth*.[8] In her essay, she uses unconventional spelling and grammar to tell the story, and she opens by emphasizing the importance of oral traditions in her childhood: "I learned to read and write in standard English at Thorpe Elementary School, but before the teachers enticed me with the clean preciseness of spelling and grammar, mine was a different language. I was no prodigy who reads at age two or three and goes bored and superior to first grade. I stared with some curiosity at the tiny black squiggles that were supposed to be words, but I did not read until I was urged to. I saw no need to hurry. I had the stories" (1998, 129).

Giardina makes clear that as a child, she valued the oral traditions of her home discourse community, but once she enters school she learns that her ways of telling stories do not align with methods sanctioned by teachers. Midway through the essay she assumes standard conventions, rhetorically aligning with her statement about the illusionary aspect of being free and independent creatures, at least when spelling, grammar, and other conventions of Standard English are involved. In the same way that Uncle Brigham's "Big Toe" story about the devil searching for his toe resonates with Giardina, it also plays an important part in Jackie's fictional adolescence. When Jackie reflects on the "silly stories" she tells Toejam, she compares them to the "dumb old hillbilly story Uncle Brigham Lloyd tells" (*TUE*, 106), and Giardina re-tells "Big Toe" once again in fictional form.

To situate Jackie's reaction to Uncle Brigham's story, Giardina first reveals that Jackie would much prefer to sit on her front porch and read Nancy Drew, a series generally popular only with young girls, but she feels obligated to cross the road and listen to Uncle Brigham. Giardina's dichotomous descriptions of Jackie's home compared with Uncle Brigham's also send a potent message to readers. Jackie comments that "it is nice on our porch with the ivy and rose bushes and flower boxes all around," while Uncle Brigham has a "bare old porch," and Jackie must walk across the road covered in red dog (a sharp and rugged by-product of mining found in slate dumps) and "open the gate that is almost off its hinges" (*TUE*, 106) in order to hear his story.

Rachel's job as a nurse allows her to rent the former company doctor's house, and Jackie knows that her home is larger and nicer than other homes in the coal camp, especially Uncle Brigham's. The red dog road functions as an especially painful liminal space in which Jackie travels from the clean, neat world of Nancy Drew's written stories to the seemingly lesser, disadvantaged oral rendering of Uncle Brigham's stories. Crossing the road Jackie takes a crucial value judgment with her that she has learned from the printed word and standard literary conventions when she thinks, "I like to sit on our front porch swing and read Nancy Drew mysteries from the library. Nancy Drew is real smart, smarter than anybody in Number Thirteen" (*TUE*, 106).

Despite her feelings about Uncle Brigham's story, out of politeness she always listens and acts as though the ending frightens her, yet Giardina highlights how "Big Toe" fails to align with what Jackie considers to be a proper story: "Every time I go to Uncle Brigham's, he tells the same dumb story about the Booger man, and no handsome prince to rescue anybody. It's not a real story like you would hear someplace else" (*TUE*, 108). Upset by the obvious divide between Uncle Brigham's story and the literary conventions Jackie encounters in her reading material, Jackie explains, "When I got back from his house I'd get a notebook and figure I would write a real story with a happy ending. But it never worked. I'm not a real writer. Real writers live in New York apartments or sit at sidewalk cafés in Paris" (108). Here Jackie also seems unable to negotiate the disparity in gender roles she finds in her own reading material (like Nancy Drew) with Uncle Brigham's stories that do not necessarily rely on patriarchal story lines in which a prince rescues a fair maidens in distress.

Since Jackie finds no representations of her home in any of the literature she reads, she tries to imagine that she lives in a different place, and in hopes of writing about that imagined space she visualizes a new reality: "In the dusk I can pretend it is not Number Thirteen, it is the German village where the Grimm brothers told their stories, and Gretel lived, cottages lit with candles and lanterns instead of cheap lamps from the five-and-ten" (*TUE*,

108). Yet despite her efforts to transport Number Thirteen into a scene from a fairy tale, "it is still the same old Number Thirteen" (108).

Ironically, Jackie's surroundings offer multiple story lines for writing, and in one succinct paragraph Giardina highlights many avenues ripe for literary rendering. From Jackie's perspective the events seem stale and boring, but by writing about people and situations that Jackie encounters as a girl, Giardina encourages readers to see that they are interesting and varied:

> In one house Homer Day reads the Bible while his wife Louella heats up bacon grease for the wild greens Toejam picked for supper. It is all they will have to eat. Nearby Homer's brother Hassel and his friend Junior Tackett sit on a vinyl couch outside Hassel's trailer. Across the street, Uncle Brigham Lloyd is getting drunk and I can hear the TV turned up loud through the open screen door. Betty and the kids are watching "Bonanza" and Uncle Brigham is hollering at them to turn down the goddamn noise. My mom is working her half-acre in the camp garden, trying to finish hoeing the tomatoes before it gets dark, and Dillon is walking the railroad track toward her. She stops hoeing to watch him come on. (*TUE*, 108)

Though Jackie seems largely oblivious to the material contained in this brief description, readers see the irony of her statement about "the same old Number Thirteen," since its stories include the Day family's struggle with hunger-producing poverty; Hassel and Junior's homosexual relationship; Uncle Brigham's battle with alcoholism and domestic violence; and her mother's incestuous relationship with Dillon, Jackie's biological father. Jackie's blindness to this artistic material echoes Gertie Nevels's inability to recognize that any of her Merry Hill neighbors would have made fine models for her carving project. *The Dollmaker*'s character Mrs. Anderson also has a similar realization when she laments that she should have painted portraits of people in the housing project, but she does not have this realization until she leaves the neighborhood. When asked about this scene in an interview, Giardina comments, "She is missing all this right under her nose, though I think she has a sense it is there. She just hasn't figured out yet that she can write about it because it doesn't fit her image of stories about princes with happy endings" (T. Douglass 2006, 246).

Unlike Jackie, readers of *The Unquiet Earth* see the literary possibilities inherent in Jackie's surroundings much sooner than she does since Giardina schools us to notice them by repeatedly juxtaposing perceived ideas of Appalachia (including a historically assumed lack of literary prowess) with a more realistic portrayal of the area. Similar to Giardina's lack of exposure to Appalachian settings in literature, Jackie cannot comprehend writing a story about her people or her place, and Jackie thinks, "So there is not a thing to write about, only hillbillies, and nobody cares to hear about hillbillies. I go inside to watch TV" (*TUE*, 108). Jackie's lack of exposure to Appalachian literary portrayals sends her to yet another source of unflattering images about the region, and her turn to television reiterates Giardina's statement about the negative cultural value judgments perpetuated on television.

Appalachia Goes Prime-Time

Television also influences Jackie's mother, Rachel, just as the Lum and Abner radio show shapes her perception of her mountain home as a child. Working as the county health nurse, Rachel encounters plenty of people in far worse condition than spry old Granny Combs, and she describes "men who had worked in the mines until their lungs filled with dust or their backs gave out, women who had cooked and scrubbed the coal dust from kitchen floors and listened for the accident whistle to blow, who finally depended upon their children for food only now their children had nothing to give" (*TUE*, 117). Rachel's adult viewpoint highlights the struggle between competing narrative voices, especially with the much different perspective of adolescent Jackie. But in both cases, media depictions of the area greatly influence these women, and Rachel recalls, "I heard President Kennedy talk about stamping out poverty in America and learned for the first time that I lived in a place called Appalachia. It was a strange feeling to think my home had been named without asking anybody who lived here, but I was glad someone was paying attention. Dillon called me naïve. I didn't care" (117).

As discussed in the introductory chapter of this project, Berea College president William Goodell Frost first named Appalachia in his 1899 essay, "Our Contemporary Ancestors." Explaining that mountain people "unconsciously stepped aside from the great avenues of commerce and of thought" and were thus "beleaguered by nature," Frost carefully describes the Appalachian mountain range and declares, "this is one of God's grand divisions, and in default of any other name we shall call it Appalachian America" (311). Frost had his own political agenda connected to Berea's mission of mountain uplift, and Appalachian scholar Henry Shapiro argues that "because

Appalachia possessed no reality independent of its conceptualization as a discrete entity, however, naming was also an act of creation, and explaining was also an act of naming" (1978, 68).

Giardina participates in a similar renaming by urging readers to evaluate stereotypes they may hold about the region. At the turn of the century officially naming the area certainly played a part in its Othering, and by the time Rachel learns that the region in which she lives is called Appalachia, much of the rest of the nation has been using the Appalachian name for more than six decades. Giardina's attention to Rachel's unawareness of naming conventions further illustrates Linda Scott DeRosier's point about government-sanctioned names for various coves and hollows in Kentucky that differ from names designated by the community. Even contemporary Appalachian residents do not always think of themselves as "Appalachian," a term that finds the most usage in academic circles.

In 2005, when Appalachian State University student Katie Gray asked Mike Mullins (the director of the Hindman Settlement School), "Did you feel that you grew up in Appalachia, or did you discover the term later?," he responded: "I never knew I lived in Appalachia until I went to Berea College. I was Mike Mullins from High Hat, in Floyd County, in Eastern Kentucky, who lived in the coalfields. If you asked my father, 'Are you Appalachian?' he would have no idea what you were talking about. He grew up at the head of Salisbury Branch in Knott County. Our place of reference was our immediate community" (2006, 315).

Rachel feels similarly about her home community, but she also indicates that if naming the region causes other Americans to see the hardship many of her mountain patients face, that makes the Othering that comes along with the name worthwhile. Similarly, in writing *The Unquiet Earth* Giardina acknowledges stereotypes of mountain illiteracy that inform much of her reading audience but then works to overcome them by illustrating the multiple literacies her characters possess, as well as the identity conflicts that they cause. Rachel takes a practical view of the region and its people, and to a certain degree she accepts demeaning portrayals of Appalachia as long as she believes that residents benefit. She demonstrates such logic when commenting on the food given by the government: "Of course it was demeaning; of course it wasn't enough. Of course Arthur Lee [Sizemore] gave cheese and butter to all his buddies, would have given it to me if I'd taken it. But children don't care for all that, and a cheese sandwich will fill a child's stomach" (*TUE*, 117). Yet Rachel's attitude changes when CBS visits her home community to make a documentary. Jackie narrates this event, and her inclusion of Rachel's comment that "they make me feel like a specimen in a jar" (123) forecasts how the camera crew makes Jackie feel as well.

The scene that unfolds as Jackie describes the following events represents how documentary directors and film crews have repeatedly singled out the most pitiful situations and people to highlight in their media depictions of Appalachia, sometimes creating an image of destitution not entirely founded in reality. As with other texts considered in this project, schools operate as a site of such manipulation, and like Rachel's nursing school and the Nevels children's school in Detroit, Jackie describes her school as a site of cultural domination and authority: "There is a fence all around the building with barbed wire strung along the top, and if you could escape over the fence you would land in the river. Adolf Hitler would have loved our school" (*TUE*, 173). In this foreboding setting Giardina depicts a media intrusion that fictionalizes a real broadcast, and she highlights its effect on Jackie.

Unbeknownst to Jackie, her teacher, or her classmates, the camera crew brings donated shoes to the school, and they plan to film their distribution. Since they will need a large space in which to give away the shoes, the camera crew director, Phil Vivanti, asks Jackie's teacher for directions to the cafeteria. When he learns that the school has no cafeteria (and children eat their lunches at their desks), he asks for the library location but also learns that the school instead stores books in individual classrooms. When he concedes, "I guess we'll just have to film in the hallway," another crew member approaches and tells him, "It's okay Phil . . . the hall has a nice bleakness" (*TUE*, 124).

Armed with donated shoes from a company in New Jersey, the camera crew creates the appearance of benevolent benefactor to these supposedly needy mountain children. Miss Cox, Jackie's teacher, does not like the idea but feels powerless against the film crew, as when Jackie narrates: "Miss Cox tries to teach about the planets but we keep looking at the door so she gives up and says that people want to see television shows about Appalachia because they think we are stupid and backward and they can't figure out why. She says we are not stupid or backward and are just as good as anybody, but she says it low and keeps glancing at the door like she thinks someone might come in and take her away" (*TUE*, 124). Although Jackie's teacher encourages self-respect in the children, she defers to the authority represented by the filming crew, and she also comments on the rest of the nation's interest in the Appalachian region.

Scholar J. W. Williamson contends that much of America remains fascinated with depictions of hillbilly mountaineers because those representations reflect their own fears about "regressing" to a hillbilly state if their own economic situations declined (1995, 41). At one point in history those portrayals were also used to raise money for uplift projects like the Moonlight Schools discussed earlier. In either case, these portrayals of mountain people permeate much that is written and said about the region, including Arnold Toynbee's history: "The children persist in going about barefoot, and their parents either cannot afford to give them shoes, or will not take the trouble to insist upon their wearing them, or are too ignorant to be aware that Hook-Worm gains entry into human bodies through sores in naked soles" (*TUE*, 311).

Giardina provides a fictional voice of agency in response to such derogatory stereotyping when Jackie raises her hand and tells Phil Vivanti, "Some of us don't need [the shoes] . . . And some of us don't want them" (*TUE*, 125). The 1964 CBS special report titled *Christmas in Appalachia*, from which Giardina draws most of her material for this scene, does not depict any children like Jackie, let alone children who do not need shoes. Instead, Charles Kuralt travels through a coal mining community in Whitesburg, Kentucky, interviewing residents while camera crews zoom in on ragged shoes, abandoned buildings, and the dirty faces of children. The report sentimentalizes the plight of its subjects, depending on pathetic appeals to the viewing audience, as when Kuralt declares that one woman, Goldie Johnson, has accepted living "a life without flowers" and goes on to describe her as "a strong woman surrounded by exhausted men."

While Giardina's portrayal of Number Thirteen in *The Unquiet Earth* includes depictions of poverty and hardship, through her writing she also grants her characters agency and voice that the CBS report does not. Even though Jackie announces that she does not need or want the free shoes, readers also understand that a number of students in her class do need the clothing items, but once she speaks out, students hesitate to accept the donations until Vivanti entices them with promises of being on television. After Jackie receives "a pair of sandals made of hard purple plastic that look like they would take all the skin off the top of your foot," she wants to tell Vivanti to give them to his daughter, but she reasons "that would be sassing a grownup" (*TUE*, 125), so she remains quiet. Similarly, despite how uncomfortable the camera crew makes her feel, Rachel remains quiet and so too does Miss Cox. Giardina soon depicts the cost of such silence when Dillon,

Rachel, and Jackie gather to watch the television broadcast. Jackie narrates their reaction to the program, and Giardina conflates several media and written depictions of the region in Jackie's description:

> We see Mom listening to a man's chest and I point and holler, "There's Mom!" "Poor health care," says a voice. Mom sighs loud like her feelings are hurt. We watch children lined up for shoes and I see Brenda Lloyd and Toejam Day. I don't see me. "Children who go barefoot," says the voice. "Schools and houses in terrible condition." The TV shows empty falling-down coal camp houses. Phil Vivanti looks at us from the TV set. He stands in front of a camp house. "There is another America hidden away in these hills," he says. "Like something out of another century," he says, "a land time forgot, a life most Americans will never experience. Why do people want to stay here? How will we bring them into the mainstream of American life?" (*TUE*, 126).

In the above passage Giardina draws from the 1964 "Christmas in Appalachia" special report, the 1989 CBS *48 Hours* episode titled "Another America," William Goodell Frost's (1899) "Our Contemporary Ancestors," and Will Wallace Harney's (1873) "A Strange Land and a Peculiar People," among others. Immediately following this paragraph Jackie comments, "We sit downhearted like we have been beat on" (*TUE*, 126).

Certainly the broadcast greatly affects Jackie's perceptions about her home and her nascent desire to become a writer, and when asked about her own reaction as a fourteen-year-old girl to the *Christmas in Appalachia* broadcast in our interview, Giardina responded: "I saw that and a number of other pieces on network TV news. I thought they were all fake in the sense of being posed, of picking and choosing scenes, what to show and what not to show (anything that showed the diversity of the place) and prompting people about what they should say. They didn't capture anything in depth. And you could cut the condescension with a knife" (2007). Here Giardina comments on her reaction to these depictions as an adult, but as an adolescent girl—both in the fictional form of Jackie and in real life—the depictions only further support negative depictions of Appalachia. Although Jackie resists the blanketed donation of shoes when she bravely tells Vivanti that not all of the children want or need them, her comments do not find their way into the broadcast. As such, the camera crew and directors wield authority over the kind of Appalachian representation that hits airwaves, further convincing the rest of the nation of Appalachia's inferiority and confirming Jackie's suspicion that "real" writers do not come from the mountains.

New, VISTA-Supported Literacies

Despite Jackie's doubts about the possibility of becoming a writer, she continues to read voraciously, even when this habit makes her unpopular at school. Like Linda Scott DeRosier's high school experience, Jackie's academic achievements distance her from many of her classmates, and she narrates, "The class treated us [her and her friend Brenda] like lepers from the Bible" (*TUE*, 174). Jackie's simile comparing herself with biblical characters further proves her literate prowess, and this tendency serves as one of the connecting points when Tom Kolwiecki, a Volunteer in Service to America (VISTA) worker, arrives in Number Thirteen. He lives with Hassel Day, the self-proclaimed mayor of Number Thirteen, and Tom tries to begin a food co-op, among other things, that he believes will help the community. Most important for Jackie, his presence encourages her reading habits when he asks if she likes poetry and then tells her that T. S. Eliot is his favorite poet. Astonished, Jackie thinks, "I never met anyone who had a favorite poet except Miss Meade my English teacher who likes Robert Frost" (182).

Similar to Richard Burlage's entry into Hoot Owl Holler in Lee Smith's *Oral History*, Tom's presence in Number Thirteen introduces Jackie to a new discursive world. Tom's Northern accent, college education, and his goal of becoming a Jesuit priest set him apart as different from other people in Jackie's community, but unlike Richard's effect on Dory Cantrell, Tom influences Jackie positively by encouraging the technical habit of reading while also introducing her to different cultural literacies.

Jackie longs to please Tom, and like her grandmother Flora, Jackie places great value on things she reads in popular magazines, as when she comments, "Once I saw in *Seventeen* magazine where you can't be a successful teenager until you have a party" (*TUE*, 182), so when Rachel agrees that Jackie can have a welcoming party for Tom, Jackie plans to serve pizza, soda, and potato chips with onion dip. However, when Jackie consults *Seventeen* to learn the proper way to throw such a party, she encounters an article entitled "Create Your Own Summer Party." Disheartened, she explains that the layout "has a big color picture of food I never heard of, like tacos and guacamole. I don't know how to pronounce them or what is in them, but the guacamole is green and looks really gross. The tacos are in little baskets with red and white checked napkins. I shouldn't have looked in *Seventeen*" (183). After reading this article featuring Mexican food, Jackie feels ashamed because she does not have the cultural capital to know about foods like those pictured in the magazine, thus she judges her own food choices substandard. Like Flora, Jackie assumes the magazine's authority over her own knowledge of appropriate party fare, but unlike her grandmother, she regrets ever having encountered the magazine at all.

Even though many of the residents of Number Thirteen resent Tom's presence, especially at the beginning, he introduces Jackie to a completely new discursive world, and it is through this new type of literacy acquisition that she eventually comes to value her home enough to believe that she can write about it. In one section Hassel explains, "Uncle Brigham is offended by the VISTA. He don't like to think we need help like they do in Africa, and he says, 'Here I am a growed man getting grayheaded and some shirttail youngen is supposed to save me? And him sent by the government and what if hit's the government I need saved from?'" (*TUE*, 176).

Dillon has a similar reaction, and in his memoir about Appalachia, John O'Brien quotes one man who echoes the sentiments of Number Thirteen's residents almost exactly: "These daggone VISTA people. Who is it sends them? Where is this Appalachia place and why do they think I live there?" (2001, 115). Like the interview response from Mike Mullins discussed earlier, this man, as well as many of the characters of *The Unquiet Earth*, think of themselves in community terms, not those created by a national, and usually academic, audience. Related to this connection to community, in a speech given to conclude Western North Carolina's 2007 "Together We Read" program, Lee Smith made a similar observation about mountain people not necessarily conceiving of themselves as Appalachian: "Also, I think one thing that some of you who are here today who are younger may not understand is that this whole idea of being proud to be an Appalachian person is brand new. When I was growing up in the mountains we were always told that culture existed somewhere else, and when the time came, we were going to be sent off to get some."

Despite the tension Tom's presence creates in Number Thirteen, Jackie becomes smitten with him, and when Toejam asks Tom if he plans on kissing Jackie at the welcoming party Jackie thinks, "I want to cry. I try to think how a *Seventeen* girl would handle the situation but I figure a *Seventeen* girl wouldn't know Toejam" (*TUE*, 185). Once again readers understand that the place and the people of Jackie's life find no representation in the printed pages of a popular magazine and instead seem to be depicted only in skewed media portrayals and written histories like Toynbee's. Consequently, like Flora and Rachel, Jackie devalues her heritage, and her constant reading habits only further enforce this devaluing.

After government officials force Tom to leave Number Thirteen, Jackie attends college, and during this time her mother, Rachel, dies of a heart condition she has had for years. Even so, Jackie has "no plans to set foot in the mountains again" because she "wanted to escape for a while to places unfamiliar to [her] people" (*TUE*, 237, 238). After graduating from Marshall University and studying abroad for a year in England, Jackie works as a press secretary for a West Virginia congressman in Washington, DC, where she "tried to close the door on [her] past" (238). Eventually she quits her job and begins work at the Cervantes Center, a Catholic charity organization where Tom works, but Jackie "travels Blackberry Creek [at home] in [her] mind at night as [she falls] asleep" (248). The longer she stays away from home, the more she seems to long for it.

Returning Home

As with other characters considered in this project, once Jackie leaves the mountains she misses home terribly, commenting, "I crave the mountains. They invade my dreams, and so do my kin, living and dead" (*TUE*, 250). Even so, she takes time to decide whether she should go home, and in an interview Giardina explains: "In West Virginia we have such an inferiority complex sometimes; we feel that if you are successful, you are going to leave. So if you don't leave, you haven't been successful; and if you do leave, you were successful, so why would you want to come back? I felt it real important to go back for that reason, just to take a position against that attitude" (T. Douglass 2006, 248).

In the same way that Giardina returns to West Virginia and reports on the Pittston Strike in 1989, Jackie moves back and takes a job as the *Justice Clarion* newspaper editor, believing that "on Blackberry Creek I would gain strength and color, like a starving person fed rich broth" (*TUE*, 263). While this job offers a different kind of creative freedom than Jackie's childhood dream of becoming a writer of fictional stories, her writing in this capacity serves an important function for the people in her community. When Dillon suspects that the slate dam holding refuse water from the coal mining process is weak, Jackie runs an editorial piece about its dangerous condition. Even though the union "said the company should do something . . . American Coal sent out a press release saying the dam is safe and the union is trying to harass the company" (327).

Jackie's editorial position allows her only so much authority, but unlike the unsure, ashamed girl of her adolescence, she now uses the power of words to speak out against political injustices inflicted upon her home community. When the dam breaks and floods the community, readers understand that Jackie's words have little sway over firmly entrenched capitalist systems that privilege profit over safety. Giardina no doubt realizes the limitations of language, especially in a political arena. She has been (and continues to be) politically active, even running for West Virginia governor in 2000, but Giardina also commented during our interview that "you reach more people with fiction than with newspaper articles or political speeches. You reach a broader group of people also" (2007). Unlike Jackie, who writes solely for newspapers, Giardina also writes about important issues, but she does so through fictional form. As with other texts considered in this project, *The Unquiet Earth* provides a viable space in which Giardina can chronicle the potentially detrimental effects of reading on writing by using fictional characters' problems to illustrate real Appalachian issues.

Near the end of the novel when Dillon begins writing his own story, he asks Jackie about her childhood dream of becoming a writer and she responds, "I do write. . . . I write every day for a living," but not satisfied with this answer Dillon counters, "That's different. . . . I'd like to see you cut loose" (*TUE*, 297). In many ways, *The Unquiet Earth* allows Giardina to "cut loose," and she depicts the technically literate ability of her characters as well as the resulting shame that ability produces. By tracing Jackie's acquisition of new literacies outside her home community, Giardina, like other authors in this project, illustrates the losses she incurs, but those losses result in a deep appreciation for home and what was lost.

In the novel the slate dam break destroys the fictional town of Number Thirteen, mirroring the real destruction of 4,000 homes and 125 lives in the 1972 Buffalo Creek Disaster, and Giardina similarly reflects that once her home town of Black Wolf coal camp was torn down that "what [she] found, to [her] sorrow, is that once those ties have been broken, once the community has been left or lost, it can never be restored or duplicated" (*TUE*, 62).

Like DeRosier, leaving her home community equipped Giardina with multiple literacies that resulted in the ability to write about that loss, and she also admits, "I've gained a larger cultural experience, yet I don't fit in in the same way. I don't know if I could ever go back to McDowell County and live quite the same way. So in a sense the mountains have spurned me. I think that is the fear of leaving and becoming different. My dad always talked about 'getting above your raising.' He always warned us, 'Don't get above your raising.' Part of that means don't put on airs, but I also took it to mean, if you get too educated and too sophisticated, then you are not quite going to fit in anymore" (T. Douglass 2006, 248).

Like Giardina, Jackie does not fit into her home community in the same way, but she uses her writing to benefit those living there. In our interview Giardina discussed what it was like moving back to McDowell County in 1980, illustrating that as in DeRosier's relationship with her mother, literacy attainment (whether technical or discursive) can strain family ties: "Even within my own family [living at home again] was difficult. I was trying to read a variety of writers, literary figures as well as popular ones. I didn't have a single relative who read those people, or who read the *New Yorker*, or who had traveled to Europe (except my dad in WWII) or were interested in doing so. And after doing those things and realizing no one else did, I began to realize I had less in common with them. This is especially hard in a culture where family is almost everything" (2007).

Giardina strives to re-create what was lost in her fiction, and while this includes a way of life no longer commonplace in twenty-first-century America, that re-creation also serves an ameliorative function in allowing Giardina to revisit a connection with her home that she lost upon gaining the literacies necessary to believe she could become an author. Giardina says that "when I go to schools now, I find that kids have read Appalachian writers" (T. Douglass 2006, 246). This observation leaves hope that perhaps the next generation of Appalachian writers will read representations of themselves in literature much sooner than Giardina's adult discovery of Lee Smith.

CHAPTER 5

Invasion of the Mountain Teachers: Literacy Campaigns and Conflicts in Lee Smith's Works

> Before [I knew that I could write about Appalachia] I thought that literature had to happen on some sort of high plane. Literally! I thought I had to write about glamorous people, stewardesses or something. Rich people, or people that I didn't know anything about. For one thing, I grew up reading voraciously, but I wasn't ever around anybody who was a writer or a serious sort of literary type, so although I read constantly—I read everything in the library—a lot of it was real schlock. . . . It was a long time, maybe a year or so after I was in college, that I realized that you didn't have to have huge Biblical plots. It was all right to write about people like Miss [Eudora] Welty wrote about, people that may have even lived in Grundy.
> (Broughton 2001, 88)

In this interview excerpt, Lee Smith's description of what she thought literature was "supposed to be" echoes Denise Giardina's adolescent thoughts about writing. In the same way that Giardina found inspiration through reading Lee Smith's *Black Mountain Breakdown*, Smith discovered similar encouragement from reading James Still's *River of Earth*. Appalachian literary critics often cite *River of Earth* as the first critically acclaimed novel about Appalachia written by an Appalachian,[1] and for Smith, the reading experience proved particularly powerful. The novel chronicles the heart-wrenching story of the Baldridge family and their constant struggle to earn a living wage in the coal mines while eking out a living in one isolated mountain cove after another. At the novel's conclusion, the father declares that the family will travel for three days and move to Lee Smith's hometown of Grundy, Virginia, where they will "start from scratch" (Still 1978, 241).

Smith discovered *River of Earth* while a student at Hollins College, and she remembers that she read the passage about Grundy "over and over. I simply could not believe that Grundy was in a novel! In print! Published! Then I finished reading *River of Earth* and burst into tears. Never had I been so moved by a book. In fact it didn't seem like a book at all. *River of Earth* was as real to me as the chair I sat on, as the hollers I'd grown up among" (1998, 280). After this experience Smith finally understood what her writing teachers meant when they advised her to write about what she knew, and she recalls: "Suddenly, lots of the things in my life occurred to me for the first time as stories: my mother and my aunts sitting on the porch talking endlessly about whether one of them had colitis or not; Hardware Breeding, who married his wife, Beulah, four times; how my uncle Curt taught my daddy to drink good liquor; how I got saved at the tent revival; John Hardin's hanging in the courthouse square; how Petey Chaney rode the flood" (280).

Once Smith felt comfortable telling stories about the kinds of people she knew growing up, she began a long and successful literary career that shows no signs of slowing down. As a senior at Hollins College, Smith published *The Last Day the Dogbushes Bloomed*, and she has since published eleven more novels and four short-story collections, seen her stories operate as the base for a musical called *Good Ol' Girls*, and edited a collection of oral histories about Grundy gathered by high school students titled *Sitting on the Courthouse Bench*. As with other authors considered in this project, literacy functions as a common trope in much of Smith's work, particularly in two of her best-known novels, *Oral History* (1983) and *Fair and Tender Ladies* (1988). During an interview with Smith in which we discussed the prominence of literacy in her literary depictions of Appalachian life she commented, "I was really interested by your characterizing literacy as including social and cultural literacies . . . Because this whole thing, I think that is absolutely central to what I've been writing about all these years" (2007).

Technical, social, and cultural literacy attainment, as well as the identity conflicts such attainment can cause, figures prominently in *Oral History* and *Fair and Tender Ladies*, since both novels feature the entrance of a non-Appalachian teacher into a mountain community. Like Arnow's Miss Whittle, DeRosier's Janis Carroll, and Giardina's Miss Kurtz, the teachers

Smith creates privilege their way of speaking, writing, and conceiving of the world over mountain discursive practices. Not unlike the film crews that descended upon Appalachia during the War on Poverty, Smith's teachers invade mountain communities, bringing with them elements of discourse communities that they assume are superior to any they might find in Appalachia. Consequently, the students of these teachers learn to devalue their mountain heritage, resulting in painful identity conflicts that Smith showcases in her fiction. By highlighting these identity-based dilemmas, Smith urges her audience to recognize the consequences of literacy acquisition for mountain women.

However, in her 2006 novel, *On Agate Hill*, Smith recasts the invasive teacher figure with the novel's protagonist, Molly Petree. Much of the novel revolves around the difficulties Molly faces as an orphan child, including her stay at the Gatewood Academy under the instruction of a strict and somewhat deranged headmistress named Mariah Snow. But instead of creating identity dilemmas for Molly, Molly's continued exposure to new literacies infuses her with a love of learning that she takes with her when she teaches at the Bobcat School in the mountains of North Carolina. In this way Smith moves past the destructive pedagogical model represented by Richard Burlage (in *Oral History*) and Miss Torrington (in *Fair and Tender Ladies*) and instead presents a more hopeful prototype of instruction for mountain students.

Whether portrayed as a positive or negative force, Smith does not introduce a new story line by writing about outsiders coming into Appalachia with the intent of social and moral uplift through classroom teaching. Since the turn of the century, missionaries have been entering and leaving Appalachia in droves, and for almost as long authors have focused on the tensions created by the entrance of those missionaries into mountain communities. Although Smith draws from this well-established literary tradition in *Oral History* and *Fair and Tender Ladies*, she also focuses specifically on gendered literacy acquisition and the dilemmas such acquisition can cause. In doing so she portrays Appalachia as a feminized space in which women function under an unyielding patriarchal system that renders literacy acquisition especially difficult. As Smith comments, "It's hard to leave, and it's even harder to come back. Tragedy is involved in both the necessity of exile and the difficulty of return" (2008, 314).

As previously discussed, a palpable fear of getting above one's raising makes leaving mountain communities difficult, but Smith also contends that the geography of the land itself also has something to do with residents' connection with it. In an interview with Rebecca Smith, Smith comments that women are "bound by family. They're bound by biology. And they're bound by place. Somehow, when I think about that, I think about the mountains, the mountains as womb. I think about geography and physiology together" (R. Smith 1994, 22). Despite these bindings, the women in both novels make themselves heard through their daughters' voices, private letter writing, or public authorship. Considering *Oral History* and *Fair and Tender Ladies* together allows us to see a progression of silenced feminine voices that gradually gain volume and empowerment—but empowerment at a cost—through literacy attainment.

Private writing and public authorship function as two of the most central ways in which Smith guides her characters to such empowerment. Smith also uses these literacy-focused topics to draw readers' attention to the access (or the lack thereof) reading audiences have historically had to balanced portrayals of Appalachia. *Oral History* and *Fair and Tender Ladies* work as correctives in which Smith formulates literacy narratives that help realign reader perceptions of Appalachia. In both novels Smith references a fictional reading audience that we understand represents the real reading audience of Smith's work. Smith formulates this traditionally defined reading audience as sharing similar access to literary and cultural instruction, thus resulting in a fairly homogeneous set of values that readers bring to literature. Although readers (both fictional and real) will no doubt have varying types of knowledge and literacies from which to draw, Smith makes clear that members of this audience all bring a similar set of cultural judgments to their reading.

As an Appalachian author, Smith is all too familiar with writing within, out of, and against mountain stereotypes, and she clearly understands that many of her readers approach her books with preconceived notions of Appalachia. To combat those notions, Smith cleverly presents a fictional reading audience contained within each book that has access to only certain types of printed materials made available to them in the story, thus fictionalizing the real literary history of Appalachia. That is, by modeling her fictional audience's exposure to limited portrayals of Appalachia, Smith comments upon the skewed image of the Southern mountains so long perpetuated in literature and popular media that her own readers have experienced and bring to her texts.

Ultimately Smith creates *Oral History* and *Fair and Tender Ladies* as counternarratives that rhetorically work to reshape her reading audience's perceptions of Appalachia, Appalachian women, and literacy. Smith models dynamically complex interactions between writers and readers, speakers and listeners in both novels, inviting readers to take on a new understanding of what "counts" as Appalachian literacy. As Smith guides readers through this process of realigning firmly entrenched cultural values and attitudes about Appalachia, she also illuminates the identity conflicts inherent in literacy acquisition, all the while repeatedly highlighting how her version of the mountains differs from the version to which her fictional reading audience has access.

Even so, such reshaping remains a challenge not only because of past literary depictions of the region, but also because of some contemporary Appalachian authors' portrayals of literacy in the mountains. For example, in Chris Offutt's memoir, *No Heroes*, while describing his return to Rowan County, Kentucky—the same county where Cora Wilson Stewart began the Moonlight Schools nearly a century before—Offutt takes his son, Sam, to the local library. He explains that he selected the same books for his son to read that he had read as a child, but "the presence of [his] signature indicated that no new card had ever been required" (2002, 69). He goes on to write, "Don't be sad, I told myself. That's why you came home—to help fix problems like this" (69).

Although it is quite possible that the books Offutt selected had not been widely circulated since he was a boy, he fails to explore why that might be the case. He does not posit that perhaps parents are buying their children books instead of acquiring them from the library, nor does he explain whether the library's cataloging system had gone digital, rendering signature cards obsolete. Most problematic, he does not cite data about literacy rates in Rowan County, data that might support his claims; instead, he blithely implies that lack of reading is an issue in the area, one that he initially believes himself capable of solving.

Yet in some of his other works, Offutt creates characters eager to learn. One of Offutt's short-story collections, *Kentucky Straight*, contains a story titled "Sawdust," about a character named Junior who wants to earn his GED but who faces resistance from his family. Junior explains, "Every night Mom claimed a worry that I was getting above my raisings. [My brother] Warren wouldn't talk to me at all" (1992, 12). Despite the internal conflict this creates for Junior, he defies his family and surprises the local VISTA worker when he takes and passes the test to receive his GED. He then refuses the VISTA worker's offer to help him find a job, instead returning to his mother's house with a new understanding that "anybody can go [to town] any time. Town's just a bunch of people living together in the only wide place between the hills" (15). In some ways writers like Offutt appear to rewrite and reshape the supposedly illiterate Appalachia that reading audiences have come to expect, but in other ways they further inscribe it.

Working to Realign Reader Perceptions of Appalachia

In *Oral History* the main story line revolves around Richmond-born Richard Burlage's five-month journey into the Virginia mountains to teach school, where he becomes romantically involved with Almarine Cantrell's daughter, Dory. Dory's character embodies almost every past stereotype of Appalachia as a fixed, feminine region: she is beautiful, docile, seemingly unchanging, and silent. Throughout the novel Smith draws from various character interactions to illustrate that although Dory never narrates her own section, the acquisition of new literacies does bring about change within and around her character. As with the entrance of outsider teachers in other stories about Appalachia, Richard represents a world into which Dory cannot enter, and the fate of their courtship seems doomed from the beginning.

The novel opens with the stilted writing of college student Jennifer, Dory's granddaughter, who has come to visit the Appalachian side of her family that she never knew in hopes of collecting data for an oral history project. Jennifer's narrative bookends the novel, making a rhetorical statement about how academic versions of Appalachia always seem to have the first and last word when chronicling the region for readers. Richard's written reflections combine with "oral" stories told from a diverse cast of mountain people to comprise the bulk of the story, but early on readers understand that the fictional reading audience contained in the book must rely on Jennifer and Richard to tell the story of Appalachia, one that remains woefully incomplete without the inclusion of "oral" stories like the ones told by Granny Younger. Conversely, Smith provides her real reading audience with the stories told by various characters surrounding Richard's narrative, a strategy that illustrates the disparity between Richard's telling of the mountains and native accounts.

Smith grants her readers access to "oral" stories told by a cast of mountain characters that differ significantly from Richard's stuffy written prose about the area and its people. Readers encounter the character of Granny Younger as their first guide, a feisty old mountain woman who announces early on, "I'll tell you a story that's truer than true, and nothing so true is so pretty . . . The way I tell a story is the way I want to, and iffen you mislike it, you don't have to hear" (*OH*, 28).[2] Granny addresses the reader directly in several other sections, prompting literary critic Katherine Henninger to speculate that Granny's "frequent asides to the audience may encourage readers' intimate participation in her oral exchange, or it may position readers as those who likely 'know' what they know from images" (2007, 164).

Granny's addresses do encourage reader participation while also positioning readers in the way that Henninger suggests, but most important for Smith's purposes in realigning audience perceptions of Appalachia, Granny's usage of "you" jolts readers out of a comfortably complacent reading position. Smith overtly plays with the caricature of the Appalachian granny figure to challenge the stereotypes in which readers have been schooled. Unlike the tired, worn-out character so long perpetuated in literature and film, Granny Younger brims with an energy that makes clear she has a story to tell. She demands that readers listen, a strategy that Smith effectively uses to alert readers to their prior perceptions of mountain women.

Since the novel's publication literary critics have theorized about the irony of a written novel containing oral stories, and Anne Goodwyn Jones observes that calling "a *written fiction Oral History* is Lee Smith's latest, best joke" (1983, 137). Dorothy Dodge Robbins argues that the thesis of *Oral History* "can be reduced to 'oral good, written bad'" (1997, 135); while Katherine Henninger posits that Smith "sets up these familiar binaries [only] to break them down," proposing that instead, "*Oral History* becomes a self-reflexive meditation not only on the politics and ethical responsibilities of storytelling but also on the place of the southern writer in the ongoing construction of southern 'place'" (2007, 162–63).

The book undoubtedly asks readers to question narrative perspective and the notion of "truth" in a postmodern world, as when Fred Hobson notes that the oral stories contained in *Oral History* are no more reliable than written records of history (1991, 28). Yet while provoking these questions about truth, history, and place, the novel also asks difficult questions about representation. Smith urges readers to ponder why Dory does not have her own narrative section, while Richard rambles for pages at a time in his journal. Smith uses characters like Richard and Jennifer to represent the literary construction of Appalachia, while Dory's character serves as a kind of cultural place marker. Like Appalachia, she has a story to tell, but readers are bewildered to learn that they never hear it from her own lips or read it from her own pen. Instead, the only version of Dory's story the fictional reading audience can access comes from Richard's memoirs, which are eventually published "to universal if somewhat limited acclaim, by LSU Press" (*OH*, 291), and whose contents Smith never makes clear, while the real reading audience hears a distilled version of what happens to Dory after Richard's departure through Dory's daughter, Sally.

Jennifer's narrative presumably makes its way into a college classroom, and when we consider that the fictional reading audience in the novel must rely only on Jennifer and Richard to narrate the story, we understand these limitations as reflective of the problem that Linda Scott DeRosier identifies in her memoirs and works to overturn: such accounts scarcely communicate a balanced account of Appalachia, and Jennifer's sophomoric prose combined with Richard's sentimentally overwrought musings about mountaineers hardly convey an accurate representation of Hoot Owl Holler and its residents. Conversely, as readers of the novel, Smith makes us privy to the long string of orally rendered stories comprising the majority of the book, and we are able to consider a more varied, and more complete, account of the region and its people.

Her careful juxtaposition of the access her fictional reading audience has to Appalachia (through Richard and Jennifer) with the access she grants her real reading audience (through the "oral" stories that surround Richard and Jennifer's writings) encourage readers to reevaluate their own perceptions of Appalachia, how those were formed, and to be troubled by it. The fact that Dory Cantrell, one of the novel's main characters, does not narrate her own section parallels the way that for roughly the first half of the twentieth century, Appalachian people did not tell their own story in printed, published form, at least not to a literary audience of much size. Near the end of *Oral History* one of Dory's daughters, Sally, fills in the gaps of Dory's life for readers, but Sally's story is an oral one and thus not one read by the fictional reading audience contained within the pages of *Oral History* (though Sally's husband does, of course, hear her story). Smith's narrative form—and Dory's silencing—are indicative of the ways in which Appalachian voices have been muted in the past, and while the fictional reading audience within the novel does not have access to Sally's story, it nonetheless operates as a corrective for Smith's real reading audience, and through Sally we glimpse the consequences of literacy acquisition for Dory.

In a later and somewhat more hopeful book, Smith continues this narrative line of fictional and real audiences in *Fair and Tender Ladies*. In this novel, like Richard Burlage's entrance into Dory Cantrell's life, a missionary teacher, Miss Gertrude Torrington, introduces a similar discursive dilemma for the novel's protagonist, Ivy Rowe. Ivy tells her story in epistolary form, and even though these personal letters to loved ones comprise the entirety of the novel, very few of her letters are read by other characters. Considering the content of some of Ivy's letters, we understand that she responds to someone reading her letters, but Smith also makes clear that within the novel, Ivy's letter writing operates within a private sphere. Even when her letters are read by other characters, that reading takes place with one other person, not a large reading audience. Consequently, the large, traditionally defined audience that Smith fictionalizes in *Oral History* and in *Fair and Tender Ladies* never reads Ivy's letters, though they do apparently read writing by Ivy's "famous author" daughter, Joli.

But in the same way that Smith grants the real reading audience access to Richard's journal entries and the oral stories in *Oral History*, she also provides us with access to Ivy's letters throughout the novel. Through these letters we learn of the discursive divide Ivy faces when Miss Torrington offers to take her to Boston to attend school, and we also witness the painful distancing that occurs between Ivy and her daughter Joli when Ivy "makes her" attend high school in town and then college away from her home on Sugar Fork. Despite the pain involved in this transition, Joli goes on to become a successful author, and she tells stories set in Appalachia drawn from the folklore and stories her mother Ivy shares with her. In this way, Joli's success with the fictional reading audience contained within the pages of *Fair and Tender Ladies* makes clear to the real reading audience that a more balanced account of Appalachia has finally found printed representation for Smith's fictional reading audience, an audience that represents readers from the early twentieth century onward.

The real reading audience hears Ivy's story through her letters, and even though Ivy never conceives of herself as a "real" writer, her beautifully wrought sentiments suggest otherwise, and Smith's epistolary form challenges readers to question their notions of literacy and authorship. Smith commented in an interview with Virginia Smith that she has "always been really interested in this notion of women's creativity as being quite different from men's. It is not public; it's so rarely public" (V. Smith 2001, 66). In *Fair and Tender Ladies* Smith takes on this notion of private female creativity, constructing a path to the public realm from Ivy's private letter writing to Joli's public authorship. Moreover, as readers we realize that this public voicing comes at a heavy cost to family relationships when Ivy writes that "Joli has broken my heart" and has "travelled far beyond me now" (*FTL*, 271).[3]

Grounded in Real-Life Examples

Smith's personal and literary experiences have exposed her to many situations similar to Joli's and Ivy's literacy-initiated distancing, and during our interview (2007) she discussed one such instance that parallels the dilemmas this project explores. As described at the beginning of this study, Smith told me that to celebrate the publication of *Sitting on the Courthouse Bench*, Grundy High School seniors who participated in the oral history project attended a banquet in their honor. By this point in the school year many of the students had applied to colleges, and according to Smith, all of them were receiving acceptances and were able to pick the college of their choice. She goes on to recall,

> And one girl from a family that had absolutely no advantages at all, her mother came, you know, to the banquet, and a whole bunch of other children. And this girl had just been accepted with full tuition to everywhere she had applied, and she was going to go to Berea. . . . Her mother came up, and this getting into Berea had just happened, and I said, "I guess you're just really proud of your daughter," and she just burst into tears. She said, "It won't never be the same after this." She said, "She'll go off, and then she'll come back and she won't know us no more." And I said, "What do you mean?" And she said, "She just won't really know us anymore. It'll all be different from now on. I've only got," whatever it was, "six more months with her." You know, and it was like, that's exactly what you're talking about.

The reaction that this girl's mother has mirrors Ivy's feelings about Joli leaving and "travelling far beyond" her, even though Ivy encourages Joli to leave home and learn new things (*FTL*, 271). Although this incident occurred after the publication of *Fair and Tender Ladies*, it points to the ways in which Smith fictionalizes reality-based conflict and change caused by literacy. Unlike this woman's sad declaration about losing ties with her daughter, in Smith's version of this story the daughter (Joli) goes on to make her voice heard, even though that voicing results in a loss of connection with her home and her family.

Examples like these characterize much of Smith's work, and the bridge that she builds through her fiction writing between imagined and real literacy situations finds grounding in her literacy work with Appalachian students. In 1995 Smith won the Lila Wallace–Reader's Digest Writers' Award, and the grant allowed her to take a three-year sabbatical from teaching at North Carolina State University to devote the majority of her time to writing. As part of the award's acceptance guidelines, she also affiliated herself with a community organization that helped expose people to language, writing, and reading in places where they might not otherwise have such experiences. For her community partnership, Smith chose to work in the adult literacy program at the Hindman Settlement School in Kentucky, an organization where she had experience teaching in the creative writing summer workshops.

Smith noted during our interview that over the span of three years in which she worked intermittently with Hindman's students, all of the pupils in her literacy classes were women. When I asked Smith whether these students faced the sort of identity conflicts similar to the women in her fiction, she responded, "Oh yeah. In fact, many of them were only able, initially, to get into the literacy program if they were able to get away from their husbands who didn't want them to learn how to read or parents who didn't want them to learn how to read or maybe, say, they'd gotten pregnant when they were real young, and they're all real religious. Nobody ever thought of an abortion it seemed like to me. You know, and they hadn't gone to school, they'd dropped out. Or they stayed at home to be the one that helped Mama take care of the other children and all these kinds of things" (2007).

Smith's reflections about why so many of her students were unable to stay in school or become technically literate connects with her previously quoted statement that women are "bound by family. They're bound by biology. And they're bound by place" (R. Smith 1994, 22), and for the majority of her students, seeking literacy instruction required a great deal of courage, fortitude, and willingness to create conflict within their own family relationships. The same holds true for the women Katherine Kelleher Sohn chronicles in her study, and these women's stories of struggle and hardship to seek literacy instruction (technical, social, and cultural) help explain why so much Appalachian literature dealing with literacy-initiated conflicts focuses on women: even though Appalachians sometimes consider literate activity "woman's work," as Anita Puckett demonstrates in her research, in other cases many mountain women must wage their own personal battle against an oppressive patriarchal system to gain access to literacy instruction, only to find that such acquisition introduces an entirely new set of conflicts, along with its liberating empowerments.

Florida Slone, one of Smith's students at the Hindman Settlement School, faced many obstacles in obtaining literacy. In addition to fulfilling the lifetime roles of wife and mother, Slone also suffered a childhood bout of typhoid fever that resulted in a lack of formal schooling. Yet once she attended the classes at Hindman she excelled, and during our interview Smith described Slone as the "shining star of the program" (2007). In 1993 Appalshop produced a documentary about Slone, and when describing Slone on their website they state, "Now that [Slone's] children are grown, and her husband has died, Florida has had to become more independent. She returned to school, learned to read and write, and got her driver's license" (Slone and DeBord 1993).

Smith provided even more context about Slone's life during our interview, explaining that one of Slone's main purposes in learning to read and write was to write down the ballads she had created and had been singing for the majority of her life. Smith worked with Slone and wrote the ballads down for her until Slone could transcribe them herself. Smith explains that Slone went on to print her songs "in a little book," make a CD, and travel to various places to speak about the importance of literacy. These achievements, coupled with Slone's obtaining her driver's license, suggest that literacy had a permanently transformative effect on her life, but Smith references the cost of living within firmly entrenched gender roles when she explains what happened to Slone after the documentary and after Smith's time with the program ended: "This is so predictable. After I left, and I'm just saying that in terms of time. It didn't have anything to do with me. She fell in love with some old man in her church, and guess what his name was. This is a great name. I could never even make this name up. His name was Virgil Lively. And he did not believe that a woman ought to be out there parading herself around in public. And he sort of stopped her signing in public and so on, and driving. . . . She was at a high school level by then, or a junior high anyway. And he said all a woman needed to read was the Bible. And she stopped coming" (2007).

Smith's retelling of Slone's story provides a strikingly similar comparison to Uncle Lot's ideas about proper reading material for Aunt Ailsie in Lucy Furman's *The Quare Women* and *The Glass Window*, but most troubling, Virgil's commands to Flordia occur in the late twentieth century, not in the 1920s fictional world of Furman's work. Consequently, Slone's driving about town on her own, public speaking about literacy, and "parading herself" came to an end, and though she never lived down her local fame as a ballad singer, in many ways she lost the voice she had worked so hard to gain as a student at the Hindman Settlement School.

Oral History

Although Smith met and worked with Slone over a decade after the publication of *Oral History*, Smith knew many women like her whose voices also remained silent, bound by the men in their lives and the sometimes claustrophobic mountains in which they lived. Smith's most salient fictional example of such silencing occurs with *Oral History*'s Dory Cantrell. When asked during our interview about why Dory does not narrate her own section, Smith responded that while she did not consciously think about Dory's lack of narrative commentary while writing the book, "I think maybe in my mind she already didn't have a voice, because she was so circumscribed by family, by circumstance." She goes on to comment, "You know, and I just couldn't imagine, exactly, her speaking. You know, getting out of her situation. And I had heard so much, and so many, many stories about . . . girls that never got more than thirty miles from where they were from and didn't even know that they were so close to home because there was a mountain in between and they'd been taken by a circular road" (2007).

Like the women Smith describes, Dory never travels far from her childhood home on Hoot Owl Holler, and once she marries Little Luther Wade she spends the remainder of her life in the Blackey Coal Camp, until she commits suicide by lying down on the train tracks. As readers we never know Dory's thoughts about her own life, but Richard Burlage's written musings about her take up much of the novel, and his perceptions reflect the attitudes and beliefs many early twentieth-century missionaries held about Appalachian people, especially mountain women. Like William Goodell Frost's infamous 1899 essay in which he called Appalachian people "America's contemporary ancestors," Richard expects to find a different world, a world of the past upon his entrance into the mountains. He writes in his journal that he "intend[s] this journal to be a valid record of what I regard as essentially a pilgrimage, a simple geographical pilgrimage, yes, but also a pilgrimage back through time, a pilgrimage to a simpler era, back—dare I hope it—to the very roots of consciousness and belief" (*OH*, 93). Richard hopes to find a sense of simplicity that he lacks at home in Richmond, where his depressed, war-scarred brother represents a modernist frustration with life. Richard's commentary also evokes typical mountain crusade rhetoric since he sees himself as someone with the capacity to teach mountain residents about life outside of Appalachia, and he places himself far above them in the social hierarchy.

Like many of the missionaries who entered Appalachia in the early part of the twentieth century, Richard assumes an Orientalist perspective in describing the region as remotely exotic and enticing. During Richard's train ride Smith provides a particularly revealing passage that casts him as a colonizing dominant male entering the womblike feminine space of the mountains: "Viewing this virtually inaccessible land from the jolting train, I was struck forcibly with a thought: seeing this, who would choose to live here? And yet there is an inescapable appeal, I find, in the very strangeness, the very inaccessibility. As our little train jolted ever farther into the rough terrain, I realized that, unwittingly, I had probably picked the most remote area still left in these United States; certainly I could not have felt more a stranger had I just entered India" (OH, 105).

Richard describes the land as "virtually inaccessible," yet as the train carries him into "the rough terrain," he accesses and enters it nonetheless, symbolizing the eventual male control he will exert over Dory, her body, and her literacy instruction. Notably the same train that brings Richard into the mountains kills Dory years later, and as in Harriette Simpson Arnow's *The Dollmaker*, the locomotive operates as a symbol of modernity, industrialization, and a discursive world to which Dory never gains complete entrance. Conversely, Richard fancies that he has full access to the mountains, and he imagines this Appalachian world as many authors described it in the early 1900s—invitingly quaint, picturesque, and beautiful. Instead he finds a rough wilderness susceptible to the extraction of its natural resources by timber and coal companies and teachers like himself.

Smith's depiction of Richard as a colonizer continues when he begins teaching school and characterizes one of his students, Jink Cantrell, as "exceptionally bright and able," and he writes to Jink's family, asking if they will allow Richard to tutor him after school (OH, 115). Jink's father, Almarine, does not want to feel obligated to Richard for his services, and he sends Jink's older sister, Dory, to convey the message to Richard. When recording this conversation exchange in his diary Richard labels the entry "September 29th—Important!," and he describes Dory as the epitome of Petrarchan beauty: "I must say without preamble that she is the most beautiful woman I have ever seen, with an ethereal, timeless, other-worldly quality about her. Her alabaster face is framed by finespun golden curls, almost like a frizz, about her head—hair like a Botticelli! Her eyes are deep, limitless violet. Her lips are red and full. When she smiles, a blush and a dimple grace her smooth fair cheeks. Her rough attire—a dark green wool skirt, brown handmade sweater, tan, nondescript coat—served only to accentuate the delicacy of her beauty" (116).

Instead of commenting on the economic circumstances in Dory's life that necessitate things like handmade clothing, Richard seems concerned only with the aesthetic effect such "rough" items have on Dory's beauty. He even goes on to call her "a girl from another world" (*OH*, 117). Richard has entered another womblike world—and another set of discursive norms—in Appalachia, and much like Jennifer's narrative that frames the novel, he appears incapable of viewing the mountains and its people in a nonromantic way. After one brief encounter with Dory in the schoolhouse Richard refers to her as "my mountain girl," and before he ever visits Dory's home in Hoot Owl Holler, Richard imagines its "high solitude" and "the clean purity of [Dory's] barren life" (119, 121). Almost immediately following their first meeting, Richard has already appropriated Dory as an object over which he exerts control, and he has created a mental image of her that he keeps throughout the remainder of the narrative. But instead of allowing readers to easily align their perceptions of Appalachia with Richard's, Smith sandwiches his journal entries with "oral" stories told from a host of mountain characters, virtually forcing readers to notice the disparity of portrayals. In doing so, Smith works to remediate the lasting effect Local Color literature had on the reading audience's perceptions of Appalachia.

In a subsequent conversation following his visit to Hoot Owl Holler, Richard becomes firmly entrenched in his superior position, and he assigns himself a great deal of importance: "I saw myself then in her eyes as some superior being from another place, with a fund of 'knowledge' beyond her ken. Thus I realized how I seem to her. I understood my position and my responsibility" (*OH*, 128). Richard also understands the difference in his Richmond-based discourse community and Dory's mountain-based one. Despite this knowledge, Richard nonetheless remains enamored with Dory, and when he tells his elderly friend Aldous Rife about his feelings, Aldous administers a stern warning to "forget her" because "she is not suitable. She is not your equal. You are a sojourner here, and the least you will do is create longings in that girl which her life can never fill. That is the least you can do. The worst you can do is far graver" (132).

Foreshadowing Dory's eventual suicide, Aldous warns Richard against crossing the discursive divide that separates Richard from Dory, since Aldous believes Dory could never achieve full membership in any discourse community other than her Appalachian one. Richard initially struggles with this advice, even making lists in his journal entitled "Reasons for pursuing Miss Dory Cantrell" and "Reasons to forget Miss Cantrell entirely" (*OH*, 134), but he eventually succumbs to his physical attraction to her, and the two engage in an affair that produces twin daughters whom Richard never learns about.

Dominating the Feminine

While Richard comments on the intellectual potential he sees in Jink, he reasons that Dory "is ignorant and largely uneducated; such a gap exists between us that it could never be truly bridged. Not even by any attempt on my part to educate her" (*OH*, 134). Richard automatically comes to this conclusion, and he never "attempts" to educate her, presumably because as a beautiful feminine possession, he either deems her incapable of learning or fears that Dory would no longer be a possession if he taught her, though he never mentions this possibility in his diary entries. Moreover, Richard wants to keep his image of Dory as a fixed, static, mountain beauty intact, and teaching her would cause change, thus destroying his image of her. Instead, Richard continues to court Dory, and literary critic Paula Gallant Eckard notes that "Burlage's exploitation destroyed [the] harmony [that Dory had with her surroundings], and Dory was ultimately cast into the unique position of being an Other in both Burlage's world and her own" (1995, 128).

Although Eckard romanticizes the "harmony" Dory had with her surroundings, she highlights an important point: the dilemma that Eckard describes mirrors the conflict faced by the people transitioning from one discourse community to another discussed by literacy scholar James Paul Gee. Both Eckard and Gee focus on the difficulties involved in this doubled othering. Anne Goodwyn Jones even declares Dory a "victim" of literacy, and Smith makes clear that Richard introduces a way of life to Dory that she comprehends and yet never achieves in her own life (A. Jones 1983, 137).

In the same way that Richard deems Dory incapable of ever spanning the gap that exists between them, he also assumes the authority to literally rewrite Dory's life experiences. When the couple makes love for the first time Richard writes in his journal that "for a second, too, I was distressed, I confess it, by Dory's apparent knowledge of lovemaking, but then I recalled her upbringing in that randy cabin with all those boys, the animals around the mountain farm, and I understood her desire to be a kind of purity" (*OH*, 146). Instead of acknowledging Dory's sexual past, Richard inscribes his own version of Dory's story in his journal. In doing so he erases her personal history and replaces it with a pastoral image of innocence and bucolic purity that echoes travel writing about Appalachia from the early part of the twentieth century.

In this same scene he goes on to portray Dory as the ultimate representation of Appalachian womblike femininity when he writes, "I try to imagine taking Dory to a picture show, walking along a sidewalk with her, as we did tonight, yet she seems to exist for me only in that shadowy setting—those three mountains, that closed valley—whence she came" (*OH*, 147). The "closed valley" from which Dory came is also the same valley that Richard enters, both literally (through Dory) and figuratively (through his teaching in the mountains), and in being able to imagine Dory only in her Appalachian home, Richard succeeds in rendering her immobile, utterly incapable of change in his view, even when exposed to new literacies. Just as missionary workers were historically invested in putting Appalachia "in its place," so too is Richard eager to keep Dory in hers, especially since in his view she represents a fixed point from which he can measure his own progress during his Appalachian journey.

Richard's progress includes efforts at culturally homogenizing his mountain pupils, and through a bathing scene Smith symbolically illustrates Richard's desire to culturally cleanse Dory. Richard's journal entry explains that he uses a washcloth from home to wash her, and Smith's description illustrates the ways in which Richard imagines Dory as a space to invade: "I see this white cloth with its pine-embroidered border, see it *there* [in Richmond], and then I see it here. I rub it across her pubic hair, between her legs. She is amused by my insistence upon these baths, used, as she is, to bathing seldom in Hoot Owl Holler. I soap her thighs, her knees, her feet, and she squeals and giggles" (*OH*, 157). In this scene Dory embodies the yonic representation of Appalachia, and geography and physiology are once again bound together.

The expensive cloth Richard brings with him from Richmond implies a wholly different set of cultural standards than Dory's mountain set of values, and by cleansing her genitalia—the essence of her femininity and Appalachia as womb—Richard attempts to sanitize and homogenize Dory's fertile womanhood and the wild, mountainous land that surrounds him, replacing them instead with the dainty, embroidered cloth representative of his life in Richmond. Likewise, by washing Dory with the cloth he submerses his Richmond-based set of beliefs within the supposed feminine wilds of Appalachia, no doubt a statement of rebellion against the middle-class set of dominant values from which he believes himself to be escaping.

Dory's family does not accept the relationship between Dory and Richard, and once Dory's family appears at the schoolhouse to take her back to Hoot Owl Holler, Richard retreats to the familiar boardinghouse in town. As he recovers from an illness he mulls over his impending return to Richmond and the possibility of Dory joining him. He has promised to take her and even sends a note asking her to join him (a note that she never receives since her jealous stepsister, Ora Mae, does not deliver it to her), yet he fails to imagine Dory anywhere else but in the mountains. He writes in his journal, "I lay in bed all that night, it seemed, imagining it, but I confess I could see her in no setting other than the lovely wilderness of her birth, against no background other than these high mountains which are her home. A failure of the imagination perhaps, or a presentiment of the sort which has characterized my journey since it first began" (*OH*, 163). Here Richard reveals a rare glimpsing of his preconceived notions of Appalachia, admitting that they have characterized his "sojourn" into the mountains. Even so, he places Dory in a fixed Appalachian setting once again, apparently incapable of imagining her any other way.

During our interview Smith commented that if Ora Mae had given Dory Richard's letter, "I think that probably Dory would've gone to Richmond and it would've been a disaster. Because I don't think Richard Burlage was smart enough or strong enough to have made it work" (2007). Here Smith notably places the onus of responsibility on Richard, not Dory. When we consider that Richard's perceptions of the mountains represent those of a large reading audience, we understand that Smith ultimately suggests that any failure to see true representations of Appalachia falls on the interpreter, not the subject.

Privileging the Masculine

Like many men during that time period, Richard not only views females like Dory as fixed in their environment, but he also considers males like her brother Jink better suited for "serious" academic subjects. Although Richard's beliefs concerning gender and literacy are at odds with findings from Puckett's study, they ultimately reflect those of mainstream culture, not those of the mountain community he enters. Consequently, Richard spends time with Jink both inside and outside the classroom, and he has a substantial effect on the way Jink perceives himself and his mountain culture. Unlike with Dory, Smith grants Jink his own narrative section, and through it readers learn that as with many literacy-initiated changes, Richard's entrance into Jink's life brings with it conflict and personal strife. While the mountains enclose and entrap many of the women in Smith's fiction, they simultaneously enclose and comfort Jink.

At the beginning of his section Jink explains that he often retreats to a spot high in the branches of a sycamore tree, and on this particular day he goes there to think over his upcoming participation in the day's hog killing. He refers to his seating area as "the mother-seat," signaling an inherent protectiveness about the branches that envelop him. As he gazes out over the mountains he imagines that he can fly, a symbolic representation of the freedom Richard introduced but did not fulfill and for which Jink desperately longs. As he takes imaginary flight, Jink remembers the poem Richard read to him about Wyncken, Blynken, and Nod, and he remembers an infamous line from book 2 of *The Odyssey* but changes it slightly to "rosy-finger dawn" instead of "rosy-fingered dawn" (*OH*, 190).

As Jink mulls over the literary themes Richard introduced to him, he also thinks about the ethical lessons Richard tried to instill in him about the immorality of slavery and racism. Suzanne Jones portrays Richard's effect on Jink as a positive one, arguing that Richard provides "Jink with a more sensitive model of manhood than that he has learned from his kinfolk," and she concludes that "after Richard leaves the hollow, Jink bemoans his departure as the loss of an alternative way of life. Soon Jink falls to imitating the violent ways of the men around him" (S. Jones 1987, 111).

While Richard does introduce Jink to a much wider world, in terms of both literature and morality, his influence is not as benevolent as Jones suggests. Instead, Richard's lessons about standard English resonate with Jink in the same way that Linda Scott DeRosier's encounter with Miss Janis Carroll linger with her. Consequently, Jink learns to devalue his native dialect and repeatedly corrects himself when narrating his own section. Eventually Jink's correction occurs "naturally" when he explains the kinds of songs sung at the hog killing he attends later in the day: "Little Luther went on singing a whole bunch of stuff you don't hear him sing when the womenfolks and girls is around. . . . Some of the time they was—were—out there at the hog-killing and some of the time they were up at the house getting ready to put up the meat" (*OH*, 199). In this passage Jink reveals his linguistic transition into the discursive world Richard represents, and at the end of his narrative readers learn about the shriveled orange Jink has saved since Richard gave it to him. While holding it, he considers the orange's Florida origins, and he thinks to himself "how I'd up and leave here after while, me and [my younger sister] Mary we'd up and leave and strike out walking as far as we could acrost the big round world" (212).

While not all markers of Jink's Appalachian dialect have disappeared,

Richard's teachings have introduced enough literacy-initiated conflict to cause self-monitoring and a deep desire to leave his mountain home. Like Reuben in *The Dollmaker*, Jink's gender grants him the ability to leave, and through Ora Mae's narration readers learn that he leaves the mountains, apparently permanently (*OH*, 221).

Bridging the Gap

Even though Smith depicts Richard as a convenient character to dislike, he also serves an important rhetorical function in the novel by chronicling the details of his entry into Appalachia for the non-Appalachian reader. Like Linda Scott DeRosier's sections in *Creeker* and *Songs of Life in Grace* in which she explains certain facets of Appalachian culture or language, Richard describes his journey into Appalachia in such a way that allows non-Appalachian readers to better understand his circumstances as he perceives them. His entries also provide basic information for reading audiences, which allows non-Appalachian readers to learn some of the native folklore and dialect presented in the "oral" sections, such as Granny Younger's.

When Richard first "sets out" for Hoot Owl Holler, his diary entry reads like a guide for the adventurous traveler, and Richard puts certain terms in quotes and then explains them, something he apparently deems necessary for his future non-Appalachian, memoir-purchasing audience (*OH*, 122). He even explains that he is "what they call a 'foreigner.' As they use it, this term does not necessarily refer to someone from another country, or even from another state, but simply to *anybody* who was not born in this area of the county" (123). He continues to describe other words specific to a mountain vocabulary, and when asked during our interview whether Smith intended Richard to serve as a guide for the non-Appalachian reader she responded, "At a certain point I realized that . . . it would be helpful [for nonnative readers] if I could have an outsider and give his perceptions as he got to know the place where he was. That that would be interesting, and particularly to tell as he went in, as he traveled by train and got into the region and what his thoughts were and what his impressions were [and I thought] that that might be helpful" (2007). While Richard does help demystify certain elements of Appalachian dialect, his character also represents the ideological attitudes Appalachian missionary workers and other visitors held about the region in the early and mid-twentieth century.

Finding a Limited Voice in the Next Generation

While both Jink and Richard leave Hoot Owl Holler, Dory remains trapped. She later marries Little Luther Wade and has two children with him (Sally and Lewis Ray), in addition to the twins (Pearl and Maggie) Richard fathered. As with Dory, the mountains confine her daughter Sally, and Sally tells her husband, Roy, that as a child she "remember[ed] us all getting in that old Dodge out in the yard and taking [an imaginary] trip to the West" (*OH*, 241). A symbol of mobility, the junk car provides an escape that Sally never finds in real life, yet she does narrate her own section. Through Sally readers learn of Dory's suicidal demise, and Sally provides the only voice Dory ever receives in the novel, explaining that there was "a place inside [Dory that] was empty that we couldn't fill" (248). Even so, Sally's story is an oral one and heard only by Sally's husband and Smith's real audience, not the fictional reading audience contained within the pages of the novel. They must instead rely on Jennifer's and Richard's versions of events. This authorial decision on Smith's part reflects the history of written representations of Appalachia, since for so long reading audiences encountered skewed portrayals of the area and its people.

At the novel's conclusion, especially after "hearing" Sally's story, readers understand all they would miss if they trusted only in Richard and Jennifer to guide them through the mountains. This understanding prompts readers to begin realigning their perceptions of the mountains, even though the novel's representative of Appalachia—Dory—never tells her own story. Conversely, in Smith's next novel, *Fair and Tender Ladies*, Ivy Rowe's daughter, Joli, works as an author and shares her version of mountain lore with the fictional reading audience within the book, while Smith gives her real audience access to Ivy's private letters.

Fair and Tender Ladies

Similar to the matriarchal line of literacy attainment Linda Scott DeRosier traces from her grandmother Emma to her mother, Grace, Smith sets up a generational model of feminized literacy acquisition and subsequent public voicing in *Fair and Tender Ladies* that begins with the storytelling sisters, Gaynelle and Virgie Cline. In a letter to her Dutch pen pal (who never responds to Ivy's letters) Ivy explains that the women are "maiden ladys" (*FTL*, 33) and live an isolated, simple life on Hell Mountain. It is notable that Ivy relies on a number of stereotypes about Dutch people when imagining how her pen pal must act and look, since such dependence on stereotypes echoes the position of many of Smith's readers when they try to imagine how an Appalachian woman must behave and look. Smith's inclusion of these stereotypical notions serves as yet another reminder to readers to consider the perceptions they bring with them when approaching Smith's work.

When describing the Cline sisters to her pen pal, Ivy goes on to speculate, "Dont nobody know how they live exackly Daddy said, they do not farm nor raise a thing but beans and flowers in the yard, nor have a cow, but folks takes them food just to hear ther storeys. I think myself they live on storeys, they do not need much food" (*FTL*, 33). In the same way that Smith earns a living by writing her stories, according to Ivy, the Cline sisters find sustenance in the stories they tell. Ivy also draws both strength and creativity from the tales that the sisters share with her family, including Old Dry Fry, Mustmag, and Whitbear Whittington. On one occasion Ivy describes the sisters' departure, and she writes that she watched "the lady sisters skitter like waterbugs over the snow, moving faster and faster it seemed until they were lost in the shadders of the trees as they headed up Hell Mountain so fast it seemed they were flying" (38).

Literary critic Dorothy Dodge Robbins notes that Ivy appropriates "the sisters' storytelling skills into her own words," and Ivy's inclusion of descriptive similes, including phrases such as "skitter like waterbugs," demonstrates an incorporation of the oral into the written that never occurs in *Oral History* (D. Robbins 1997, 142). Although Jennifer and Richard both spend time in the mountains immersed in oral traditions, their literary renderings of those encounters still display written conventions and a strict adherence to Standard English, except when Richard tries to "capture" mountain dialect. Neither writer masters the kind of oral telling Smith presents in sections like Granny Younger's, Rose Hibbitts's, or Sally's; and Ivy's integration of the Cline sisters' storytelling conventions into her letters represents a blending of the oral and the literate that marks a progression in voice for readers.

Learning New Divides

By the time Ivy describes the Cline sisters' stories in a letter, she is already a voracious reader and deep into a textual world, as when she tells her pen pal in an early letter that she loves reading "bettern anything and mostly poems such as Thanatopses and the little toy soldier is covered with dust but sturdy and staunch he stands and the highwayman came riding up to the old inn door. I love that one the bestest" (*FTL*, 14). Yet despite Ivy's fondness for reading, as in *Oral History*, Smith presents literacy (technical, social, and cultural) as a potentially dangerous skill. In the same way that Aldous Rife warns Richard not to become involved with Dory since at best he can only create longings that her life can never fulfill, Ivy's mother becomes upset with Ivy's constant reading and says it "will just fill [Ivy's] head with notions" that "will do [Ivy] no good in the end" (15).

One of the notions that results from Ivy's reading is her idea to become an author, and she tells her pen pal, "I want to be a writer, it is what I love the bestest in this world" (*FTL*, 15). A few letters later she restates her professional goal, this time adding fame as a qualifier of success: "I want to be a famous writter when I grow up, I will write of Love" (21). Ivy soon learns that her teacher, Mrs. Brown, censors student letters to pen pals, telling Ivy that her first letter to Hanneke is too long and not appropriate. This message confuses Ivy, along with the fact that she seems to read only of "love" and never stories focused on Appalachia. In the same way that Denise Giardina learned about "acceptable" subject matter and topics through her reading, so too does Ivy Rowe.

Ivy's letters, particularly the ones written during her adolescent years, contain unconventional spelling and grammar since she first writes as a young girl who does not have many years of educational training. Even so, Ivy values a school-based education, and she tells her pen pal Hanneke, "I am smart thogh I go to school when I can and try to better myself" (*FTL*, 17). Smith uses these writer-reader interactions to make Ivy's intellectual curiosity clear to readers, working to reshape any notions they may have about ignorant mountaineers. Even at a young age, Ivy understands the inherent changes involved in gaining an education and new literacy skills. As the novel progresses, her spelling and grammar become more standard as she continues to learn both inside and outside a classroom.

Ivy's first teacher, Mrs. Brown, plays a significant role in Ivy's education, especially when she invites Ivy to stay with her while Mrs. Brown's niece (Molly) visits. Ivy's family allows her to go, and one of Ivy's letters to her family reveals the beginning of a discursive divide that continues as the novel progresses. While describing her new friend, Molly Bainbridge, in her letter home she also writes, "Now as I write this letter I am sad all of a sudden, I dont know what has come over me, I think of you All so. Please do not think I am fancy, nor spoilt, nor putting on Airs. It is not so, as I will tell you direckly" (*FTL*, 51). Through this letter Ivy voices her concerns about socializing with Molly, a child who has many more material advantages than Ivy. Ivy's worry over "putting on airs" signals her entry into a different social class and discourse community and also an awareness of the impending conflicted family relationships resulting from that transition. Although *Oral History*'s protagonist, Dory, remains silent throughout the novel, Ivy's voice reaches the readers of Smith's novel, signaling a certain sense of progress from Dory to Ivy. Whereas Dory never expresses her feelings about literacy-initiated identity conflicts and must instead rely on an oral telling through Sally, Ivy writes her concerns down on paper both for her family and for Smith's audience of readers.

Gender, Literacy, and Conflict for Ivy

One source of contention for Ivy revolves around her gender, and before she becomes pregnant—and physically bound by her womanhood and her mother's insistence on keeping the baby—she believes that literacy-centered learning will provide the most viable avenue for escape from what she considers a stagnant life. After her father dies and she moves to town with her mother and siblings, Ivy begins to understand that as a female, she has limited physical mobility. She observes the men in town riding logs down the river to a distant town or joining the army to fight in World War I, neither of which Ivy can do as a woman. This realization troubles her, and in a letter to her sister Silvaney Ivy writes, "But the logs go out on the river, and oh Silvaney, I wuld give a million dollars to go along.... I wuld give anything to be one of them boys and ride the rafts down to Kentucky on the great spring tide!" (*FTL*, 91). Ivy even considers dressing as a man and "trying to sneak along" but reasons that "Momma and Geneva [her mother's friend] wuld have a fit," and she decides to stay home (91).

As an alternative to riding down the river, she attends school and proudly tells her sister Beulah in a letter that she is "the very first pupil," even though her mother "does not seem to care one way or the other" (*FTL*, 100). Ivy studies under Miss Gertrude Torrington, a Presbyterian missionary who Ivy knows has come to "describe the conditions," though Ivy writes to Beulah, "I cannot immagine what she will say. It seems to me that conditions are very good" (100).

Compared to Ivy's life on Sugar Fork, the conditions of Majestic represent a vast material improvement, but Miss Torrington and her missionary-focused agenda instead see a mountain town in need of educational uplift.

Miss Torrington occupies an important role both in the novel and in Ivy's life, and in casting her as a single female missionary, Smith echoes the historical profiles of many female missionary teachers. Like those who preceded her in history, Miss Torrington envisions Appalachia as a space to invade and "save" along with its inhabitants like Ivy, echoing Richard Burlage's goals when he first arrived in Appalachia. Miss Torrington's goals for the community and Ivy also parallel those of missionaries who traveled into Indian territory to recruit pupils for boarding schools, as discussed in this project's introductory chapter.

Gender functions as the most notable difference between Richard Burlage from *Oral History* and Miss Torrington in *Fair and Tender Ladies*. Richard's invasion into the feminized space of the mountains parallels his relationship with Dory, but in pairing Ivy with a female teacher, Smith adds a new dynamic to their student-teacher relationship. Even more interesting, Miss Torrington makes a sexual advance toward Ivy, and in this way she represents the masculine ideological dominance over mountain ways that Richard also symbolizes for Dory. Miss Torrington's gender allows her to take greater public (not private, as occurs when Richard sleeps with Dory) liberties with Ivy than Richard can take with Dory, and Smith suggests that Ivy's family and friends would not suspect sexual interaction between a female teacher and a female student.

Smith describes Miss Torrington as the stereotypical schoolmarm: "Her forehead is wide and white. She pulls her hair strate back in a bunch and wears no jewelry of any kind" (*FTL*, 100). Stripped bare of typical, stereotypical markers of femininity, Miss Torrington seems outwardly de-sexed, her womanhood divorced from her role as a teacher. In Ivy's community none of her family members seem concerned about the time she spends with Miss Torrington, and literacy scholar Sarah Robbins notes that in the nineteenth century, females were preferred teachers for a host of reasons, one of which "cast schoolteaching as a mother-in-training activity" and another "held that women's empathetic moral sense made them especially adept at teaching young children" (2004, 98).

Hardly a comforting model for motherhood for Ivy, Miss Torrington instead represents a judgmentally different discursive world that introduces a host of dilemmas into Ivy's life. Moreover, within their relationship Miss Torrington occupies the top of an unequal power structure that she establishes once she knows that Ivy desires the knowledge Miss Torrington possesses. Ivy gushes to Beulah that Miss Torrington tells her she is "remarkable"

(*FTL*, 100) and wants her to return to Boston with her to attend school. Ivy desperately wants to go, since even though she cannot ride a log down the river or join the army, she can attend school. She tells Beulah, "How often I try to immagine the world beyond this town" (101). Ivy also reveres Miss Torrington and the learning she represents, even imagining the classroom as a kind of holy, sacred space in a letter to Silvaney in which she describes

> the big recitation hall with all the little panes of glass frosted over by the cold and the new steam radiators hissing. Oh Silvaney, I love this room! It is the room I love bestest in the whole world next to mine! The cielings are very high here, and the woodwork is old and curly around the big windows and the cieling and the door. I love the big slates on the wall and the way the eraser dust hangs in the air, and the oak table with the globe on it, and the pictures of Jesus Blessing the Little Children and Jesus Asending in Light. I love the way the schoolroom smells, the dusty somehow holy air. It seems as if the lessons quiver in the air, the sums and poems and conjugations we have learned by hart are all still there. (*FTL*, 104)

For Ivy the "somehow holy air" represents a rebirth that she can find only through acquiring new literacies, but as with other texts considered in this project, that acquisition comes at a price.

Similar to other authoritative teachers this project discusses, including Arnow's Miss Whittle, DeRosier's Janis Carroll, and Giardina's Miss Kurtz, Miss Torrington denigrates Ivy's mountain speech patterns; this alters not only the way Ivy speaks but also the way she conceives of her home and her family. When Ivy responds to one of Miss Torrington's comments by saying "Yessum," Miss Torrington corrects her by saying, "Say, <u>Yes Miss Torrington</u>, when will you learn to drop these backward customs?" (*FTL*, 105). After diminishing Ivy's confidence, Miss Torrington immediately bolsters it again, calling her "remarkably tallented [and] so extraordinarily gifted in language," finally telling Ivy, "I confess to you I feel that God has sent me here to save you Ivy, to offer you a life which will enable you to use your gifts to his glory" (105).

Like Richard Burlage, Miss Torrington views herself far above Ivy in every way, and she tells her, "I am perhaps espeshally suited to help you fulfill your destiny, Ivy. I can educate you, I can dress you, I can take you to Europe. For there is everything, everything to learn! I am a woman of some means Ivy. I can give you the world" (*FTL*, 106). Certainly Miss Torrington represents a life that is in some ways better than the one Ivy has, since she could give her access to more material things. Ivy comprehends the benefits of going with Miss Torrington to Boston and becomes especially excited when she thinks of the books to which she would have access, telling Silvaney, "I thought of all the stories I dont know yet, of books and books full of stories in Boston. I immagined their lether bindings and their deep rich covers and the pretty swirling paper inside the covers, like the snow" (106–7). Acquiring books has always been a hardship for Ivy, and Miss Torrington's offer provides learning opportunities Ivy has never experienced before.

Despite feeling excited about those books, almost immediately after considering what she would gain from going with Miss Torrington, Ivy feels guilty because from Miss Torrington she has also learned contempt for her Appalachian family and the ways in which they speak. In her letter to Silvaney Ivy explains that she was standing outside the school talking with one of the teachers when her grandmother (Granny Rowe) and aunt (Tennessee) came to visit her at school on one of their ginseng-selling trips to town: "<u>Lord God, how ye doing honey,</u> Granny said, and I confess that for a minute I drew back, for here was Granny smoking her pipe and wearing her old mans hat, and Tennessee behind her giggling and clutching that filthy dirty crazy bead purse. I drew back. For all of a sudden they seemed to me strange people out of another time" (*FTL*, 107).

Ivy knows that Miss Torrington would never approve of a greeting like "Lord God, how ye doing honey," and Ivy's initial reaction to "draw back" illustrates that Ivy has successfully learned Miss Torrington's demeaning judgments about mountain people. In addition to adding to a growing literary repertoire, like Clytie and Enoch in *The Dollmaker*, Ivy has also learned to be properly ashamed of mountain cultural markers. Even so, Ivy laments her reaction and tells Silvaney, "I was ashamed of myself," and in her letter she considers the downside of going with Miss Torrington: "If I go to Boston, I will not see [Granny Rowe and Tennessee], nor Beulahs new baby, nor Ethel grinning behind that big cash register in Stoney Branhams store, nor see my little momma any more, and I pictured her there in her rocking chair. Nor will I see Silvaney agian I thought" (*FTL*, 107). Ivy's pendulum-like train of thought represents the great divide that new literacies introduce to many of the characters' lives discussed in this project. Although Miss Torrington offers a new way of life for Ivy, the path to that life is fraught with painful identity conflicts and decisions to willfully separate herself from her family. Even so, when she considers the books she can read if she goes to Boston, she decides that she will go.

Soon after Ivy makes the decision to go with Miss Torrington, she also writes in a letter to Silvaney that when Miss Torrington spoke to her "it was like she owned me" (*FTL*, 109). In accepting the offer to go to Boston Ivy has given over many of her liberties to Miss Torrington, and she realizes that the opportunities that await will come at a great sacrifice. This realization intensifies when Miss Torrington suggests that Ivy follow her to her room to conduct drawing lessons and Ivy agrees immediately since "this was something I had been hoping for" (109). At first the lesson proceeds without incident, but as Ivy draws, Miss Torrington stands near her, places her hand on her shoulder, and then kisses her neck. Ivy instantly jumps up, and Miss Torrington sinks "down on her bed with her mouth in a wide round O" (110). In this one brief scene, Smith casts Miss Torrington not only as an invasive teacher with a dominant system of ideological beliefs to teach her pupils but also as a controlling sexual figure. Although she regrets her actions and later writes an apologetic note to Ivy encouraging her to come to Boston with her, she assumes the same position of sexual authority as Richard does with Dory.

Maternal Entrapment

Despite this incident, Ivy accepts Miss Torrington's apology and decides to accompany her to Boston; however, soon after making this decision, she learns that she is pregnant. Even though her soon-to-be daughter (Joli) will go on to accomplish what Ivy had hoped to achieve in her own life, including becoming an author, leaving home, and even traveling to Paris, upon first realizing that she is pregnant, Ivy feels trapped. In a letter to Silvaney she laments that "all is lost," and even though she almost has an abortion, she acquiesces to her mother's demands to keep the baby since "Momma has been through so much" (*FTL*, 121, 124). Although Ivy's mother does not use biblically-supported scripture to buttress her request (as does Gertie Nevels's mother in *The Dollmaker* when she convinces Gertie to follow Clovis to Detroit), she does wield a substantial influence over Ivy's decision. In a previously discussed letter to Beulah, Ivy made a comment about her mother's blasé attitude about her academic achievements, and it seems plausible that her mother's demand to have a baby and stay at home functioned as a ploy to keep Ivy in Majestic.

In deferring to her mother's insistence to keep the baby, Ivy feels helplessly bound to her body and place, and she tells Silvaney in a letter that she "could see that baby clear as day, tiny and pink and all curled up, and then it started beating with its little fists against my stomach, trying to escape. It hurt me. And then, I cannot explain it Silvaney, I <u>was</u> that little baby caught inside of my own self and dying to escape. But I could not. I could never ever get out, I was caught for ever and ever inside myself" (*FTL*, 122). While Miss Torrington's offer to attend school in Boston was problematic and would have no doubt introduced many difficult identity conflicts for Ivy, the biological function of her body combined with a devotion to her mother's wishes has revoked the choice to go or stay. Not only has Ivy's gender kept her from joining the army or riding logs out of town to a different place, it has also grounded her within her own feminine reproductive capacity and kept her from pursuing one avenue of potentially empowering escape offered by Miss Torrington.

Autodidactic Ivy

In 1918 Ivy gives birth to her daughter Joli, and while she receives no formal educational training, she embarks upon her own literacy campaign that lasts the majority of a lifetime. By this point in the novel the grammar, spelling, and overall organization of her letters have vastly improved, and she borrows six books a week from the company store in the coal mining town where she lives with her sister Beulah. In a letter to her mother's friend Geneva, Ivy tells her, "I read and read, you know how I love to read! I remember you and Momma saying it was foolishness. Well Beulah thinks so too, I can tell I am getting on her nerves. I know she thinks I ought to go out and get a job soon and so I will have to, but I can not bear to leave Joli just yet.... And so I sit and rock her, and sit and read and watch her sleep" (*FTL*, 144).

After Joli's birth Ivy no longer feels the terrifying feeling of motherly entrapment, and she finds her escape through both reading and mothering. Her letters bear no indication that her current reading produces the kind of conflict Denise Giardina's adolescent reading caused for her or for *The Unquiet Earth*'s protagonist Jackie, and Ivy's hobby of reading has clear implications for her writing. In Pierre Bourdieu's terms, Ivy operates as an "autodidact" (1984). James Paul Gee argues that "autodidacts are precisely people who, while often extremely knowledgeable, trained themselves and thus were trained outside of a process of group practice and socialization. They are almost never accepted as insiders [by members of a secondary discourse community], as members of the club" (1996, 140). Gee's statement might apply to Ivy if she ever left Appalachia, but she does not. Instead, she remains in the mountains and even moves from the coal town of Diamond back to her childhood home on Sugar Fork after marrying her adolescent friend Oakley Fox. Consequently, her literacy campaign operates within her primary discourse community, and after her early encounters with Miss Torrington, she never again encounters the kind of literacy-initiated conflicts that later haunt her daughter, Joli.

The inherent problem with Ivy's literacy campaign is that it never prompts her to gain elements of a secondary discourse community in the same way tit does for Denise Giardina, Jackie, Joli, or a host of other characters considered in this project. While this allows Ivy to avoid the perils of attaining multiple literacies, it also limits her empowerment. Instead of forging into unknown discourse communities, where she would experience both gains and losses, Ivy reads her books in a cabin high on Sugar Fork mountain, safe within the cultural boundaries of Appalachia. Ivy's literacy development seems like part of a fantasy story line that explores the possibilities of literacy attainment without the recognizable discursive dilemmas that so often characterize it.

Other Forms of Escape

Although reading provides a sense of freedom for Ivy, her sexual relationships with men also grant her a refreshing escape from societal gender norms. While living in Majestic with her sister Beulah and brother-in-law Curtis, Ivy begins seeing Franklin Ransom, the son of a wealthy coal operator. Ivy enjoys spending time with reckless, wild Franklin, and she reflects in a letter to Silvaney, "It is a fact that if you are ruint, like I am, it frees you up somehow" (*FTL*, 167). Many years later, after she marries Oakley Fox and has several more children, Ivy laments that mothering takes time away from her beloved activity of reading, and she writes in a letter to Miss Torrington (whom she still keeps in contact with through writing), "To answer your question, I do not read much any more. I do not have the time" (192). Ivy feels too physically and mentally exhausted to enjoy reading, and she instead finds comfort in the arms of Honey Breeding, a nomadic beekeeper who visits her cabin to help Oakley begin his own beehives.

In the same way that reading both defines and sustains Ivy, so too does her extramarital affair with Honey. In a deeply personal letter to Silvaney

Ivy explains, "We are exactly the same size. It's like he is me, or I am him" (*FTL*, 218). By describing Honey as a masculine mirror image of Ivy, Smith suggests the kind of character Ivy might have been, had she been male. In an interview with Rebecca Smith, Lee Smith explains, "[Ivy] had all those children, and she had to stay put. But he was a bee man. . . . And the thing about them is that they were travelers. They were not from anywhere. And I think that's the main thing that fascinated Ivy about Honey Breeding—his enormous freedom, his traveling, whereas she was put. She stayed put because of the children. But he was her other self, her alter ego, and being with him was somehow her expressing or living out that kind of male principle that she was unable to live in her own life—like going to the top of the mountain. She could never go if a boy didn't go with her" (R. Smith 1994, 21).

Literary critic Linda Byrd (2001) has noted that like the bees he tends, Honey floats from feminine flower to flower, but instead of feeling jealous about his promiscuity, Ivy discovers a great freedom with Honey, especially when sharing stories. She writes that "my own voice sounded funny in my ears. It sounded rusty. I felt like I hadn't used it in such a long time except to say something like, The wooden paddle is broke or Close the door" (*FTL*, 224). In the same way that stories flow from Ivy's pen into her letters, so too do they pour from her mouth once she begins telling them to Honey. She also enjoys listening to his stories and begs him to tell her more, saying, "*I am starved for stories*" (226).

During this process of sharing orally rendered stories, Ivy has an epiphany similar to the one literacy attainment brought to the women Smith taught at the Hindman Settlement School—she truly discovers her own independence for the first time. Ivy comments, "I felt I had got a part of myself back that I had lost without even knowing it was gone. Honey had given me back my very soul" (*FTL*, 232). The missing component within her soul is a belief in herself and her own abilities, and she tells Silvaney, "All of a sudden I thought, *I could of climbed up here by myself, anytime!* . . . And I had got up there myself at long last with a man it is true, but not a man like any I had ever seen before in all my life" (233). For a brief time, Ivy escapes the entrapment of her life, trappings that even reading cannot liberate. Through her time spent with Honey on top of the mountain Ivy becomes a fuller version of herself, and though her actions have dire consequences (she misses the death of her daughter and inflicts much emotional pain upon her husband, Oakley), she tells Silvaney, "I would of stayed up there. I would of stayed with him until I starved to death and died, I reckon, living on love. I would have stayed right there with him if he hadn't of made me leave, and that's a fact" (236).

Two years elapse between the letter in which Ivy tells Silvaney about her affair with Honey and her next letter. By this point in the novel Ivy has undergone many significant identity changes, and Smith reflects those transitions in the way Ivy signs her letters. As a young girl she signs virtually all of them "Ivy Rowe," and once she marries Oakley she signs them "Ivy R. Fox." After the couple moves from Majestic back to Ivy's adolescent home on Sugar Fork, Ivy considers herself completely immersed in her married life and drops her middle initial, simply signing her letters "Ivy Fox." Once Ivy's depression begins she signs two letters to Silvaney with only her first name, and after her affair with Honey Breeding, Ivy signs off with "Ivy Rowe," her maiden name (*FTL*, 207, 221, 240). This reversion symbolizes both Ivy's newfound independence and the guilt she feels over the affair and the tragic death of her daughter.

Throughout the remainder of the novel Ivy seems more comfortable in her own skin, and she signs the rest of her letters "Ivy," "Ivy Fox," "Mama," "Mamaw," and even "Ivy Rowe" (*FTL*, 294) in a letter to her childhood friend Molly after Oakley has died. Ivy's signatures reveal how she conceives of herself during various points in her life, and in her final letter to Silvaney she reflects, "I used to think I would be a writer. I thought then I would write of love (Ha!) but how little we know, we spend our years as a tale that is told I have spent my years so. I never became a writer atall. Instead I have loved, and loved, and loved. I am fair wore out with it" (315).

A Continued Realignment of Reader Perceptions

The sheer volume and insightfulness of Ivy's letters are a testament to her authorship, yet like the letters Linda Scott DeRosier's mother and grandmother exchange, Ivy's writing never sees publication, at least within the fictional confines of the novel. In an interview with Pat Arnow, Smith comments, "There's less an emphasis upon the end product in the artistic work that women do, so often the process is what's important rather than the product. It's why in [*Fair and Tender Ladies*] I was trying to show that the writing of the letters was more important than the letters. It's like the knitting of a sweater, the making of the quilt, and that kind of thing, you know, that something is art even though it's not perceived as public art. It's the difference between monumental sculpture and needlepoint" (2001, 63).

Certainly the process of writing sustains Ivy throughout some of the most difficult phases in her life. She repeatedly comments on how writing helps her reflect on what has happened, saying, "Sometimes I despair of ever understanding anything right when it happens to me, it seems like I have to tell it in a letter to see what it was, even though I was right there all along!" (*FTL*, 183). Writing even solidifies events in Ivy's life and renders them real, as when she tells Joli about Oakley's death and writes, "I have to stop now. Because I have written this letter to you, it is real now" (274). Writing functions as a necessary activity for Ivy, and just as she works through the discursive divide introduced by Miss Torrington in her letters, she also writes about the conflicted feelings she has about her daughter Joli leaving home to fulfill many of the same dreams Ivy held as a child.

When encountering *Fair and Tender Ladies*, Smith's readers also understand that she grants them access to private letters that Ivy never intended for a large reading audience. In granting that kind of access, Smith works to realign readers' perceptions of Appalachian women, echoing the effect of many authorial strategies in *Oral History*. Through Ivy's private thoughts we learn of her early intellectual curiosity, her increasing ability to write, and her steady desire to become an author who writes for public audiences. By making readers aware of Ivy's most private—and most intelligent—thoughts, Smith makes it increasingly difficult for readers to keep any preconceived notions they may have about ignorant hillbillies.

Recently literacy scholar Katrina Powell has made a similar observation about letters written by real Appalachian people who wrote to government officials protesting their forced removal from the Shenandoah National Park in the 1930s. Powell argues that "the rhetorics employed in these letters by the mountain families counter monolithic discourse written *about* them," and "the representations contained in mountain families' letters directly counter those constructed for them" (2007, 7, 56; italics in original). Smith draws on a similar vein in constructing Ivy's character, who ultimately speaks out against a literary and media tradition that assumes Appalachian illiteracy. Knowing that Ivy's "private" letters will speak to a real reading audience, Smith's strategy has an effect similar to her inclusion of "oral" stories in *Oral History*: not only does Smith's rhetorical approach call readers' attention to their own stereotypes about Appalachia, but it also causes them to be troubled by knowledge of their own prejudices.

Literacy's Effects for Mothers and Daughters

Similar to the story Smith shared during our interview in which a young girl prepares to leave home to attend Berea College and her distraught mother worries about how college will change their relationship, Ivy harbors the same fears for her daughter Joli. After Ivy's brief exposure to Miss Torrington and a much different discourse community, Ivy knows that Joli will encounter incredibly different circumstances once she moves to town and then on to college and beyond. Ivy wants to ensure that Joli remembers her home, its culture, and its storytelling traditions, so she insists that they hike up Hell Mountain in search of Gaynelle and Virgie Cline's cabin. Joli protests, arguing that the expedition was "crazy," but the pair makes the trek, only to discover the remnants of the Cline home site. While the sisters and their cabin are gone, their stories continue to live on in Ivy's memory, and on that day she shares the sisters' stories with Joli.

By retelling the stories to her daughter, Ivy connects the oral traditions of the Cline sisters, Ivy's private letter writing, and Joli's eventual public authorship. Although unaware of her impact at the time, incidents like this fuel Joli's later writing endeavors and support her literary success. When writing about the day to Silvaney, Ivy explains why she felt so strongly about taking Joli to the Cline home site, and she predicts the eventual divide that occurs between them: "For I had got it in mind to go up there and take her. Before she left, before she went down off the mountain for good—for when Joli comes back she will be all different. I know. So I took her up on Hell Mountain while she was still mine" (*FTL*, 200).

Once Joli leaves home she graduates from high school, and although Ivy bursts with pride at her accomplishments, she also feels a twinge of remorse, remarking in a letter to her sister Ethel, "It will be such a good thing for her, in the long run" (*FTL*, 207). Like Ivy, Joli performs well in school, and she graduates from Radford Normal Institute. She also meets and becomes engaged to Taylor Cunningham III, a man from an elite family in eastern Virginia. In the scene where Ivy and Oakley discuss whether they should attend Joli's wedding, Smith illustrates one of the most painfully divisive conversations caused by competing discourse communities that this project considers. Ivy explains in a letter to Silvaney that declining to go to the wedding has "fair broke [her] heart," because she "would love to go, and travel across Virginia on a train paid by Taylor Cunninghman the Third, and see what there is to see!" (268).

Ivy goes on to reason that Oakley does not physically feel well enough to make the trip, but she also confesses, "And it is more than that. Oakley feels we <u>ought not</u> to go, and in my heart of hearts I know he is right" (*FTL*, 268). Ivy has even planned what she would wear on such an exciting trip to see her firstborn daughter get married, and when she asks Oakley why he does not think they should go, even though Joli's fiancé has agreed to pay their train fare, Oakley responds, "She could of come here and got married if she had chose" (269).

Ivy understands that Joli has entered a new discursive realm after her experiences in college, and now she has chosen to marry into that world in eastern Virginia, not Appalachia. Even though Ivy cherishes Joli's accomplishments, like the girl's mother Smith discussed during our interview, Ivy feels that she has lost Joli because "Joli has broken my heart. For she is the child of my childhood, and in losing her, I have lost my youth. I can not say it better than that. I wanted her gone, I wished her godspeed, but now I am about to die because she has took me up on it! Oh, I am contrary. It is true! She has travelled far beyond me now" (*FTL*, 271).

Finding Voice

Despite the pain this divide causes for Ivy and presumably for Joli as well, Joli goes on to achieve what no Appalachian character manages in *Oral History*: she brings her stories—stories representative of the mountains—to print for Smith's fictional reading audience. Dory remains silent, Sally shares her stories orally for the real audience but not the fictional reading one, the Cline sisters' oral stories reach both audiences, Ivy's letters are read by us, but it is Joli's writing that finds public voice within fictional form, representing the impact Smith's own writing has had for contemporary readers.

Notably, Joli uses Appalachia as the setting for many of her best-selling books, and Ivy also functions as an active source for Joli's stories. In a letter to Joli Ivy tells her, "Oh Joli! It is no time atall that you and me were sitting out together in the sweet long grass and I knew what all you had read and what you'd not. And now you have gone on past me down the road. It is too late for you to turn back, honey. You have got past the point where you can do that, past the point where you could ever come back here and live. I know it and you know it. So you have got to keep on keeping on. I know it is hard sometimes" (*FTL*, 280). Although Ivy insists that Joli has "gone on past [her] down the road," she still suggests books that Joli should read, including *Gone With the Wind*, and she repeatedly tells her to include more romantic plotlines in her books, since "people don't like to have too much thinking in a book" (293).

Like Denise Giardina, who thought that "real" writers lived in New York or Paris, Ivy has similar ideas about where "real" books take place, and she warns Joli against placing her novels in Appalachia, telling her in a letter, "Oh honey, I am real proud of you! But I wonder, why don't you write about New York City, since you have been up there for so long? Or about Norfolk and the newspaper life? It seems like that would be more exciting than these mountains which nobody wants to read about, honey" (*FTL*, 290). The vast success of Smith's literary career, which includes a large number of works set in Appalachia, highlights the irony of Ivy's statement, yet during our interview Smith also commented that her father held beliefs similar to Ivy's. Smith said that her father "didn't like it when [she] came back and started writing about the mountains." When asked to elaborate about why her father felt this way Smith responded, "Well my daddy said again and again, he said, 'I did not send you off to those fine schools,' because he never got a college education himself, but he went for a year. He said, 'I did not send you off to those fine schools to come back here and be writing bad English [laughs] and up in the hollers talking to Ava McClanahan and Granny Rowe' and so on. You know, because I was gathering materials for my books and talking to the people I'd always loved. He wanted me to 'rise above'" (2007). Like so many of the people and characters considered in the project, Smith's father had learned to devalue his mountain heritage, and Smith echoes this sentiment in Ivy's suggestions for Joli.

Like Smith, Joli ignores her family's advice and continues to draw from her Appalachian heritage to create popular works of fiction. Even though Joli never returns to the mountains to live, she stays in close contact with Ivy. While Joli's acquisition of new literacies permanently changes their relationship, by the novel's end readers understand that the two share an unbreakable bond, and without Ivy, Joli's public authorship would never have been possible. Near the novel's conclusion Ivy even writes to Joli explaining an Appalachian folk remedy that no doubt finds its way into one of Joli's stories, though Ivy cannot imagine why it would make appropriate subject matter: "It was *chicken gizzards*, but why you need to know is beyond me. Are you going to put it in a book? Or have you got one? Anyway, what you do is peel the outside off of the chicken gizzard and rub it on the wart. Then you bury the gizzard and forget all about it. When you forget, the wart will be gone. If you <u>don't</u> forget, I won't promise a thing!" (*FTL*, 301). Remedies like this one pepper Smith's fiction, and Joli's methodology clearly reflects Smith's own research tactics, especially for *Oral History*, as when she told Edwin T. Arnold in an interview, "I did all this research, all this reading, and I'd been taping my relatives for years and I knew all this material that I wanted to do something with" (1984, 246).

In the same way that the Cline sisters "live on stories," Ivy lives on her letters. In Ivy's penultimate letter she explains to Joli that she always knew that her beloved sister Silvaney died in the 1920s flu epidemic, but that she wrote to her anyway because "the letters didn't mean anything. Not to the dead girl Silvaney, of course—<u>nor to me</u>. Nor had they ever. It was the <u>writing</u> of them, that signified" (*FTL*, 313). To prepare for her own death Ivy burns her collection of letters, and she tells Joli, "With every one I burned, my soul grew lighter, lighter, as if it rose too with the smoke" (313). Having fulfilled her role as author (though she never conceives of herself as such), mother, wife, and the link between the oral traditions of the Cline sisters and the public voicing that Joli achieves, in a final letter to Silvaney Ivy writes that she has "got so much on [her] mind these days, and no time to waste on talking" (314). Instead, she writes until the moment of her death, and she tells Silvaney in a previous letter that "Joli is the writer which I always wanted to be" (303).

More Real-Life Inspiration

As with much of her fiction, Smith found inspiration for *Fair and Tender Ladies* from real life. In an interview with Pat Arnow, Smith explains that when she purchased a packet of letters at a flea market in Greensboro, North Carolina, she began thinking about writing an epistolary novel. She tells Arnow that she was interested in them because "they were from a woman to her sister, and she was a woman who had not had any particular education. I was just struck how every now and then she'd have this real literary image, or striking turn of phrase or something. And I just got real interested in the idea of somebody's letters being a sort of work of art. You know, letters over their whole lifetime. Is it art because there's a critic somewhere who perceives it as art? Or is it art because it just is? I don't know. It's just some sort of aesthetic thing I've had in my mind for a while that interests me" (63). In keeping with this woman's writing style, Smith highlights Ivy's lack of formal education in the beginning of *Fair and Tender Ladies* through heavy dialect and unconventional spelling, and readers become increasingly aware of the literary progressions Ivy makes as she continues to read and write. Ivy's refusal to consider herself an author also resonates with readers.

Smith worked to overturn this same notion in the life of Lou Crabtree, Smith's model for Ivy Rowe. Smith encountered Crabtree when teaching a writing workshop in Abingdon, Virginia, and she discovered that Crabtree had been writing stories her entire life without any thought of publication. During our interview Smith said, "Yeah, [Lou Crabtree is] where I got the idea of someone who just simply writes for the love of it because it's necessary to keep her soul alive, you know, as a way to make it through the night. . . . When I first encountered her she had literally suitcases full of writing that she'd done all her life" (2007). Smith was amazed at Crabtree's talent, and after working with her, reviewing her pieces, and helping her polish selected stories, in 1984 LSU Press published Crabtree's collection of short stories titled *Sweet Hollow*.

In an interview with Jeanne McDonald, Smith remembers, "Once I said to her, 'Lou, what would you do if somebody told you that you weren't allowed to write anymore?' 'Well,' Lou replied, 'I reckon I'd just have to sneak off and do it'" (2001, 188). Ivy treats writing similarly, and it soothes her in much the same way it functioned as a cathartic exercise for Smith, who wrote the novel while her mother was dying. Smith operates as the catalyst that allows Crabtree a public voice, and Ivy does the same for Joli. Smith's fiction, as well as the other works considered in this project, repeatedly focuses on the identity conflicts necessitated by the acquisition of new literacies, yet those literacies make possible the public voicing that these authors and characters like Joli achieve.

During our interview Smith reflected that "by the very act of writing . . . you put yourself outside of whatever you're writing about. . . . The very act of writing makes you no longer a part of whatever community or relationship or whatever it is you're writing about" (2007), but that painful distancing remains necessary in order to give public voice to these Appalachian women's stories of literacy-initiated conflict.

Interview with Lee Smith

EAL: Thank you for allowing me to send you some materials before the interview. I'm very interested in these conflicted identities that happen as a result of literacy attainment and how that's happened in your own life and in the life of your characters.

LS: You're welcome. First, I wanted to say that I was really interested by your characterizing literacy as including social and cultural literacies. Because this whole thing, I think that is absolutely central to what I've been writing about all these years.

EAL: I'm so glad to hear you say that, because it sort of depends which side of the camp you're on. Some literacy theorists don't like that inclusion, and I think it's very important to talk about.

LS: Oh, I think it's really, really important, and I think it's just interesting to think about this approach with regard to being a writer. I think you can think about these ideas in terms of insider/outsider too. You know, and that too is interesting to me. By the very act of writing you put yourself outside of whatever you're writing about.

EAL: Oh, absolutely.

LS: You know, you become an outsider. I mean, the very act of writing makes you no longer a part of whatever community or relationship or whatever it is you're writing about. This is really interesting. I mean, I've always felt a little bit of an exile myself. I think from the time I was really little, partially because of growing up there in Grundy, which when I was there, was so insular and so literally, geographically cut off by these straight-up-and-down mountains and very poor roads at that time and many people that had never been outside the county. And then here was my mother, who had come there.

EAL: She was the foreigner.

LS: She was the foreigner, yeah, and that, I think that in a certain way is what made me a writer, because I came from a big family of storytellers and language lovers, but it's that perspective. And I think that's what happens when you become sort of culturally literate in any way. It puts you outside of your culture.

EAL: Yes!

LS: Do you see what I'm saying?

EAL: Completely. And you used the word "exile." Do you find that there's pain associated with that?

LS: Well, there often is. I mean, in my case, there wasn't so much. I remember being very hurt. I was having a talk with Mike Mullins, who runs the Hindman Settlement School where I've worked so much, and he told me, he said, "Well, in a certain way, you're different" from just about everybody who was there at that particular session. He said, "Because you were raised to leave."

EAL: Well gosh.

LS: Yeah, and I think that's absolutely true, that phrase "raised to leave" really struck me, because my parents really didn't want me to live in Grundy for my whole life. They wanted me to go elsewhere and live and have what they considered a better life. And actually, they sent me off to prep school because they were afraid I was going to run off and marry my high school boyfriend, which I probably would have.

EAL: Right.

LS: So you know, this has all been really close to me and interesting. You can even think of it in terms of language. You know, the kind of dialect my father's family had was very different from my mother's very refined eastern Virginia accent, with not one grammatical mistake and so on.

EAL: That's very interesting. So when you were sent off to St. Catherine's, and then you went to Hollins, and then you did leave, was there some resentment on the part of your family that you did not come back, even though that was the idea all along?

LS: No, well that was what they all sort of—I think—wanted me to do and expected me to do. I mean, my parents were clearly raising me to leave. They sent me off in the summer to camps, you know, not just Girl Scout or 4-H camps, although I went to those too, but like monthlong camps. Like fancy camps [laughs]. I mean, my mother had these notions, you know, because of how she had grown up and where she'd grown up. Her family had lost their money, but they had a lot of notions and sort of grandiose ideas and so on. So I was being raised in a way to kind of fit in with those ideas of the kind of future they hoped I would have.

EAL: I see.

LS: They didn't like it when I came back and started writing about the mountains.

EAL: Why not?

LS: Well, my daddy said again and again, he said, "I did not send you off to those fine schools," because he never got a college education himself, but he went for a year. He said, "I did not send you off to those fine schools to come back here and be writing bad English [laughs] and up in the hollers talking to Ava McClanahan and Granny Rowe" and so on. You know, because I was gathering materials for my books and talking to the people I'd always loved. He wanted me to "rise above."

EAL: But what about the fact that you were very successful?

LS: Isn't it interesting? I remember he called me once from the dime store, and I'd written I guess *Oral History*, and he said "I'm sitting here in the dime store, and I'm looking at this book that's sold nine million copies," he was reading off the outside of it, and he said, "Why can't you write a book like this?" I said, "What is it, Daddy?" And it was *Scruples* by Judith Krantz. [Laughs]

EAL: [Laughs] Did he ever change his mind?

LS: He did change his mind, because he got a big crush on, after Mama died but not a serious crush, on the woman who did the one-woman play of *Fair and Tender Ladies*. A fabulous actress, named Barbara Smith, came to do it in Grundy, and she and I of course stayed with Daddy. And he was just taken, I mean really enamored of Barbara Smith. [Laughs] And after Barbara Smith's visit, he decided he was going to be proud of it. I went and picked him up in the car to take him up to the high school to see the show, and he didn't read my book. He just didn't read fiction, you know. So he's all dressed up, right, and we're in the car, and he turned over to me and he said, "All right. What the hell is this thing about anyway?" And I said [laughs], "Well, it's about the life of a mountain woman, just like a whole lot of the women that we know and knew growing up here," and he kind of nodded. And in a little while he said, "Well, has it got any sex in it?" [Laughs] I said, "Well, it's got a little bit, but I think you'll like it." He didn't mind it at all, and everybody clapped and stood up and rushed forward you know, to hug Barbara and all this, and he was amazed.

EAL: You know, that took awhile.

LS: And then he decided that he loved Barbara and it was all going to be okay. It was just outside of what he had had in mind, you know.

EAL: Of course. No, I understand. You know, people have these notions of "high" literature, and sometimes regional literature is different and lovable and wonderful.

LS: That's right, and I think he began to be really proud.

EAL: That's good to know.

LS: He was a really sweet man. It wasn't that he was mean or anything; he just, you know, just wished that I would've had, chosen a life that he would've understood more.

EAL: I understand completely.

LS: And let me just tell you this one other story that happened not too long ago.

EAL: Oh, please do.

LS: I was so moved, and I knew exactly what she meant, and of course this is really a whole different approach from the sort of dynamic that was going on with me and my dad. But I was back up in Buchanan County to do a book named *Sitting on the Courthouse Bench*, which is an oral history. Did you ever see that?

EAL: Not yet, but I read about it in an interview; it sounded wonderful.

LS: Well, it was just because they were getting ready to destroy the town and so on, as part of this flood project. So I went up there and did a book of oral histories of people who had been active in the town, the downtown merchants like my dad. And it was with high school students; one of my good friends still teaches senior English at Grundy High School. And so her students all participated, and we arranged so they would all get high school credit for their work, which was a lot of work. And we did that, and their book was published, and you know they just did such a good job. And then we had a banquet for them, and they were all by then applying to colleges, and it really helped that they had published a book.

EAL: Yeah, I would think so!

LS: And they were all real smart, and they were getting in everywhere they applied. And one girl from a family that had absolutely no advantages at all, her mother came, you know, to the banquet, and a whole bunch of other children. And this girl had just been accepted with full tuition to everywhere she had applied, and she was going to go to Berea. They were just thrilled to get her. Her mother came up, and this getting into Berea had just happened, and I said, "I guess you're just really proud of your daughter," and she just burst into tears. She said, "It won't never be the same after this." She said, "She'll go off, and then she'll come back and she won't know us no more." And I said, "What do you mean?" And she said, "She just won't really know us anymore. It'll all be different from now on. I've only got," whatever it was, "six more months with her." You know, and it was like, that's exactly what you're talking about.

EAL: That's my project! If I had an oral history summary of the whole project, that's it. That's beautiful.

LS: She said, "She won't know us no more." And I just thought, "Oh my gosh." And I know they will be, are by now, so proud of her.

EAL: Of course.

LS: But you know, it can just be really, really hard, and you don't quite fit in anywhere. That's what I mean by the sense of exile. You know, I didn't quite fit in at St. Catherine's, and you didn't quite fit in at Hollins, but then you certainly don't fit in back home really anymore. There's an outsiderness, which, I guess, is good for being a writer, or a critic, or a student. But it's a little hard on you.

EAL: It's definitely hard.

LS: It's a lot harder on some people than others, just depending upon the attitude your family takes. And I've had students too who dealt with this, in particular if they were the only ones in their families to go off to school or to go off to a really good school. There's a lot of jealousy and resentment, and you know, a lot of people I know have had a lot of trouble with that.

EAL: I wanted to ask you about your work in the adult literacy programs at the Hindman Settlement School. What can you tell me about that?

LS: Oh man, now there are some major stories. I had always been involved with literacy, but suddenly out of the blue I was awarded a Lila Wallace–Reader's Digest grant, and at that time that meant that they would give me three years off from teaching.

EAL: Wow.

LS: And pay me the same thing I would make if I was teaching.

EAL: That's incredible.

LS: Uh-huh. My school was really mad at me [laughs], but I did it, of course. But the deal was, the artist, or writers then I guess it was, the writers who were chosen for this had to affiliate with some sort of a nonprofit organization and help bring literacy of some sort, including the sorts you're talking about, to a population which usually didn't have access to it. This was really interesting, and you might even look into the Lila Wallace Reader's Digest Foundation and look at the list of kinds of "literacy" that the various writers who were chosen over the years have affiliated with. Because there would be like prison populations, maybe a Native American population, all kinds of things, and mine was the Hindman Settlement School. It wasn't their creative writing program that I had been affiliated with in the summers; it was their literacy program. And so I went and worked for three years, you know, for parts of the year. And it was really, really interesting. Because I worked with a lot of the same women, and it was all women in this group that had to do with writing. And we wrote a lot of books, little books, and me and Kinko's published them [laughs], and they've been used in a lot of other literacy programs. Because for people to be able to tell their own story is finally what they really want to do.

EAL: And as these women learned to write, and you worked with them, and they gained these new literacies, did you see in them the kind of conflicts that we've been talking about?

LS: Oh yeah. Oh yeah. In fact, many of them were only able, initially, to get into the literacy program if they were able to get away from their husbands who didn't want them to learn how to read or parents who didn't want them to learn how to read or maybe, say, they'd gotten pregnant when they were real young, and they're all real religious. Nobody ever thought of an abortion it seemed like to me. You know, and they hadn't gone to school, they'd dropped out. Or they stayed at home to be the one that helped Mama take care of the other children and all these kinds of things. And so their whole sense of themselves was totally dependent and wrapped up in other people. This one woman came in there with her head hung down, and she wouldn't even look at any of us. And [she] just sat there without saying a word for months and months and months, and she gradually began to speak up and to write. And at the end of three years she was wearing nail polish, she'd left her husband [laughs], and she was getting a job. She was able to write a letter to sue him for child support.

EAL: Oh, that's wonderful!

LS: And the whole thing was all about empowerment through literacy. And I saw it in a lot of different ways. You know, we had some of the women in different groups at different levels. And some of them were getting their GED, and other ones were literally, just at a third-grade level or something. So we had all kinds of levels and all kinds of senses of self. I mean, they were working with some women who were too shy and full of shame and embarrassment to even work in a group. They just were working with them one-on-one or in their own home, and then I did some of that and had the writing group too. And so I went there at intervals for three years and really got to see so much change in each of these women as a result of literacy.

EAL: That's so wonderful. You know, Katherine Kelleher Sohn has got a book called *Whistlin' and Crowin' Women of Appalachia*, and it's about literacy practices since college. And it's a whole lot of the same sort of thing.

LS: What is her name? I need to write this down.

EAL: Katherine, but she goes by Kathy.

LS: Okay, I'm going to look at that, because I would be really interested in that. One of the women in the program was Florida Slone. She was fabulous, and she was a ballad singer who made up a ballad for everything that happened in the community. She was like the sort of soul and voice of this community, the county there. She was just locally really famous, real religious and so on. She couldn't really learn to read and write until her husband died, but when he did, she showed up over there. She was very motivated, and the main things she wanted to do were learn to drive a car, get a license, and learn to write those songs down that she'd been making up and singing all of her life. I worked with her even before she learned to read and write well enough to do that. She would say them to me, and I would write them down.

EAL: Well, did she do it? Did it work?

LS: Yeah! Yeah, it worked great, and she wrote them, and she would put them into a little book, you know. And printed it up, and then she made a CD of her songs. She went around speaking about literacy and so on. She was really funny and fun, and she used to do the quilting over at the community center with the other ladies, and then she was just kind of the soul of the program. But then guess what.

EAL: What?

LS: This is so predictable. After I left, and I'm just saying that in terms of time. It didn't have anything to do with me. She fell in love with some old man in her church, and guess what his name was. This is a great name. I could never even make this name up. His name was Virgil Lively. And he did not believe that a woman ought to be out there parading herself . . .

EAL: Oh no.

LS: . . . around in public. And he sort of stopped her singing in public and so on, and driving. She was at about at the sixth- or seventh-grade level, and her intention had been to get her GED. She was at a high school level by then, or a junior high anyway. But he said all a woman needed to read was the Bible. And she stopped coming.

EAL: Do you know Anita Puckett?

LS: Uh-unh. I knew some Pucketts growing up in Grundy, but I don't know Anita Puckett.

EAL: She does anthropological work, and she's got this fabulous essay called "Let the Girls do the Spelling and Dan will do the Shootin."

LS: [Laughs] That sounds great!

EAL: It's about literacy practices, and she says at the beginning of the article that it's an isolated experience and ethnographic data.

LS: Well, so is this.

EAL: But, her findings are exactly what you said. It was sanctioned for women to read and write and read the Bible and do the checkbook and things like that, but not too much. And Lord knows, no man is supposed to be reading that much, unless he's a preacher. And that's okay, but otherwise that's just odd.

LS: Yeah, and I think so. And I think for boys if they want to be boys, or a man's man, they're not supposed to be good at reading and writing, which is sort of awful for them.

EAL: There's this other great researcher in Cincinnati, I think she's still there, Victoria Purcell-Gates, and she worked with this mother and son in a literacy program. Both were completely illiterate technically, not socially and culturally, obviously, but the mother learns to read and write. But the son is very resistant, and she finally figures out that it's because his father doesn't read and write, and he wants to be just like his dad.

LS: It's awful to know more than your dad, in a way.

EAL: Of course.

LS: It's hard, particularly if you're still a child.

EAL: And I was just delighted to read about the Moonlight Schools in *On Agate Hill*. And I wanted you to, if you didn't mind, tell me about your research, and how you know about Moonlight Schools and where you found out about them.

LS: Well a lot of work has been done on isolated rural education, and so really, I just did a whole lot of reading in the Southern Historical Collection and the books are listed, actually, in the back of *On Agate Hill*.

EAL: I saw those; they're great.

LS: And also, I was just talking to a whole lot of people. You know, we spend a lot of time up in Ashe County, and I talked to a whole lot of people who had attended the one-room schools. And also in Buchanan County, where I grew up, there were so many of them, and I had great aunts who taught in them, and so on. And they told me about them, and I'd always heard about the Moonlight Schools.

EAL: That's just fascinating. I came to Louisiana State University thinking that was my dissertation topic.

LS: Oh really?

EAL: My grandmother taught in a Moonlight School on Big Sandy Mush, about forty-five minutes west of Asheville. And there are all of these great documents and photographs and letters from students; it's definitely a future project. Well, can I ask you a question about *Oral History*?

LS: Sure, yeah.

EAL: Okay, I have thought and thought about it, and why does Dory not get her own section?

LS: Well you know, I just never thought about that. It's so funny. I read what you had written [in the draft of interview topics e-mailed beforehand] concerning that, and I remember when the book came out, several critics mentioning that you know, and commenting on it one way or the other. I don't know why. I think maybe in my mind she already didn't have a voice, because she was so circumscribed by family, by circumstance. The circumstances of her life were not going to give her a voice, I guess. I don't know. I never thought about it when I was writing it.

EAL: That's just incredibly interesting. I've thought a lot about how she had no voice.

LS: Yeah, absolutely she doesn't. You know, and I just couldn't imagine, exactly, her speaking. You know, getting out of her situation. And I had heard so many stories about girls that never got more than thirty miles from where they were from and didn't even know that they were so close to home because there was a mountain in between and they'd been taken by a circular road, and just all that stuff, you know.

EAL: Yeah, I always wondered too, and I know this is an unanswerable question, because you didn't write the book that way, but what would've happened if Ora Mae had not intercepted?

LS: No, I did think about that, and actually, I didn't know what was going to happen when I got to that point in the novel. I just was real surprised when Ora Mae did that. Except Ora Mae was a type that I had thought about a lot and had seen in a lot of families. You know, the one who was like "I just have to stay home and take care of all the rest of them," but was really jealous of ones who were able to have a sexual life, a life beyond the family.

EAL: Yes.

LS: And so on, but I think that probably, Dory would've gone to Richmond and it would've been a disaster. Because I don't think Richard Burlage was smart enough or strong enough to have made it work.

EAL: I loved it when the old preacher was talking to Justine, and I love

Justine too, and says that he's a total innocent. It's not Dory that's the innocent; it's him, it's Richard.

LS: Right, right, absolutely. And again, I read just so many accounts at the time of various people, it was usually under some auspices of a church, a missionary preacher or a do-gooding person who would go into the mountains to do good. And they would always keep these diaries because they wanted to record it, how good they were doing in whatever way. And that tone, that sort of flighty, highfalutin kind of tone, you know, and then in a way he was much, much more innocent.

EAL: And naive.

LS: And [more] naive than Dory, yeah. That was exactly what he was.

EAL: I know that you really enjoyed writing Richard's sections, and I read that you enjoyed the voice. And it seems to me that his sections would kind of rhetorically help along readers who don't know anything about Appalachian culture.

LS: Well I was thinking that too, and at a certain point I realized that it would be helpful if I could have an outsider and give his perceptions as he got to know the place where he was. That that would be interesting, and particularly to tell as he went in, as he traveled by train and got into the region and what his thoughts were and what his impressions were that that might be helpful.

EAL: I think it is. Because I chose to teach *Fair and Tender Ladies* to a group of undergraduates in Baton Rouge, and that was absolutely hilarious. They had the hardest time with the dialect.

LS: I'm sure they did. You know, if I were doing it again today, I would not have it be as heavy.

EAL: Really?

LS: I think so. I was just in love with it, you know. In love with it, and I still am. I think one person who does a very good job with getting dialect exactly right but also not ever making it sound like a foreign language is Denise Giardina.

EAL: Oh absolutely.

LS: Isn't she good?

EAL: Yeah she's good. One of my chapters is on her.

LS: That's right! I think she came along a little bit later than me, and by then, you know, she was more aware of not overdoing it. I mean, I'm glad I did it just like I did, but I think if I'm writing Appalachian dialect or something now, I don't go quite so much into it. I was just recording it. I was in love with it.

EAL: Oh me too. It's home. It's the voice of home.

LS: Yeah, and all those really old ones in my family were dying, you know, so I was just getting it down. And they have died, so I'm glad I did.

EAL: I am too. I know you've answered this question a million times, but is *Fair and Tender Ladies* still your favorite book that you've written?

LS: Umm . . . maybe. Yeah, I mean, I loved it. But I am also really, really partial to *On Agate Hill*, which I just finished. Again, like with *Fair and Tender Ladies*, it was a very, very emotional writing experience, and there is something that Molly Petree and Ivy Rowe have in common, you know that just kind of pulls at my heart. But I was going to say one other thing about *Oral History* before we just leave it entirely. I do think that I was always aware of people that would come into the mountains and take things away. And use up our stuff. You know, whether it was people coming in with the big lumber companies buying up our trees or companies looking to excavate the coal or the natural gas and oil. And now there are things like mountaintop removal, things that literally destroy our mountains. Although he certainly didn't mean to be, I think that just in the same way that all these outsiders would come and rape the land, I think in a certain way Richard Burlage was taking advantage of Dory.

EAL: Absolutely. I'm glad to hear you say that, because I'd always thought that.

LS: Oh yeah.

EAL: And the thing that I hadn't really thought about until recently and discovered that a lot of people have written about, is how the stripping of the land in Appalachia is a kind of colonization. You know, postcolonial theory really does apply.

LS: Yeah, it does.

EAL: It's frightening.

LS: It is. And you know, it's continuing. It's just amazing.

EAL: Well I'm glad you went back to that, thank you. *Fair and Tender Ladies*—these were two questions that my students had: How do you pronounce Silvaney's name? Is it Sil-vain-ee?

LS: Yes, Sil-vain-ee. And actually, that's just a name that I had heard a lot, as a child.

EAL: And does Babe sexually abuse her?

LS: I think so.

EAL: I think so too, because she's so upset when he comes back.

LS: I don't think that Ivy knew it when she reported it, or understood it. It's just one of those instances where the narrator is telling what she can understand at that point.

EAL: I so enjoyed learning and reading about Lou Crabtree.

LS: Oh, she's *so* great.

EAL: I've ordered her book. I had not read it in the past. One person mentioned her to me, a year or two ago, but I didn't know the story. So anyway, it's on its way, and I can't wait.

LS: Great! I'm so glad. She was a person of such influence on me and so many, many other people. There's just nobody like her. She's just a really rich person.

EAL: Now was she like Ivy in that . . .

LS: Yeah, she's where I got the idea of someone who just simply writes for the love of it because it's necessary to keep her soul alive, you know, as a way to make it through the night. And it's writing, just purely for herself without any thought of publication. And that's what Lou was doing. When I first encountered her she had literally suitcases full of writing that she'd done all her life.

EAL: And was that the distinction for her between just writing and being a "real" writer? The publishing and not publishing, or was it something else?

LS: Well, yeah, it was almost typing and not typing [laughs]. She had not typed stuff up before, and we had to do that and Xerox them. I like to have everybody to be able to look at everything.

EAL: Sure.

LS: And she'd say, "Well that looks real good." [Laughs] "That looks real good, don't it?" I think it's also just letting other people read it is a big part of that and having more than just yourself looking at what you're writing.

EAL: One of the things I've always wondered about is the way Ivy signs her letters.

LS: Oh yeah, you mentioned that, and see, I wasn't aware of that until I read that, because I guess the way she signs them does have to do with her own concept of herself. And there's a difference when she's married and then gaining her sort of sense of selfhood back, and so I thought that was a very astute observation. I wasn't even thinking about it [laughs].

EAL: One part that really just knocked my socks off is after she runs off with Honey, she goes back to her maiden name.

LS: Yeah! I wasn't aware of that. Yeah.

EAL: And then she's Mama, and she's Mamaw.

LS: The book sort of took off, and I guess that's one reason that I loved it. It just, I didn't really have to write it, it was like I was just showing up, and that was the case with *On Agate Hill* too. That's the only two times that that's really happened to me. So I wasn't thinking through that. I was just writing whatever seemed to fit; it was like channeling, or something. I didn't think through that, that it had anything to do with her sense of identity, I have to say.

EAL: That's really interesting. I read in an interview that you said that she starts out with this very colloquial way of speaking and writing, and then as she reads more it becomes more standard, and then it kind of goes back to the way she was before.

LS: I was real struck by that. Because my dad, and a number of other people in my family, were really conscious of their language and had really tried to stop being so country. I mean, tried consciously to not use the double negatives and not do this and not do that. And it was real important to them. And then what I noticed with my dad in particular, and with most of them, was as they got older, they slipped back into what had more been the speech of their youth.

EAL: Why do you think that is?

LS: I absolutely don't know. I just noticed it, and I have since noticed it. It's like there's a kind of speech you adopt, it's almost like, it's not like it's fake, but you know that other people in other places will respect you more.

EAL: Oh, absolutely.

LS: And for business and for dealing with business, my dad would go up to Baltimore and buy toys and things from the makers, you know at the toy fair and stuff like that, and he didn't want to sound like a country guy. You know, a hillbilly. He dressed really well by that point, and he had made some money, and he just wanted to sound cultured and educated. And so I think you're conscious of it for a while, and then maybe when you sort of get older, and what you think people are thinking of you doesn't matter so much, maybe you just kind of let your guard down.

EAL: Yes, like a surer sense-of-self sort of thing, about what's important. And I love it when some of your characters get older, it's like, "Well, I'm old now, so I'm going to do what I want."

LS: I think that's what people do [laughs].

EAL: You had this other beautiful, wonderful quote about the Honey Breeding section which I love and adore.

LS: I am so glad. I have gotten more letters from these book clubs, saying, "Our book club was very much enjoying your book until we got to that section, and we just closed the book."

EAL: "Oh, get over yourself!" you should write back to them! It's the best thing in literature, as far as I'm concerned.

LS: [Laughs] Well you know, right now, this book is up for being banned and somebody is trying to ban it in Abington [Virginia] and the whole county, Washington County.

EAL: Oh, Lord have mercy.

LS: The school board has called for this review and wants all of my books taken out of the public schools.

EAL: Well, I guess that means you've arrived!

LS: It is because of that, because of *Fair and Tender Ladies*, and they said it "encourages adultery" and that it was written by a "literary pornographer."

EAL: My goodness.

LS: Yeah, I mean, twenty, twenty-five years ago when this was new, you know, that was one thing. But now? I mean, good Lord, these high school seniors can go right on the Internet or turn the TV on to any channel, you know?

EAL: Yes, Honey Breeding is very tame compared to a lot of things.

LS: I know!

EAL: I love the quote that you had in an interview about the reason, one of the reasons Ivy loves him so much is because of his freedom. And he represents that thing that she doesn't have. And you went on to talk about the mountains and the mountains as womb and geography and physiology together, and I'm really trying to work through this notion of Appalachia as a feminized place. In other people's views it's always been submissive. It's been the object of pity and outreach. And I wondered if you could talk a little bit more about that, either Ivy and her feminized ties or the mountains in general.

LS: Well that is really, really, really interesting. I mean, I think it has existed in people's minds as a sort of separate and enclosed space, and then there would be that outsider, the male, somebody with an agenda. Somebody coming in, like we were saying, the outsider, you know, except for the settlement ladies. But that's true, the notion of a place as something to be saved, something to come into sort of, you know, that is very interesting. I had never thought about it like that. I think that's really a fruitful sort of approach for you. I think it's great.

EAL: I'm glad. You know, since good old William Goodell Frost had his essay about "Our Contemporary Ancestors," everybody tried to make Appalachia sound like this fixed thing, to put it in its place sort of, much like that whole notion of womanhood. This is what a woman is; this is what she does.

LS: That's right.

EAL: Okay, I have one more question about *Fair and Tender Ladies*, and then I've got to ask you some things about *On Agate Hill*. You know when Joli wants the quilt from Ivy, did you get that idea from the Alice Walker short story ["Everyday Use"]?

LS: You know, no, but I have now read Alice Walker's short story, which is a fabulous short story, of course. No, I just, we had so many quilts all the time, and they were such a perfect symbol. You know, of the whole family and the whole place. Joli, of course wanted what she could have. I mean, she had left, but she wanted what she could take, what she could have.

EAL: No, I understand. That makes sense to me.

LS: And I always, I've got so many quilts here, and I always wanted them. And again, my mother never put them on beds.

EAL: Really?

LS: No, she had fancy bedspreads.

EAL: Oh, I see.

LS: [Laughs] There was also a lot of beautiful handmade furniture. Because in my dad's family, he had two uncles that were furniture makers, and this is great, their names were both Bill Smith, and one was called Near Bill, cause he lived close to town, and other one was Far Bill [laughs]. But my mother, as soon as they could afford to buy these fancy reproduction furniture from Williamsburg, and so on, that's what they had in their house. They really didn't have, I mean, they had saved a few things. Like I have a spinning wheel and a few things, but it was just really interesting. Anyway, go ahead.

EAL: Okay, these are just some plot questions that I'm dying to know. I've read *On Agate Hill* twice, and the first thing I wanted to tell you is all along I thought that Simon Black was Molly's biological father.

LS: Oh really?

EAL: Yeah, and then I got to his letter at the end, and I started this whole Faulknerian line of thought: Is he a reliable narrator? Are we supposed to trust his letter?

LS: I did mean that he is a reliable narrator and that we are to trust his letter. I guess that's a plotline that I sort of started the book with and then moved away from, that plotline of somebody who is so much in love with the mother that he then gets all psychologically involved with the daughter. He loves the daughter beginning with the mother, because that's a story that I found when I moved into this house in Hillsborough. Everybody came over; that's the story associated with this house.

EAL: Can you tell me about that?

LS: Yeah, it's a story of obsessive love and he fixates on the daughter because he could never have the mother, sort of. That's the way it translated into *On Agate Hill*, but the original story was more complicated, so it's all about that story, and it was sort of something that I started with. I don't know if I was clear enough, but that was where I started.

EAL: I think you were, and it's a good mystery too. The other thing I wanted to know was, does Simon Black have this sort of intimate relationship with Mariah Snow, before she ever meets Cinncinatus, or is that all in her head? I mean, is she just imagining it?

LS: [Laughs] I think she's nuts.

EAL: Okay, because I thought, "I really don't think we're supposed to trust Mariah, but *maybe*."

LS: No, we can't trust her [laughs].

EAL: Okay, and then one last plot question: Did BJ shoot Jacky?

LS: Yeah.

EAL: Okay, and that's the same whole want, can't have sort of thing, right? Okay, well, we got that cleared up.

LS: Yeah, he had been in love with Molly, I think all along. I mean, lots of people would like to have motive.

EAL: The thing that struck me about *On Agate Hill* is that it seems to be so much more a Southern book in terms of The South, as in capital letters, you know, than some of your other fiction. Juney is just so much like a Flannery O'Connor character to me.

LS: That's so funny to me! And I don't know, I never wrote about or was interested in the Civil War at all, ever before. And I guess that's about as Southern as you can get.

EAL: And the plantation house that's like Sutpen's Hundred, I just loved it. I wondered, was it a conscious thing, like "I'm going to write a book about the South?"

LS: No, it's just because I had just moved into this house. And it's a house right next door to the Civil War cemetery, and it has this legend associated with it. In the corner of my yard, literally, is the Orange county historical museum with all of the soldiers' diaries and stuff. You know, I just got interested.

EAL: Now can you tell me, just briefly, the legend?

LS: Yeah. It is that right after the Civil War, the real story is, right after the Civil War, there were two lawyers here in Hillsborough who fell in love with the same girl, and her name was Annie Gray. And she was from Tarboro, North Carolina. And one of the lawyers was this old, he may have been all of forty-five [laughs], he was this older guy and very sort of saturnine and not a pleasant person, Allen Ruffin, a lawyer. The other one was a war hero, named Sam Nash, who had walked home from the war. And his family owned an estate right here on Queen's Street named Pilgrim's Rest. And he came back to Pilgrim's Rest, to his family's farm and so on. And he fell in love with Annie Gray, and so did Allen Ruffin. So they would both go down to Tarboro and court her. And of course she picked the young, dashing hero, Sam Nash. And Allen Ruffin couldn't stand it, so he bought up this huge property right across from the family's house, Pilgrim's Rest, and he made additions to a little house on the property as close as possible to their house. So he lived right across from the young couple [laughs]. He just moved in literally, right across the road. I mean, it's not a hundred yards. And so that's my house, Allen Ruffin's house.

EAL: Oh, so you're living across the road from the young couple.

LS: Yeah! And when she had a daughter, a baby, who she also named Annie Gray, the story is that old Allen Ruffin went and knocked on the door and when she opened the door with babe in arms, he said, "If I could not have you my darling, then I shall have your daughter." Oooo . . . but then he did. When Annie Gray, the baby, was sixteen he married her.

EAL: Eww!

LS: I know, what were these people thinking? All of them, what in the hell were they thinking? And brought her across the street, and so she lived in my house. She had a child here in what is now the TV room, and that child was named Peter Brown Ruffin, and he grew up to become the United States ambassador to France. And so on, but Allen Ruffin died very soon after, or not long after his marriage, and so Annie Gray went down to Wilmington, sort of a geographic cure for heartbreak, you know, she went down there and the guy who owned Orton Plantation, which is the grandest plantation in North Carolina, fell in love with her, and she became the mistress of Orton Plantation.

EAL: My goodness.

LS: Peter Brown Ruffin grew up with a very fine education and so on and became this noted individual.

EAL: Wow. Well I'm really glad that Molly didn't marry Simon.

LS: No!

EAL: I think that concludes my questions for you; thank you again for making time to talk with me.

LS: I've enjoyed talking to you; send me a copy of what you come up with, especially the feminization of Appalachia part, okay?

EAL: I absolutely will, and thank you so much.

Epilogue

Stereotypes associating Appalachia with illiteracy have plagued the region for well over a century, yet the women writers in this project disrupt such cultural judgments by repeatedly encouraging readers to consider characters' multiple literacies, as well as the conflicts that accompany them. Though this project has highlighted what literacy proponents seldom acknowledge—the very real losses sometimes incurred through literacy acquisition—characters also clearly benefit by transitioning from one discourse community to another. If Harriette Simpson Arnow's protagonist never learns the power of negotiated identity, her readers do; after leaving home to pursue a secondary education, Linda Scott DeRosier questions the sexist system that governed (and to some extent still governs) much of Appalachia; new literacies allow Denise Giardina and *The Unquiet Earth*'s protagonist, Jackie, to write about social injustices; and literacy acquisition grants Lee Smith's characters in *Oral History* and *Fair and Tender Ladies* a voice fueled by literacy attainment.

Perhaps one of the most inspiring real-life examples of empowerment through new literacies occurs at the New Opportunity School for Women in Berea, Kentucky. As discussed at the beginning of this project, in many ways Berea College has been central in defining Appalachia to the rest of the nation, thanks in large part to president William Goodell Frost's publications, including "Our Contemporary Ancestors" in 1899. Frost was president of the college from 1892 until 1920, and roughly six decades later, John Stephenson served as president from 1984 until 1994. In 1987 John's wife, Jane Stephenson, founded the New Opportunity School for Women (NOSW), an organization that aims to "improv[e] the educational, financial, and personal circumstances of low-income, middle-aged women in Kentucky and the south central Appalachian region."[1] The NOSW website explains that twice a year fourteen low-income women from south-central Appalachia are selected to participate in a residential program at Berea College where they can choose from various classes, receive health-care services, and participate in community internships. The site boasts that "in the past 20 years, over 513 women have completed the school's three-week residential program," and a second location is in operation at Lees-McRae College in Banner Elk, North Carolina.

Like Frost and missionary groups from the earlier part of the century, founder Jane Stephenson is saddled with the same responsibility to raise money to support her efforts, but she goes about doing so in a much different way. Whereas earlier efforts to increase education levels in the mountains depicted Appalachians as in dire need of help, Stephenson instead openly discloses the difficult situations from which her students come, but she then focuses on their incredible achievements and on the positive changes that learning brings into their lives. Unlike past representations of mountain people that suggested an inherent degeneracy, Stephenson's promotional materials about the school make clear that life circumstances have created a hard existence for the women who attend her school, not some genetic or cultural deficiency.

Stephenson demonstrates this kind of respect clearly in her (1995) book *Courageous Paths: Stories of Nine Appalachian Women*, an edited collection of interviews from past NOSW students. Considered together, the women's stories included in the book tell a heartbreaking story of family illiteracy, alcohol and substance abuse, physical violence, poverty, dominating men, and shame. But the interviews also tell the stories of truly courageous women, women who were able to confront potentially debilitating circumstances, overcome them, and share with a larger audience the role that the NOSW played in transforming their lives.

As with the women discussed in this project, some—but notably, not all—of the women interviewed for Stephenson's collection experienced varying levels of resistance from family and community members when they expressed a desire to further their educations. One woman, Crystal, explains that her husband, Joe, "told [her] time and time again that he wants the old Crystal back. He can't accept this new one" (1995, 49). She goes on to lament, "That makes me very sad because the more I change I'm growing more away from him. I know my marriage is ending and I can't stop it. . . . My family, all of them—since I've started changing—say I'm just an outsider to all of them. I am not accepted by any of them" (49).

The information following the interview reveals that Joe and Crystal do eventually file for divorce, and Crystal's comment that her family "makes [her] feel guilty and it really hurts [her]" makes clear that this empowerment has come at a price (50). But like some of the women from Katherine Kelleher Sohn's study, Crystal also seems simultaneously excited and nervous about what lies ahead, reflecting that "the growing has begun and there's no stopping it. Whether I like it or not I can't stop it so I'm just going with the flow and see where I'll land" (50). A woman named Bea experiences a similar conflict with her husband, especially when she begins attending college classes after her experience at the NOSW, but he eventually supports her learning endeavors.

Unlike the women in Sohn's study, the women interviewed for Stephenson's collection openly discuss the conflicts that new literacies introduce into their lives after attending the NOSW and in some cases college, whereas the women in Sohn's study discuss such fears only before attending college. Without questioning each interviewee, we cannot know for certain why this is the case, but perhaps it has something to do with the fact that the women in Stephenson's book literally speak for themselves. At the end of the interviews Stephenson includes a section entitled "Interview Methods" where she explains that "all interviews with the nine women were tape recorded and later transcribed. . . . All interviews began with [her] talking to each woman about the book project and asking her for permission to tape her story for it. Each woman was told that she would have an opportunity to read her completed story and make any deletions or changes" (135).

While Sohn granted the same opportunity to the women in her study, her narrative voice, while respectful, framed her subjects' voices, and in Stephenson's collection this is not the case, with the exception of a brief preface by Stephenson and introduction by Kentucky poet laureate Gurney Norman. The authority to tell one's own story, outside of an academic frame, seems likely to have liberated these women to honestly chronicle both the perils and the empowerments of new literacies. Moreover, most of the interviews end on a positive, uplifting note, one meant to inspire any readers who feel that they might also benefit from attending the NOSW, as when Ada says: "I've got some stories to tell that are not so good, but maybe they'd help somebody else. I definitely want to help other people" (101).

Like Ada, other former NOSW students also want to advocate for the school to recruit women who might benefit from attending a session there. At the 2010 Appalachian Studies Association meeting, Jane Stephenson delivered the keynote address, alongside two former NOSW students. One of them, George Ann Greene Lakes, recounted her extraordinarily difficult childhood and early adult years, explaining the tremendous difference that the NOSW made in her life. She received her GED in 1992, her BA in social work in 1999, and her master's in social work in 2004, when she was sixty-one years old. I was so moved by George's story that I asked her if she would be willing to answer some of my questions about how her experiences at the NOSW affected her life, and she graciously agreed.

When asked about how her family reacted to her decision to attend college as an adult, George writes that her mother, "even today at 89 years of age, still believes that it is more appropriate for a man to have an education than a woman" (2010). Upon first consideration this statement seems at odds with the findings Anita Puckett reported in her 1992 article on gendered literacy practices in an Appalachian community, but education and frequency of literate practices are not necessarily synonymous activities. It seems that education, in the reference that George's mother makes, refers to a broad, often life-changing journey, whereas literate practices might involve a similar ideological shift or might not, depending on the circumstances in which they take place. According to George's mother, it is "more appropriate" for men to have an education than women, and according to Puckett, literate activities like letter writing and bill keeping are more appropriate for women than for men. These sentiments are not necessarily in conflict with one another since Puckett's findings also suggest that literate practices were sanctioned for women as long as they did not encourage learners to break from conventional gender norms.

As George writes, many women she knew were "expected to be the work horse for whomever might need us, mainly the men in our lives" (2010), but her experience at the NOSW changed that outlook, perhaps reconciling her mother's views on education and findings from Puckett's (1992) study: education often introduces new literacies that can and do change Appalachian women, often making them less willing to function within a male-dominated family system.

George also comments at length about the effect that reading Appalachian literature had on her self-esteem. She reflects, "The best part of going to NOSW was the rewarding experience of getting to know about the Appalachian Literature that Jane Stephenson taught us. The books she sent us before we ever got to the campus made me realize that I was more than just a 'second class citizen'" (2010). Similarly, in *Courageous Paths: Stories of Nine Appalachian Women*, former NOSW student Crystal discusses taking Appalachian literature with Gurney Norman at the school: "Here I was, ashamed of who I was and where I come from and here he is teaching classes on the same people from the same background—people that I was ashamed of being part of. After awhile, I felt proud—and not ashamed of where I come from" (Stephenson 1995, 47).

These comments not only illustrate the changes fiction can produce for real-life Appalachian women learners, but they also bridge the real and the fictional by demonstrating the power that Appalachian writers wield when depicting mountain people, especially those in search of new literacies. While this project has worked to highlight the often difficult conflicts that learning can produce for Appalachian women, the benefits are often immeasurable. As George writes near the end of her e-mail, she "never regretted a moment of it. Wow, what a trip for a woman who thought she was stupid and could not learn" (2010).

Notes

Introduction

1. These include: Purcell-Gates, *Other People's Words*; Powell, *The Anguish of Displacement*; Puckett, "Let the Girls Do the Spelling"; Sohn, *Whistlin' and Crowin' Women of Appalachia*; Webb-Sunderhaus, "A Family Affair"; Merrifield, *Life at the Margins*; and Donehower, Hogg, and Schell, *Rural Literacies*.

2. Shapiro, *Appalachia on Our Mind*; Batteau, *The Invention of Appalachia*; and Algeo, "Locals on Local Color."

3. To learn more about how Appalachians react to such pervasive stereotypying, see Billings, Norman, and Ledford, *Back Talk from Appalachia*; and Smith, *Strangers and Kin*.

4. Following the example set by Native American scholars, I use Native American and Indian interchangeably. I recognize that those from India generally claim the term Indian, but since many Native Americans self-identify as Indian, I use it here to also mean Native American.

5. Refer to the following to see a small sampling of what has been written about Indian boarding schools and their effects on Indian identity: Coleman, *American Indians*; Spack, *America's Second Tongue*; Child, *Boarding School Seasons*; Adams, *Education for Extinction*; Katanski, *Learning to Write "Indian"*; Cobb, *Listening to Our Grandmothers' Stories*; Lomawaima, *They Called It Prairie Light*; Stromberg, *American Indian Rhetorics of Survivance*; and Archuleta, Child, and Lomawaima, *Away from Home*.

6. According to Native American scholar Ruth Spack (*America's Second Tongue*), Zitkala-Ša attended a Yankton Agency day school, White's Institute, Santee Normal Training School, and Earlham College (144–45).

7. Geller and Evans, *The Appalachians*; to learn more about the African American presence in Appalachia, see Inscoe, *Appalachians and Race*; and Dunaway, *Slavery in the American Mountain South*.

8. A few of these include: Villanueva, *Bootstraps*; Lubrano; Welsch, *Those Winter Sundays*; Dews and Law, *This Fine Place so Far from Home*; Young, *Minor Re/Visions*; and Ryan and Sackrey, *Strangers in Paradise*.

Chapter One: Appalachia on Our Pages

1. For more information, see Hanna, "Representation and the Reproduction of Appalachian Space."

2. Appalachian literary scholar Elizabeth Engelhardt takes issue with the way Murfree's work has been used, "taken as fact by her contemporaries and later scholars, generalized to apply to all of Appalachia, and reduced to one or two repeatedly anthologized stories" (2003, 103). Engelhardt argues that while Murfree's stories do produce some regional stereotypes, they also help overturn those same notions, especially in her later work, which Engelhardt claims scholars often dismiss. To learn more, see *The Tangled Roots of Feminism, Environmentalism, and Appalachian Literature*.

3. "Another America," *48 Hours* (CBS, December 14, 1989).

4. Lewis, Johnson, and Askins, *Colonialism in Modern America*; and Cunningham, "Appalachianism and Orientalism."

5. Harvey Graff conducted a sociological study of the effects of literacy for industrialized workers in nineteenth-century Canada, concluding that workers oftentimes did not need to know how to read and write to complete job tasks; furthermore, learning to read and write generally failed to make any noticeable impact in workers' socioeconomic standing. For more, see Graff, *The Literacy Myth*; and Graff, *The Labyrinths of Literacy*.

6. Florida Slone is a locally well-known ballad singer and storyteller from Knott County, Kentucky. The Appalshop group filmed a documentary about her life titled *Homemade Tales: Songs and Sayings of Florida Slone*. To read a description or to order a copy, visit http://appalshop.org/store/index.php?main_page=product_info&products_id=256.

7. Freire and Macedo, *Literacy*; and Freire, *Pedagogy of the Oppressed*.

8. To learn more about the history of the hillbilly stereotype, see Harkins, *Hillbilly*; and Williamson, *Hillbillyland*; for a documentary that juxtaposes historical portrayals of hillbillies with reflections by mountain people, see Smith and Appalshop, *Strangers and Kin*.

9. To learn more about the Hindman Settlement School, see Stoddart, *Challenge and Change in Appalachia*; and Whisnant, *All That is Native and Fine*.

Chapter Two: Shaping Biscuit Dough and Rolling Out Steel

1. The abbreviation *TD* will be used to denote future references in this chapter to Harriette Simpson Arnow's *The Dollmaker*.

2. Arnow's maternal grandmother (Grandmother Denney) greatly resembles the portrayal of Gertie's mother in the novel. According to Eckley's (1974) biography, Grandmother Denney "did her best to make ladies out her granddaughters; and, while she lived, they wore fine tucked, lace-trimmed, stiffly starched underwear, kept their hair in curls, [and] sat often with books on their heads to make them straight" (21). Similar to these biographical facts, Arnow describes a scene in the novel in which Gertie's mother tortures her with "required" feminine garments appropriate for church attendance: "Her thighs, that could endure the jolting of a mule's back or long hours on the iron seat of the iron-wheeled mowing machine,

cried to her in church with unceasing agony at their confinement in the encircling bands of knitted or crocheted lace and tucks, all starched and ironed until each toothed edge seemed so much iron cutting into her sweating flesh" (63).

3. For more information, see Taylor, *Toxic Literacies*.

4. For more information, see Harkins, *Hillbilly*, 17; and Arnow, "On Being Harriette Arnow's Son."

5. For a more in-depth discussion of America's interest in mountain handicrafts and folkways, see Shapiro, *Appalachia on Our Mind*; and Whisnant, *All That Is Native and Fine*.

6. Gee makes it clear that this mastery must occur through acquisition, not learning (as he defines those terms). In short, "literacy (fluent control or mastery of a secondary Discourse) is a product of acquisition, not learning, that is, it requires exposure to models in natural, meaningful, and functional settings, and (overt) teaching is not liable to be very successful" (*Social Linguistics and Literacies*,144). For more information, see the sections titled "The Acquisition Principle" and "The Learning Principle" on pages 144 and 145.

7. It is worth noting here that while Purcell-Gates relies heavily on the theories of Gee in her work, she also accuses him of "discourse determinism," stating that theories based on discourse sometimes lock individuals into a pre-determined path, denying them the agency that exists in actuality. Instead, Purcell-Gates aligns her work more closely with that of Lisa Delpit, claiming that Delpit's research chronicles those who have gained a secondary discourse, almost despite a primary discourse (*Other People's Words*, 192).

Editors James Collins and Richard Blot similarly accuse Gee of denying the existence of agency within discourses. For more, see Collins and Blot, *Literacy and Literacies*, 105.

I argue that while Gee's treatment of discourse somewhat predetermines the way an individual operates in the world, that determination does not preclude individuals from gaining secondary discourses through acquisition.

8. To read one version of the tale, see Throne-Thomsen, *East O' the Sun and West O' the Moon*.

Chapter Three: Narrating Socialization

1. The abbreviation *CAWJ* will be used to denote future references in this chapter to Linda Scott DeRosier's *Creeker: A Woman's Journey*.

2. The abbreviation *SLG* will be used to denote future references in this chapter to Linda Scott DeRosier's *Songs of Life and Grace*.

3. For more information about the differences and similarities between Decoration Day and Memorial Day celebrations in mountain communities, see Jabbour and Jabbour, *Decoration Day in the Mountains*.

4. Namely, Harriette Simpson Arnow's Miss Whittle; Denise Giardina's depiction of Rachel's nursing teacher, Miss Kurtz; and Lee Smith's Richard Burlage and Miss Torrington.

5. Many development experts have theorized about why young women sometimes discredit their own knowledge. To learn more about this phenomenon, consult the following texts as starting points for further research: Gilligan, Lyons, and Hanmer, *Making Connections*; and Gilligan, Rogers, and Tolman, *Women, Girls, and Psychotherapy*.

Chapter Four: "Overcoming Backgrounds"

1. To learn more about the Battle of Blair Mountain, see Shogan, *The Battle of Blair Mountain*; Corbin, *Life, Work, and Rebellion in the Coal Fields*; the second episode of the public television series by Geller and Evans, *The Appalachians*; and the History Channel's film by Moore Huntley Productions et al., *Hillbilly the Real Story*. To learn more about the Buffalo Creek Disaster, see Erikson, *Everything in Its Path*; Stern, *The Buffalo Creek Disaster*; and Pickering and Appalshop Films, *The Buffalo Creek Flood an Act of Man*.

2. The abbreviation *TUE* will be used to denote future references in this chapter to Denise Giardina's *The Unquiet Earth*.

3. During our (2007) interview I asked Giardina, "Given the pervasive stereotypes about Appalachian incest, what was your purpose in making [Rachel and Dillon] relatives?" She responded: "I didn't have any choice because I had already made them cousins at the end of *Storming Heaven*, when I didn't have any intention of writing about them, or of having them fall in love. And it was in print. So once that was the case, I was forced to deal with it. I really resisted it for a long time. But finally I realized I shouldn't let the stereotype keep me from writing the book. And it was the stereotype which finally killed their relationship. I didn't think it should kill my book too. I also really resented that Jane Austen could suggest Mr. Darcy marry his first cousin without batting an eye, and yet I wasn't supposed to have my characters have a relationship. Talk about a double standard."

4. Like the fictional characters of Carrie and Rachel, Giardina's mother also worked as a nurse. To read more about her family, see Giardina, "Appalachian Images."

5. To read a largely positive history of the Lum and Abner program, see Hall, *Lum and Abner*.

6. Southern and Appalachian literature depicting strong connections with the earth abound, but to read one that aligns especially well with Rachel's description of Granny Combs, see Rash's *One Foot in Eden*.

7. For her treatment of the Moffett and larger literacy issues, see Donehower, Hogg, and Schell, *Rural Literacies*.

8. To listen to a 1949 audio recording of one version of "Big Toe," visit this website: "Digital Library of Appalachia," http://www.aca-dla.org/; To read a written version of that same story, see Roberts, *South from Hell-fer-Sartin*.

Chapter Five: Invasion of the Mountain Teachers

1. For an interesting take on the created literary persona of James Still, see Crum, "Constructing a Marketable Writer." Crum argues that the reading public's conception of Still as a romanticized rugged mountaineer was more fiction than fact, and Crum suggests that Still purposely emphasized and marketed his role as an isolated Appalachian author, even though he was quite worldly.

2. The abbreviation *OH* will be used to denote future references in this chapter to Lee Smith's *Oral History*.

3. The abbreviation *FTL* will be used to denote future references in this chapter to Lee Smith's *Fair and Tender Ladies*.

Epilogue

1. "New Opportunity School for Women," http://www.nosw.org.

Works Cited

A Hidden America: Children of the Mountains. 2009. *20/20*, hosted by Diane Sawyer. CBS. February 10.

Adams, David Wallace. 1995. *Education for Extinction: American Indians and the Boarding School Experience, 1875–1928*. Lawrence: University Press of Kansas.

Alderman, L. R. 1927. "Buncombe County's Excellent Work for Adult Illiterates." *School Life: Organ of the United States Bureau of Education, Department of the Interior* 12 (9): 176–79.

Algeo, Katie. 2003. "Locals on Local Color: Imagining Identity in Appalachia." *Southern Cultures* 9 (4): 27–54.

"Another America." 1989. *48 Hours*. CBS. December 14.

Archuleta, Margaret L., Brenda J. Child, and K. Tsianina Lomawaima, eds. 2004. *Away from Home: American Indian Boarding School Experiences, 1879–2000*. 2nd ed. Phoenix, AZ: Heard Museum.

Arnold, Edwin T. 1984."An Interview with Lee Smith." *Appalachian Journal* 11 (3): 240–54.

Arnow, Harriette Simpson. 2003. *The Dollmaker*. New York: Perennial. First published 1954.

Arnow, Pat. 2001. "Lee Smith: An Interview." In *Conversations with Lee Smith*, edited by Linda Tate, 57–64. Jackson: University Press of Mississippi.

Arnow, Thomas L. 2005. "On Being Harriette Arnow's Son." *Appalachian Journal* 32 (4): 460–67.

Bakhtin, M. M. 1986. *Speech Genres and Other Late Essays*. Edited by Caryl Emerson and Michael Holquist. Translated by Vern W. McGee. Austin: University of Texas Press.

Baldwin, Yvonne Honeycutt. 2006. *Cora Wilson Stewart and Kentucky's Moonlight Schools: Fighting for Literacy in America*. Lexington: University Press of Kentucky.

Bassard, Katherine Clay. 1992. "Gender and Genre: Black Women's Autobiography and the Ideology of Literacy." *African American Review* 26, no. 1 (Spring): 119–29.

Batteau, Allen. 1990. *The Invention of Appalachia*. Tucson: University of Arizona Press.

Billings, Dwight B., Gurney Norman, and Katherine Ledford, eds. 2000. *Back Talk from Appalachia: Confronting Stereotypes*. Lexington: University Press of Kentucky.

Bjerre, Thomas Ærvold. 2007. "The Natural World is the Most Universal of Languages: An Interview with Ron Rash." *Appalachian Journal* 34 (2): 216–27.

Bourdieu, Pierre. 1984. *Distinction: A Social Critique of the Judgement of Taste*. Translated by Richard Nice. Cambridge, MA: Harvard University Press.

Brandt, Deborah. 1990. *Literacy as Involvement: The Acts of Writers, Readers, and Texts*. Carbondale: Southern Illinois University Press.

———. 2001. *Literacy in American Lives*. Cambridge: Cambridge University Press.

Bridwell-Bowles, Lillian. 1997. *Identity Matters: Rhetorics of Difference*. Upper Saddle River, NJ: Prentice Hall.

Broughton, Irv. 2001. "Lee Smith." In *Conversations with Lee Smith*, edited by Linda Tate, 78–91. Jackson: University Press of Mississippi.

Byrd, Linda J. 2001. "The Reclamation of the Feminine Divine: 'Walking in My Body Like a Queen' in Lee Smith's *Fair and Tender Ladies*." In *He Said, She Says: An RSVP to the Male Text*, edited by Micha Howe and Sarah Appleton Aguiar, 42–56. Madison: Fairleigh Dickinson University Press.

Cattell, James McKeen, ed. 1932. *Leaders in Education: A Biographical Directory*. New York: Science Press.

Child, Brenda J. 1998. *Boarding School Seasons: American Indian Families, 1900-1940*. Lincoln: University of Nebraska Press.

Christmas in Appalachia. 1964. CBS. Hosted by Charles Kuralt. December 21.

Chung, Haeja K. 1995. "Harriette Simpson Arnow's Authorial Testimony: Toward a Reading of *The Dollmaker*." *Critique* 36 (3): 211–23.

Clabough, Casey. 2007. "The Imagined South." *Sewanee Review* 115 (2): 301–7.

Cobb, Amanda J. 2000. *Listening to Our Grandmothers' Stories: The Bloomfield Academy for Chickasaw Females, 1852–1949*. Lincoln: University of Nebraska Press.

Coleman, Michael C. 2007. *American Indians, the Irish, and Government Schooling: A Comparative Study*. Lincoln: University of Nebraska Press.

Collins, James, and Richard K. Blot. 2003. *Literacy and Literacies: Texts, Power, and Identity*. Cambridge, UK: Cambridge University Press.

Corbin, David. 1981. *Life, Work, and Rebellion in the Coal Fields: The Southern West Virginia Miners, 1880–1922*. Urbana: University of Illinois Press.

Crum, Claude Lafie. 2005. "Constructing a Marketable Writer: James Still's Fictional Persona." *Appalachian Journal* 32 (4): 430–39.

Cunningham, Rodger. 1989. "Appalachianism and Orientalism: Reflections on Reading Edward Said." *Journal of the Appalachian Studies Association* 1:125–32.

Day, Della M. 1933. "Buncombe County Night Schools Carry On." *Mountain Life and Work, Council of the Southern Mountains* 9, no. 1 (April): 7–11.

———. 1938. "The History of the Adult Education Movement in North Carolina." North Carolina Collection, Pack Memorial Library.

Denning, Michael. 1996. *The Cultural Front: The Laboring of American Culture in the Twentieth Century*. London: Verso.

DeRosier, Linda Scott. 1999. *Creeker: A Woman's Journey*. Lexington: University Press of Kentucky.

———. 2003. *Songs of Life and Grace*. Lexington: University Press of Kentucky.

———. 2007. Phone interview with author, March 2.

Dews, C. L. Barney, and Carolyn Leste Law, eds. 1995. *This Fine Place so Far from Home: Voices of Academics from the Working Class*. Philadelphia: Temple University Press.

"Digital Library of Appalachia." http://www.aca-dla.org/.

Donehower, Kim, Charlotte Hogg, and Eileen E. Schell. 2007. *Rural Literacies*. Edited by Robert Brooke. Carbondale: Southern Illinois University Press.

Douglass, Frederick. 1960. *Narrative of the Life of Frederick Douglass, an American Slave*. Edited by Benjamin Quarles. Cambridge, MA: Belknap Press of Harvard University Press. First published in 1845.

Douglass, Thomas. 1993. "Interview: Denise Giardina." *Appalachian Journal* 20 (4): 384–93.

———. 2006. "Denise Giardina: Resurrecting the Dead, Recognizing the Human: Interview by Thomas Douglass (1998)." In *Appalachia and Beyond: Conversations with Writers from the Mountain South*, edited by John Lang, 241–58. Knoxville: University of Tennessee Press.

Dunaway, Wilma A. 2003. *Slavery in the American Mountain South*. Cambridge: Cambridge University Press.

Eckard, Paula Gallant. 1995. "The Prismatic Past in Oral History and Mama Day." *MELUS* 20 (3): 121–35.

Eckley, Wilton. 1974. *Harriette Arnow*. New York: Twayne Publishers.

Egan, Marcia. 1993. "Women: The Path from the 'Hollows' to Higher Education." *Affilia* 8 (3): 265–76.

Eldred, Janet Carey. 1991. "Narratives of Socialization: Literacy in the Short Story." *College English* 53 (6): 686–700.

Eldred, Janet Carey, and Peter Mortensen. 1992. "Reading Literacy Narratives." *College English* 54 (5): 512–39.

Emerson, Miss D. E. 1883. "Bureau of Woman's Work: The Paper Mission and What Came of It." *The American Missionary* 37, no. 10 (October): 310–12.

Engelhardt, Elizabeth Sanders Delwiche. 2003. *The Tangled Roots of Feminism, Environmentalism, and Appalachian Literature.* Athens: Ohio University Press.

———. 2005. *Beyond Hill and Hollow: Original Readings in Appalachian Women's Studies.* Athens: Ohio University Press.

Erikson, Kai T. 1978. *Everything in Its Path: Destruction of Community in the Buffalo Creek Flood.* New York: Simon & Schuster.

Fetterley, Judith, and Marjorie Pryse. 2003. *Writing Out of Place: Regionalism, Women, and American Literary Culture.* Urbana: University of Illinois Press.

Fishman, Andrea. 1990. "Becoming Literate: A Lesson from the Amish." In *The Right to Literacy*, edited by Andrea A. Lunsford, Helene Moglen, and James Slevin, 29–38. New York: Modern Language Association of America.

Flexner, Hortense. 1919. "Are You Too Old to Learn?." *Red Cross Magazine*.

Foley, Barbara. 1993. *Radical Representations: Politics and Form in U.S. Proletarian Fiction, 1929–1941.* Durham, NC: Duke University Press.

Foote, Stephanie. 2001. *Regional Fictions: Culture and Identity in Nineteenth-Century American Literature.* Madison: University of Wisconsin Press.

Frazier, Charles. 1998. *Cold Mountain: A Novel.* 1997 New York: Vintage Books.

Freire, Paulo. 1970. *Pedagogy of the Oppressed.* New York: Continuum.

Freire, Paulo, and Donaldo Pereira Macedo. 1987. *Literacy: Reading the Word and the World.* Westport, CT: Greenwood Publishing.

Frost, William Goodell. 1899. "Our Contemporary Ancestors in the Southern Mountains." *The Atlantic Monthly* 83, no. 497 (March): 311–20.

Furman, Lucy S. 1923. *The Quare Women: A Story of the Kentucky Mountains.* Boston: Atlantic Monthly Press.

———. 1926. *The Glass Window: A Story of the Quare Women.* Boston: Little, Brown.

Gee, James Paul. 1996. *Social Linguistics and Literacies: Ideology in Discourses.* 2nd ed. London: Taylor & Francis.

Geller, Phylis, and Mari-Lynn C. Evans. 2005. *The Appalachians.* DVD. Home Video Ltd.

Giardina, Denise. 1992. *The Unquiet Earth.* New York: Ivy Books.

———. 1998. "No Scapin the Booger Man." In *Bloodroot: Reflections on Place* by *Appalachian Women Writers*, edited by Joyce Dyer, 128–31. Lexington: University Press of Kentucky.

———. 1999. "Appalachian Images: A Personal History." In *Back Talk from Appalachia: Confronting Stereotypes*, edited by Dwight Billings, Gurney Norman, and Katherine Ledford, 161–73. Lexington: University Press of Kentucky.

———. 2007. E-mail interview with author. "Re: Questions about The Unquiet Earth," August 26.

Gilligan, Carol, Nona P. Lyons, and Trudy J. Hanmer, eds. 1990. *Making Connections: The Relational Worlds of Adolescent Girls at Emma Willard School*. Cambridge: Harvard University Press.

Gilligan, Carol, Annie G. Rogers, and Deborah L. Tolman, eds. 1991. *Women, Girls, and Psychotherapy: Reframing Resistance*. New York: Haworth Press.

Graff, Harvey J. 1979. *The Literacy Myth: Literacy and Social Structure in the Nineteenth-Century City*. New York: Academic Press.

Gray, Katie, Dare Cook, Ashley Crabtree, Aaron Davis, and Michael Troy. 2006. "'It's Not a Job to Me': Mike Mullins and the Hindman Settlement School." *Appalachian Journal* 33 (3–4): 310–42.

Green, Chris. 2009. *The Social Life of Poetry: Appalachia, Race, and Radical Modernism*. Palgrave Macmillan.

Hall, Randal L. 2007. *Lum and Abner: Rural America and the Golden Age of Radio*. Lexington: University Press of Kentucky.

Hamilton, Sharon J. 1995. *My Name's Not Susie: A Life Transformed by Literacy*. Portsmouth, NH: Boynton/Cook.

Hanna, Stephen P. 2000. "Representation and the Reproduction of Appalachian Space: A History of Contested Signs and Meanings." *Historical Geography* 28: 179–207.

Harkins, Anthony. 2004. *Hillbilly: A Cultural History of an American Icon*. New York: Oxford University Press.

Harney, Will Wallace. 1873. "A Strange Land and a Peculiar People." *Lippincott's Magazine* 12 (October): 429–38.

Heath, Shirley Brice. 1983. *Ways with Words: Language, Life, and Work in Communities and Classrooms*. Cambridge, MA: Cambridge University Press.

———. 2001. "Protean Shapes in Literacy Events: Ever-Shifting Oral and Literate Traditions." In *Literacy: A Critical Sourcebook*, edited by Ellen Cushman, Eugene R. Kintgen, Barry M. Kroll, and Mike Rose, 443–66. Boston: Bedford/St. Martin's.

Henninger, Katherine. 2007. *Ordering the Facade: Photography and*

Contemporary Southern Women's Writing. Chapel Hill: University of North Carolina Press.

Hobson, Fred. 1991. *The Southern Writer in the Postmodern World*. Athens: University of Georgia Press.

Hoganson, Kristin L. 2007. *Consumers' Imperium: The Global Production of American Domesticity, 1865–1920*. Chapel Hill: University of North Carolina Press.

hooks, bell. 2000. *Where We Stand: Class Matters*. New York: Routledge.

Hsiung, David C. 1997. *Two Worlds in the Tennessee Mountains: Exploring the Origins of Appalachian Stereotypes*. Lexington: University Press of Kentucky.

Inscoe, John C. 2001. *Appalachians and Race: The Mountain South from Slavery to Segregation*. Lexington: University Press of Kentucky.

Jabbour, Alan, and Karen Singer Jabbour. 2010. *Decoration Day in the Mountains: Traditions of Cemetery Decoration in the Southern Appalachians*. Chapel Hill: University of North Carolina Press.

Jacobs, Harriet A. 2000. *Incidents in the Life of a Slave Girl*. Enl. ed. Cambridge, MA: Harvard University Press. First published 1861.

Jones, Anne Goodwyn. 1983. "The World of Lee Smith." *Southern Quarterly: A Journal of the Arts in the South* 22 (1): 115–39.

Jones, Suzanne W. 1987. "City Folks in Hoot Owl Holler: Narrative Strategy in Lee Smith's *Oral History*." *The Southern Literary Journal* 20 (1): 101–12.

Jordan, Rebecca. 2010. "DeRosier Info." E-mail, August 6.

Katanski, Amelia V. 2007. *Learning to Write "Indian": The Boarding School Experience and American Indian Literature*. Norman: University of Oklahoma Press.

Kennedy, Rory, and Moxie Films. 1999. *American Hollow*. Home Box Office.

Kephart, Horace. 1913. *Our Southern Highlanders*. New York: Outing Publishing.

Kristeva, Julia. 1984. *Revolution in Poetic Language*. Translated by Margaret Waller. New York: Columbia University Press.

Lakes, George Ann Greene. 2010. E-mail correspondence with author, August 2.

Lawson, Willie. 1924. Letter, September 9. North Carolina Collection, Pack Memorial Library.

Lenski, Lois. 1959. *Coal Camp Girl*. Philadelphia: J. B. Lippincott.

Lewis, Helen Matthews, Linda Johnson, and Donald Askins. 1978. *Colonialism in Modern America: The Appalachian Case*. Boone: Appalachian Consortium Press.

Lomawaima, K. Tsianina. 1994. *They Called It Prairie Light: The Story of Chilocco Indian School*. Lincoln: University of Nebraska Press.

Lubrano, Alfred. 2004. *Limbo: Blue-Collar Roots, White-Collar Dreams*. Hoboken, NJ: Wiley.

McDonald, Jeanne. 2001. "Lee Smith at Home in Appalachia." In *Conversations with Lee Smith*, edited by Linda Tate, 178–88. Jackson: University Press of Mississippi.

Merrifield, Juliet, Mary Beth Bingman, David Hemphill, and Kathleen P. Bennett deMarrais. 1997. *Life at the Margins: Literacy, Language, and Technology in Everyday Life*. New York: Teachers College Press.

Moffett, James. 1988. *Storm in the Mountains: A Case Study of Censorship, Conflict, and Consciousness*. Carbondale: Southern Illinois University Press.

Moore Huntley Productions, New Video Group, History Channel (Television network), and Arts and Entertainment Network. 2007. *Hillbilly: the Real Story*. Moore Huntley Productions for the History Channel, A&E Television Networks.

Morgan, Thomas. 1890. "Which Should have the Best Chance for Education Indian Boys or Girls?." *Indian Helper*, January 17.

Morriss, Elizabeth Cleveland. 1927. *Citizens' Reference Book: A Textbook for Adult Beginners in Community Schools*. Chapel Hill: University of North Carolina Press.

Mortensen, Peter. 1994. "Representations of Literacy and Region: Narrating 'Another America.'" In *Pedagogy in the Age of Politics*, edited by Patricia A. Sullivan and Donna J. Qualley, 100–120. Urbana, IL: National Council of Teachers of English.

———. 1999. "Figuring Illiteracy: Rustic Bodies and Unlettered Minds in Rural America." In *Rhetorical Bodies*, edited by Jack Selzer and Sharon Crowley, 143–70. Madison: University of Wisconsin Press.

Myers, Miles. 1996. *Changing Our Minds: Negotiating English and Literacy*. Urbana, IL: National Council of Teachers of English.

"New Opportunity School for Women." http://www.nosw.org.

O'Brien, John. 2001. *At Home in the Heart of Appalachia*. New York: Alfred A. Knopf.

Offutt, Chris. 1992. *Kentucky Straight*. New York: Vintage Contemporaries.

———. 2002. *No Heroes*. New York: Simon & Schuster.

Olney, James. 1984. "'I Was Born': Slave Narratives, Their Status as Autobiography and as Literature." *Callaloo* 20:46–73.

Olsen, Tillie. 1978. *Silences*. New York: Delacorte Press/Seymour Lawrence.

Parrish, Nancy C. 1994. "'Ghostland': Tourism in Lee Smith's Oral History." *Southern Quarterly* 32 (2): 37–47.
Pickering, Mimi, and Appalshop Films. 2006. *The Buffalo Creek Flood: An Act of Man / Buffalo Creek Revisited*. Appalshop.
Powell, Douglas Reichert. 2007. "'Bluewashing' the Mountaineer: A Recent Television Trend." *Appalachian Journal* 34 (2): 206–15.
Powell, Katrina M. 2007. *The Anguish of Displacement: The Politics of Literacy In the Letters of Mountain Families in Shenandoah National Park*. Charlottesville: University of Virginia Press.
Puckett, Anita. 1992. "Let the Girls Do the Spelling and Dan Will Do the Shooting: Literacy, the Division of Labor, and Identity in a Rural Appalachian Community." *Anthropological Quarterly* 65, no. 3 (July): 137–47.
Pudup, Mary Beth, Dwight B. Billings, and Altina L. Waller, eds. 1995. "Taking Exception with Exceptionalism: The Emergence and Transformation of Historical Studies of Appalachia." In *Appalachia in the Making: The Mountain South in the Nineteenth Century*, 1–24. Chapel Hill: University of North Carolina Press.
Purcell-Gates, Victoria, ed. 1995. *Other People's Words: The Cycle of Low Literacy*. Cambridge, MA: Harvard University Press.
———. 2007. *Cultural Practices of Literacy: Case Studies of Language, Literacy, Social Practice, and Power*. Mahwah, N.J: Lawrence Erlbaum Associates.
Qoyawayma, Polingaysi (Elizabeth Q. White), and Vada F. Carlson. 1964. *No Turning Back: A True Account of a Hopi Indian Girl's Struggle to Bridge the Gap Between the World of Her People and the World of the White Man*. Albuquerque: University of New Mexico Press.
Rash, Ron. *One Foot in Eden: A Novel*. Charlotte, NC: Novello Festival Press.
Reid, Herbert. 2003. "From the Director." *Appalachian Center News*, April.
———. 2007. E-mail. "Re: A Quick Question," August 7.
Robbins, Dorothy Dodge. 1997. "Personal and Cultural Transformation: Letter Writing in Lee Smith's Fair and Tender Ladies." *Critique* 38 (2): 135–44.
Robbins, Sarah. 2004. *Managing Literacy, Mothering America: Women's Narratives on Reading and Writing in the Nineteenth Century*. Pittsburgh: University of Pittsburgh Press.
Roberts, Leonard W. 1955. *South from Hell-fer-Sartin: Kentucky Mountain Folktales*. Lexington: University Press of Kentucky.
Rodriguez, Richard. 1983. *Hunger of Memory: The Education of Richard Rodriguez: An Autobiography*. New York: Bantam.
Rose, Mike. 1989. *Lives on the Boundary: The Struggles and Achievements of America's Underprepared*. New York: Free Press.

Royster, Jacqueline Jones. 2000. *Traces of a Stream: Literacy and Social Change Among African American Women*. Pittsburgh: University of Pittsburgh Press.

Rubin, Rachel Lee. 1998. "'My Country Is Kentucky': Leaving Appalachia in Harriette Arnow's *The Dollmaker*." In *Women, America, and Movement: Narratives of Relocation*, edited by Susan L. Roberson, 176–89. Columbia: University of Missouri Press.

Ryan, Jake, and Charles Sackrey, eds. 1995. *Strangers in Paradise: Academics from the Working Class*. Lanham, MD: University Press of America.

Schafer, William J. 1986. "Carving Out a Life: The Dollmaker Revisited." *Appalachian Journal* 14 (1): 46–50.

Semple, Ellen Churchill. 1995. "The Anglo-Saxons of the Kentucky Mountains: A Study in Anthropogeography." In *Appalachian Images in Folk and Popular Culture*, 146–74. Knoxville: University of Tennessee Press.

Shapiro, Henry D. 1978. *Appalachia on Our Mind: The Southern Mountains and Mountaineers in the American Consciousness, 1870–1920*. Chapel Hill: University of North Carolina Press.

Shogan, Robert. 2004. *The Battle of Blair Mountain: The Story of America's Largest Labor Uprising*. Boulder, CO: Westview Press.

Slone, Anthony, and Mary Angelyn DeBord. 1993. *Homemade Tales: Songs and Sayings of Florida Slone*. http://appalshop.org/store/index.php?main_page=product_info&cPath=44&products_id=256.

Smith, Herby, and Appalshop, Inc. 1984. *Strangers and Kin*. Appalshop.

Smith, Lee. 1983. *Oral History*. New York: Ballantine.

———. 1988. *Fair and Tender Ladies*. New York: Putnam.

———. 1998. "Terrain of the Heart." In *Bloodroot: Reflections on Place by Appalachian Women Writers*, edited by Joyce Dyer, 277–81. Lexington: University Press of Kentucky.

———. 2000. *Sitting on the Courthouse Bench: An Oral History of Grundy, Virginia*. With Grundy high school students. Chapel Hill, NC: Tryon Publishing.

———. 2006. *On Agate Hill*. Chapel Hill: Algonquin Books of Chapel Hill, 2006.

———. 2007. Phone interview with author, October 24.

———. 2008. "Dancing with the One That Brung You." *Appalachian Journal* 35 (4): 310–17.

Smith, Rebecca. 1994. "A Conversation with Lee Smith." *Southern Quarterly* 32 (2): 19–29.

Smith, Virginia A. 2001. "On Regionalism, Women's Writing, and Writing as a

Woman: A Conversation with Lee Smith." In *Conversations with Lee Smith*, edited by Linda Tate, 65–77. Jackson: University Press of Mississippi.

Sohn, Katherine Kelleher. 2006. *Whistlin' and Crowin' Women of Appalachia: Literacy Practices Since College*. Carbondale: Southern Illinois University Press.

Spack, Ruth. 2002. *America's Second Tongue: American Indian Education and the Ownership of English, 1860–1900*. Lincoln: University of Nebraska Press.

Standing Bear, Luther. 1928. *My People the Sioux*. Lincoln: University of Nebraska Press.

Stephenson, Jane B. 1995. *Courageous Paths: Stories of Nine Appalachian Women*. Berea, KY: New Opportunity School for Women.

Stern, Gerald M. 1976. *The Buffalo Creek Disaster: The Story of the Survivors' Unprecedented Lawsuit*. New York: Random House.

Stewart, Cora Wilson. 1922. *Moonlight Schools for the Emancipation of Adult Illiterates*, New York: E. P. Dutton.

Still, James. 1978. *River of Earth*. Lexington: University Press of Kentucky. First published 1940.

Stoddart, Jess. 2002. *Challenge and Change in Appalachia: The Story of Hindman Settlement School*. Lexington: University Press of Kentucky.

Stromberg, Ernest, ed. 2006. *American Indian Rhetorics of Survivance: Word Medicine, Word Magic*. Pittsburgh, PA: University of Pittsburgh Press.

Taylor, Denny. 1996. *Toxic Literacies: Exposing the Injustice of Bureaucratic Texts*. Portsmouth, NH: Heinemann.

Thompson, Tommy R. 1993. "The Image of Appalachian Kentucky in American Popular Magazines." *Register of the Kentucky Historical Society* 91:176–202.

Throne-Thomsen, Gudrun. 1912. *East O' the Sun and West O' the Moon with Other Norwegian Folk Tales*. Chicago: Row, Peterson.

Villanueva, Victor. 1993. *Bootstraps: From an American Academic of Color*. Urbana, IL: National Council of Teachers of English.

Vincent, David. 2003. "Literacy Literacy." *Interchange* 34 (2): 341–57.

Webb-Sunderhaus, Sara. 2007. "A Family Affair: Competing Sponsors of Literacy in Appalachian Students' Lives." *Community Literacy Journal* 2, no. 1 (Fall): 5–24.

Weller, Jack E. 1965. *Yesterday's People; Life in Contemporary Appalachia*. Lexington: University of Kentucky Press.

Welsch, Kathleen A. 2004. *Those Winter Sundays: Female Academics and Their Working-Class Parents*. Illustrated edition. Lanham, MD: University Press of America.

Whisnant, David E. 1983. *All That Is Native and Fine: The Politics of Culture in an American Region*. Chapel Hill: University of North Carolina Press.

Williams, Cratis D. 1976. "The Southern Mountaineer in Fact and Fiction: Part IV." *Appalachian Journal* 3 (4): 334–92.

Williams, John Alexander. 2002. *Appalachia: A History*. Chapel Hill: University of North Carolina Press.

Williamson, J. W. 1995. *Hillbillyland: What the Movies Did to the Mountains and What the Mountains Did to the Movies*. Chapel Hill: University of North Carolina Press.

Young, Morris. 2004. *Minor Re/Visions: Asian American Literacy Narratives as a Rhetoric of Citizenship*. Carbondale: Southern Illinois University Press.

Zitkala-Ša. 1921. *American Indian Stories*. Lincoln: University of Nebraska Press.

Index

Adams, David Wallace, 8–9
African American literacies, 15–18
Alderman, L.R., 44
American Indian Stories, 9–10
American Missionary Association, 17, 44, 150
Appalachian exceptionalism, 4
Appalachia; and whiteness, 17–18; media portrayals of, 27–28, 143, 145–48, 164–69; and ethnicity, 71–73; and vernacular and dialect, 101–6, 109, 130, 132–33, 141; being Appalachian, 165; pronunciation of, 102; and orality, 160–64
Arnold, Edwin T. 210
Arnow, Harriette Simpson, 3, 13, 25, 50, 51, 53–54, 56–91
Arnow, Pat, 205, 210

Bakhtin, Mikhail, 112
Baldwin, Yvonne Honeycutt, 31–35, 44, 48, 152
Bassard, Katherine Clay, 16
Batteau, Allen, 4, 26
Billings, Dwight, 4
Black Mountain Breakdown, 143, 174
Blot, Richard, 6, 104
Brandt, Deborah, 5, 58, 62
Bourdieu, Pierre, 78, 111, 117, 202
Bridwell-Bowles, Lillian, 123
Byrd, Linda, 204

Child, Lydia Maria, 15
Chung, Haeja, 82, 88
Clabough, Casey, 53
Coal Camp Girl, 142
Collins, James, 6, 104
commodification; of literacy, see literacy; of whittling, 84–87
Courageous Paths: Stories of Nine Appalachian Women, 230–33
Crabtree, Lou, 211
Creeker: A Woman's Journey, 27, 50, 54, 92–141
cultural capital, 78, 81, 117, 146, 152, 170
Cunningham, Rodger, 28

Day, Della 35–48
Decoration Day, 99
Denning, Michael, 58
DeRosier, Linda Scott, 3, 10, 11, 13, 19, 25, 27, 28, 48–51, 54, 92–141, 156, 165, 172, 173, 181, 192–94; interview with, 127–41
Discourse communities, 5–6
Donehower, Kim, 6, 160
Douglass, Frederick, 15

Eckard, Paula Gallant, 189
Eckley, Wilton, 56, 57, 59, 61, 66
Egan, Marcia, 49
Eldred, Janet Carey, 50, 52, 94–95, 111–14, 125, 144

Eller, Ronald, 154
Engelhardt, Elizabeth, 155, 236

Fair and Tender Ladies, 10, 19, 49, 51, 55, 111, 161, 174–211
Fetterley, Judith, 25
Fisher, Dexter, 10
Fishman, Andrea, 50–51, 81
Flexner, Hortnese, 31
Foley, Barbara, 59
Foote, Stephanie, 25
Fox Jr., John, 4, 24
Freire, Paulo, 14, 34, 49, 58, 75, 80–81, 98
Frost, William Goodell, 26–28, 32, 164–65, 186, 229
Furman, Lucy, 29–31, 115, 185

Garrison, William Lloyd, 15
Gee, James Paul, 5–6, 48, 49, 58, 73, 77, 79–82, 98, 103, 156, 159, 189, 202
gender roles, 133
"getting above your raising," 2, 48, 110, 156, 173, 178, 216, 230–33
Giardina, Denise, 3, 13, 19, 25, 49, 50, 51, 54–55, 142–73
Giroux, Henry, 49
Goody, Jack, 5, 62
Graff, Harvey, 28, 77, 236
Green, Chris, 17

Hamilton, Sharon Jean, 112
Hampton Normal Institute, 8
Hanna, Stephen, 24
Harkins, Anthony, 72, 73, 147
Havelock, Eric, 5
Heath, Shirley Brice, 5, 63, 65, 70, 93
Henninger, Katherine, 179
Hindman Settlement School, 184, 204
Hobson, Fred, 180
Hoganson, Kirstin, 46
Hogg, Charlotte, 6

hooks, bell 18
Hsiung, David, 18, 26

illiteracy; stereotypes of, 4, 23–29, 56, 71, 104, 127–30; defining, 64
Indian Helper, 12

Jacobs, Harriet, 16
Jones, Anne Goodwyn, 180, 189
Jones, Suzanne, 192
Jordan, Rebecca, 94

Kanawha County, 159–60
Katanski, Amelia, 11, 14
Kennedy, Rory, 27, 92
Kephart, Horace, 102
Kristeva, Julia, 159
Kuralt, Charles, 92, 167

La Flesche, Francis, 9
Lakes, George Ann Greene, 231–33
Lauer, Janice, 49
Law, Carolyn Leste, 18–19, 121
Lawson, Willie, 44
Lenski, Lois, 142–43
literacy; and gender, 29–31, 58, 63, 65–66, 88, 106–10, 122–26, 155–57, 191–93, 197–201; and patriotism, 46–48; commodification of, 67–78; resistance to, 80–83, 87–89, 148–49; narratives, 93, 94–95; discouraging writing, 158–59; and autodidacticism, 202–3
literacy and literacies; definitions of, 5–7, 60–68; consequences of, 2
Local Color writing, 4, 24, 25, 32, 43, 51–53, 55, 92, 188
Lum and Abner, 146–147

Macedo, Donaldo, 34, 80
McDonald, Jeanne, 211
Merrifield, Juliet, 70
Moffett, James, 160
moonlight schools, 31–48
Morriss, Elizabeth, 35–48

Mortensen, Peter, 28, 52, 95, 112, 144
Mullins, Mike, 165, 170, 213
Murfree, Mary Noailles, 4, 24

narratives of socialization, 94–95
Native American boarding schools, 7–15
Native American literacies, 7–15; and gender, 11–12
New Literacy Studies (NLS), 5
New Opportunity School for Women (NOSW), 229–33
Norman, Gurney, 232–33

O'Brien, John, 25, 28, 170
Oates, Joyce Carol, 86, 90
Offutt, Chris, 178
Olney, James, 15
Olsen, Tillie, 57
On Agate Hill, 176
Ong, Walter, 5
Oral History, 19, 51, 55, 169, 174–211
Orientalism; in *Oral History*, 186–87

Parrish, Nancy, 147–48
Phillips, Wendell, 15
Powell, Douglas Reichert, 51
Powell, Katrina, 206
Pryse, Marjorie, 25
Puckett, Anita, 3, 12, 16, 29, 102, 148–49, 184, 191, 232
Pudup, Mary Beth, 4
Purcell-Gates, Victoria, 6, 63, 65, 83–84, 219

Qoyawayma, Polingaysi, 9, 12–15

Rash, Ron, 23
Rather, Dan, 27, 92
Reid, Herbert, 94
Robbins, Dorothy Dodge, 180, 195
Robbins, Sarah, 12, 198
Rodriguez, Richard, 18, 98
Rose, Mike, 18

Royster, Jacqueline Jones, 16
Rubin, Rachel Lee, 71–72, 82

Said, Edward, 28
Sawyer, Diane, 28, 92
Schafer, William, 57, 72, 91
Schell, Eileen E., 6
self-monitoring, 120–126, 136–37
Semple, Ellen Churchill, 17
Seventeen, 169–71
Shapiro, Henry, 4, 24, 25, 26, 164–65
Sitting on the Courthouse Bench: An Oral History of Grundy, Virginia, 1
Slone, Florida, 29, 184–185, 218
Smith, Lee, 1, 2, 3, 10, 13, 19, 20, 25, 29, 49, 50, 51, 55, 143, 161, 169, 170, 174–211; interview with, 212–28
Smith, Rebecca, 177, 204
Smith, Virginia, 182
social class, 18
Sohn, Katherine Kelleher, 2–3, 18, 19, 27, 48–50, 110, 184, 218, 231–33
Songs of Life and Grace, 27, 50, 54, 93–141
Standing Bear, Luther, 11
Stephenson, Jane, 229–33
Stewart, Cora Wilson, 31–35, 44, 48, 112
Still, James, 25, 174–75, 239
Stowe, Harriet Beecher, 15
Street, Brian, 5, 102–5
Stromberg, Ernest, 9

The Dollmaker, 13, 19, 53, 54, 56–91, 115, 148, 150, 163, 187, 193; and proletarian fiction, 58–60
The Unquiet Earth, 19, 49, 54, 142–173
Thompson, Tommy, 26
Toynbee, Arnold, 150–153, 167, 171

UK 101, 93–94
unions, 58, 89–90

Villanueva, Victor, 18
Vincent, David, 6–7
VISTA, 169–71

Waller, Altina, 4
Washington, Booker T., 8
Watt, Ian, 5, 62
Webb-Sunderhaus, Sara, 19
Weller, Jack, 27

Williams, Cratis, 25, 58
Williams, John Alexander, 17, 26, 102
Williamson, J.W., 148, 167
Wolfe, Margaret Ripley, 96

Young, Morriss, 52

Zitkala-Ša, 9–12

Acknowledgments

I am humbled by the level of support that so many people have shown me throughout this process. Without their help, writing this book would not have been possible.

First, I want to thank the American Association of University Women. An American Fellowship from their Educational Foundation fully funded my dissertation research and writing during the 2007–2008 academic year, and for that I will always be grateful. I am similarly indebted to the National Endowment for the Humanities 2008 Summer Institute at Ferrum College, "Regional Study and the Liberal Arts: Appalachia Up-Close," where I was able to finish an initial draft of this manuscript's proposal. At that institute I was lucky enough to meet Catherine Halverson; she read and commented on my work and has been a valuable supporter and friend during these last few years. I also owe a great deal to Gillian Berchowitz and all of the other fine people at Ohio University Press for their sustained interest in this project. Since I first spoke with Gillian about my work at the 2007 Appalachian Studies Association conference in Maryville, Tennessee, she has patiently answered my questions about the manuscript process, and I am thankful that she believed in my work so early on.

I still find it difficult to believe that all of the living, primary authors considered in this project—Linda Scott DeRosier, Denise Giardina, and Lee Smith—were willing to correspond with me, sometimes at length, about their work. The stories and thoughts they shared with me during our interviews added invaluable insights to this study, and I am grateful for their kindness, their approachability, and for their willingness to help me develop my ideas.

I was also fortunate enough to have a great deal of professional support. My colleagues at the University of North Carolina at Asheville have been extremely helpful: from reading portions of my manuscript (Lori Horvitz, in particular), to asking about my progress, to helping me balance my teaching, research, and service responsibilities, my department and university have been outstanding supporters of my efforts to bring this project to fruition. Lorena Russell and Gwen Ashburn deserve a heartfelt thank you for their administrative support during this process. My dissertation director at Louisiana State University, Katherine Henninger, also warrants special recognition for her help with this project, as do other committee members: Lillian Bridwell-Bowles, Richard Moreland, and Brannon Costello. Shannon Wilson at Berea College was kind enough to read my introduction and provide me with feedback. Chris Green unselfishly shared segments of his recent book, *The Social Life of Poetry: Appalachia, Race, and Radical Modernism*, with me before its publication, and I am deeply thankful for his encouragement. A host of other scholars have been equally gracious with their time and help. To David Whisnant, Herb Reid, Phillip Obermiller, Sandy Ballard, and many more: Thank you.

My primary research on the Moonlight School project in Buncombe County, North Carolina, would not have been possible without the help of Ann Wright and Zoe Rhine, two gracious and knowledgeable North Carolina Collection librarians at Pack Memorial Library in Asheville, North Carolina. They patiently fulfilled my repeated requests to see the same materials, and I am especially grateful that they helped me digitize images from the collection to use in this project. I am also greatly indebted to Patricia O'Cain. During the spring semester of 2009 she completed an undergraduate research project with me about Appalachian literacies, and her meticulous research in the North Carolina Collection at Pack Memorial Library helped me more than she could ever imagine. Helen Wykle, Special Collections librarian of the Ramsey Library at UNC Asheville, has been an invaluable resource, and I greatly appreciate Sallie Klipp's help and support as well.

Finally, I am thankful for a host of loving family and friends whose steady support helped me revise and finish this project. My parents, Bert and Darlene Abrams, taught me what it means to know and cherish your mountain heritage; my husband, Mark Locklear, believed in me and my writing, even when I worked through countless weekends and holidays; and my best friend, Kirstin Squint, helped me remember why I love what I do. Thank you to you all.

www.ingramcontent.com/pod-product-compliance
Lightning Source LLC
Chambersburg PA
CBHW031238290426
44109CB00012B/349